Entity Framework Core Cookbook

Second Edition

Leverage the full potential of Entity Framework with this collection of powerful and easy-to-follow recipes

Ricardo Peres

BIRMINGHAM - MUMBAI

Entity Framework Core Cookbook
Second Edition

First published: March 2012

Second edition: November 2016

Production reference: 1031116

Published by Packt Publishing Ltd.
Livery Place
35 Livery Street
Birmingham B3 2PB, UK.

ISBN 978-1-78588-330-9

www.packtpub.com

Credits

Author

Ricardo Peres

Reviewer

Jason De Oliveira

Commissioning Editor

Kunal Parikh

Acquisition Editor

Chaitanya Nair

Content Development Editor

Siddhi Chavan

Merint Mathew

Technical Editors

Bhavin Savalia

Dhiraj Chandanshive

Copy Editor

Safis Editing

Project Coordinator

Suzanne Coutinho

Proofreader

Safis Editing

Indexer

Tejal Daruwale Soni

Graphics

Abhinash Sahu

Production Coordinator

Melwyn Dsa

Cover Work

Melwyn Dsa

About the Author

Ricardo Peres is a Portuguese developer, blogger, and occasionally an e-book author. He has more than 17 years of experience in software development, using technologies such as C/C++, Java, JavaScript, and .NET. His interests include distributed systems, architectures, design patterns, and general .NET development.

He currently works for London-based Simplifydigital as a technical evangelist, and was first awarded as MVP in 2015.

Ricardo maintains a blog, *Development With A Dot*, where he regularly writes about technical issues. You can read it here: `http://weblogs.asp.net/ricardoperes`.

He has reviewed *Learning NHibernate 4* for Packt.

You can catch up with him at `@RJPeres75`.

I'd like to thank my family, Zézinha, Francisco, and Madalena, for their love and patience and my friends and colleagues at Simplifydigital for all their support.

This book is dedicated to my parents, Irene (1947-2005) and Jorge Peres (1941-2015), with love and "saudades."

About the Reviewer

Jason De Oliveira works as a CTO for MEGA International (http://www.mega.com), a software company in Paris (France) that provides modeling tools for enterprise architecture, enterprise governance risk, and compliance management. He is an experienced manager and senior solutions architect with a lot of skills in software architecture and enterprise architecture.

He loves sharing his knowledge and experience via his blog, by speaking at conferences, writing technical books, writing articles in the technical press, giving software courses as MCT, and coaching co-workers in his company. He frequently collaborates with Microsoft, and you can quite often find him at the Microsoft Technology Center (MTC) in Paris. Microsoft awarded him in 2011 with an MVP in C# for his numerous contributions to the Microsoft community. Microsoft seeks to recognize the best and brightest from technology communities around the world with the MVP award. These exceptional and highly-respected individuals come from more than 90 countries, serve their local online and offline communities, and have an impact worldwide. Jason is very proud to be one of them. Please feel free to contact him via his blog (http://www.jasondeoliveira.com) if you need any technical assistance or want to discuss technical subjects.

Jason has worked as a reviewer on *.NET 4.5 Expert Programming Cookbook*, *WCF 4.5 Multi-tier Services Development with LINQ to Entities*, *.NET 4.5 Parallel Extensions Cookbook*, and *WCF 4.5 Multi-layer Services Development with Entity Framework, Third Edition* by Packt. He has also worked as an author on *Visual Studio 2013: Concevoir, développer et gérer des projets Web, les gérer avec TFS 2013* by Editions ENI.

I would like to thank my lovely wife, Orianne, and my beautiful daughters, Julia and Léonie, for supporting me in my work and for accepting long days and short nights during the week and sometimes even during the weekend. My life would not be the same without them!

www.PacktPub.com

eBooks, discount offers, and more

Did you know that Packt offers eBook versions of every book published, with PDF and ePub files available? You can upgrade to the eBook version at www.PacktPub.com and as a print book customer, you are entitled to a discount on the eBook copy. Get in touch with us at customercare@packtpub.com for more details.

At www.PacktPub.com, you can also read a collection of free technical articles, sign up for a range of free newsletters and receive exclusive discounts and offers on Packt books and eBooks.

https://www.packtpub.com/mapt

Get the most in-demand software skills with Mapt. Mapt gives you full access to all Packt books and video courses, as well as ind]ustry-leading tools to help you plan your personal development and advance your career.

Why subscribe?

- ▸ Fully searchable across every book published by Packt
- ▸ Copy and paste, print, and bookmark content
- ▸ On demand and accessible via a web browser

Table of Contents

Preface

This book is about the new Entity Framework Core 1.0. In here, you will find recipes that will hopefully make your life easier when working with Entity Framework Core. If all goes well, you will also have some fun while doing it.

It has something for both beginners as well as more seasoned developers.

What this book covers

Chapter 1, Using Entity Framework in the Real World, introduces you to the structure of the sample project, and we will see some examples of how to use Entity Framework in a real MVC application.

Chapter 2, Mapping Entities, presents the way to configure the mapping of entities and properties and relations between entities.

Chapter 3, Validation and Changes, talks about how Entity Framework detects modifications made to entities, and how we can intercept those modifications, or apply our custom validation logic to it.

Chapter 4, Transactions and Concurrency Control, covers ACID transactions and optimistic concurrency control.

Chapter 5, Querying, covers the many querying options available to Entity Framework Core, some of which are quite new.

Chapter 6, Advanced Scenarios, presents some more advanced scenarios.

Chapter 7, Performance and Scalability, introduces you to some tips related to how we can make our application more responsive and scalable.

Appendix, Pitfalls, presents a list of pitfalls, or anti-patterns, regarding Entity Framework Core usage.

What you need for this book

All you need is .NET Core, including Entity Framework Core, together with an edition of Visual Studio 2015 that supports it (the free Community Edition will work).

We will be using SQL Server as the relational database (any version starting with 2012 will do, in any edition), including Express.

Who this book is for

This book is for .NET developers who work with relational databases on a daily basis and understand the basics of Entity Framework, but now want to use it in a more efficient manner. You are expected to have some prior knowledge of Entity Framework.

Sections

In this book, you will find several headings that appear frequently (Getting ready, How to do it, How it works, There's more, and See also).

To give clear instructions on how to complete a recipe, we use these sections as follows:

Getting ready

This section tells you what to expect in the recipe, and describes how to set up any software or any preliminary settings required for the recipe.

How to do it...

This section contains the steps required to follow the recipe.

How it works...

This section usually consists of a detailed explanation of what happened in the previous section.

There's more...

This section consists of additional information about the recipe in order to make the reader more knowledgeable about the recipe.

See also

This section provides helpful links to other useful information for the recipe.

Conventions

In this book, you will find a number of text styles that distinguish between different kinds of information. Here are some examples of these styles and an explanation of their meaning.

Code words in text, database table names, folder names, filenames, file extensions, pathnames, dummy URLs, user input, and Twitter handles are shown as follows: "Create an entity with the name `MyEntity` in the `BusinessLogic` project."

A block of code is set as follows:

```
namespace BusinessLogic
{
  public class Post : BlogContent
  {
    public string Body { get; set; }
  }
}
```

When we wish to draw your attention to a particular part of a code block, the relevant lines or items are set in bold:

```
namespace BusinessLogic
{
  public class Post : BlogContent
  {
    public string Body { get; set; }
  }
}
```

New terms and **important words** are shown in bold. Words that you see on the screen, for example, in menus or dialog boxes, appear in the text like this: "Open **Using EF Core Solution** from the included source code examples.

 Warnings or important notes appear in a box like this.

 Tips and tricks appear like this.

Reader feedback

Feedback from our readers is always welcome. Let us know what you think about this book—what you liked or disliked. Reader feedback is important for us as it helps us develop titles that you will really get the most out of.

To send us general feedback, simply e-mail `feedback@packtpub.com`, and mention the book's title in the subject of your message.

If there is a topic that you have expertise in and you are interested in either writing or contributing to a book, see our author guide at `www.packtpub.com/authors`.

Customer support

Now that you are the proud owner of a Packt book, we have a number of things to help you to get the most from your purchase.

Downloading the example code

You can download the example code files for this book from your account at `http://www.packtpub.com`. If you purchased this book elsewhere, you can visit `http://www.packtpub.com/support` and register to have the files e-mailed directly to you.

You can download the code files by following these steps:

1. Log in or register to our website using your e-mail address and password.
2. Hover the mouse pointer on the **SUPPORT** tab at the top.
3. Click on **Code Downloads & Errata**.
4. Enter the name of the book in the **Search** box.
5. Select the book for which you're looking to download the code files.
6. Choose from the drop-down menu where you purchased this book from.
7. Click on **Code Download**.

You can also download the code files by clicking on the **Code Files** button on the book's webpage at the Packt Publishing website. This page can be accessed by entering the book's name in the **Search** box. Please note that you need to be logged in to your Packt account.

Once the file is downloaded, please make sure that you unzip or extract the folder using the latest version of:

- ▶ WinRAR / 7-Zip for Windows
- ▶ Zipeg / iZip / UnRarX for Mac
- ▶ 7-Zip / PeaZip for Linux

The code bundle for the book is also hosted on GitHub at `https://github.com/PacktPublishing/Entity-Framework-Core-Cookbook`. We also have other code bundles from our rich catalog of books and videos available at `https://github.com/PacktPublishing/`. Check them out!

Errata

Although we have taken every care to ensure the accuracy of our content, mistakes do happen. If you find a mistake in one of our books—maybe a mistake in the text or the code—we would be grateful if you could report this to us. By doing so, you can save other readers from frustration and help us improve subsequent versions of this book. If you find any errata, please report them by visiting `http://www.packtpub.com/submit-errata`, selecting your book, clicking on the **Errata Submission Form** link, and entering the details of your errata. Once your errata are verified, your submission will be accepted and the errata will be uploaded to our website or added to any list of existing errata under the Errata section of that title.

To view the previously submitted errata, go to `https://www.packtpub.com/books/content/support` and enter the name of the book in the search field. The required information will appear under the **Errata** section.

Piracy

Piracy of copyrighted material on the Internet is an ongoing problem across all media. At Packt, we take the protection of our copyright and licenses very seriously. If you come across any illegal copies of our works in any form on the Internet, please provide us with the location address or website name immediately so that we can pursue a remedy.

Please contact us at `copyright@packtpub.com` with a link to the suspected pirated material.
We appreciate your help in protecting our authors and our ability to bring you valuable content.

Questions

If you have a problem with any aspect of this book, you can contact us at `questions@packtpub.com`, and we will do our best to address the problem.

1

Improving Entity Framework in the Real World

In this chapter, we will cover the following topics:

- ▸ Improving Entity Framework by using a code-first approach
- ▸ Unit testing and mocking
- ▸ Creating databases from code
- ▸ Creating mock database connections
- ▸ Implementing the repository pattern
- ▸ Implementing the unit of work pattern

Introduction

If we were to buy the materials to build a house, would we buy the bare minimum to get four walls up and a roof, without a kitchen or a bathroom? Or would we buy enough material to build the house with multiple bedrooms, a kitchen, and multiple bathrooms?

The problem lies in how we define the *bare minimum*. The progression of software development has made us realize that there are ways of building software that do not require additional effort, but reap serious rewards. This is the same choice we are faced with when we decide on the approach to take with Entity Framework. We could just get it running and it would work most of the time.

Customizing and adding to it later would be difficult, but doable. There are a few things that we would need to give up for this approach. The most important among those is control over how the code is written. We have already seen that applications grow, mature, and have features added. The only thing that stays constant is the fact that at some point in time, in some way, we will come to push the envelope of almost every tool that we leverage to help us. The other side is that we could go into development, being aware of the value-added benefits that cost nothing, and with that knowledge, avoid dealing with unnecessary constraints.

When working with Entity Framework, there are some paths and options available to us. There are two main workflows for working with **Object-Relational Mapper** (**ORM**) tools such as Entity Framework:

- **Database first**: We start by defining our database objects and their relations, then write our classes to match them, and we bind them together
- **Code first**: We start by designing our classes as **Plain Old CLR Objects** (**POCOs**) to model the concepts that we wish to represent, without caring (too much!) how they will be persisted in the database

 The model-first approach was dropped in Entity Framework Core 1.0.

While following the database-first approach, we are not concerned with the actual implementation of our classes, but merely the structures—tables, columns, keys—on which they will be persisted. In contrast, with POCOs or code first, we start by designing the classes that will be used in our programs to represent the business and domain concepts that we wish to model. This is known as **Domain-Driven Design** (**DDD**). DDD certainly includes code first, but it is much more than that.

All of these approaches will solve the problem with varying degrees of flexibility.

Starting with a database-first approach in Entity Framework means we have an existing database schema and are going to let the schema, along with the metadata in the database, determine the structure of our business objects and domain model. The database-first approach is normally how most of us start out with Entity Framework and other ORMs, but the tendency is to move toward more flexible solutions as we gain proficiency with the framework. This will drastically reduce the amount of code that we need to write, but will also limit us to working within the structure of the generated code. Entities, which are generated by default here, are not 100% usable with WCF services, ASP.NET Web APIs, and similar technologies – just think about lazy loading and disconnected entities, for example. This is not necessarily a bad thing if we have a well-built database schema and a domain model that translates well into **Data Transfer Objects** (**DTOs**). Such a domain and database combination is a rare exception in the world of code production. Due to the lack of flexibility and the restrictions on the way these objects are used, this solution is viewed as a short-term or small-project solution.

Modeling the domain first allows us to fully visualize the structure of the data in the application, and work in a more object-oriented manner while developing our application. Just think of this: a relational database does not understand OOP concepts such as inheritance, static members, and virtual methods, although, for sure, there are ways to simulate them in the relational world. The main reasons for the lack of adoption of this approach include the poor support for round-trip updates, and the lack of documentation on manipulating the POCO model so as to produce the proper database structure. It can be a bit daunting for developers with less experience, because they probably won't know how to get started. Historically, the database had to be created each time the POCO model changed, causing data loss when structural changes were made.

Coding the classes first allows us to work entirely in an object-oriented direction, and not worry about the structuring of the database, without the restrictions that the model-first designer imposes. This abstraction gives us the ability to craft a more logically sound application that focuses on the behavior of the application rather than the data generated by it. The objects that we produce that are capable of being serialized over any service have true persistence ignorance, and can be shared as contract objects as they are not specific to the database implementation. This approach is also much more flexible as it is entirely dependent on the code that we write. This allows us to translate our objects into database records without modifying the structure of our application. All of this, however, is somewhat theoretical, in the sense that we still need to worry about having primary key properties, generation strategies, and so on.

In each of the recipes presented in this book, we will follow an incremental approach, where we will start by adding the stuff we need for the most basic cases, and later on, as we make progress, we will refactor it to add more complex stuff.

Improving Entity Framework by using a code-first approach

In this recipe, we start by separating the application into a **user interface** (**UI**) layer, a data access layer, and a business logic layer. This will allow us to keep our objects separated from database-specific implementations. The objects and the implementation of the database context will use a layered approach so we can add testing to the application. The following table shows the various projects, and their purpose, available for code-first approach:

Project	Purpose
BusinessLogic	Stores the entities that represent business entities.
DataAccess	Classes that access data and manipulate business entities. Depends on the BusinessLogic project.

Project	Purpose
UI	User interface – the MVC application. Makes use of the BusinessLogic and DataAccess projects.
UnitTests	Unit tests. Uses both the BusinessLogic and DataAccess projects.

Getting ready

We will be using the NuGet Package Manager to install the Entity Framework Core 1 package, Microsoft.EntityFrameworkCore. We will also be using a SQL Server database for storing the data, so we will also need Microsoft.EntityFrameworkCore.SqlServer.

Finally, xunit is the package we will be using for the unit tests and dotnet-text-xunit adds tooling support for Visual Studio. Note that the UnitTests project is a .NET Core App 1.0 (netcoreapp1.0), that Microsoft.EntityFrameworkCore.Design is configured as a build dependency, and Microsoft.EntityFrameworkCore.Tools is set as a tool.

Open **Using EF Core Solution** from the included source code examples.

Execute the database setup script from the code samples included for this recipe. This can be found in the DataAccess project within the Database folder.

How to do it...

Let's get connected to the database using the following steps:

1. Add a new C# class named Blog with the following code to the BusinessLogic project:

    ```
    namespace BusinessLogic
    {
        public class Blog
        {
            public int Id { get; set; }
            public string Title { get; set; }
        }
    }
    ```

2. Create a new C# class named BlogContext with the following code in the DataAccess project:

    ```
    using Microsoft.EntityFrameworkCore;
    using BusinessLogic;
    namespace DataAccess
    {
    ```

```
public class BlogContext : DbContext
{
    private readonly string _connectionString;
    public BlogContext(string connectionString)
    {
        _connectionString = connectionString;
    }
    public DbSet<Blog> Blogs { get; set; }
    protected override void OnConfiguring
      (DbContextOptionsBuilder optionsBuilder)
    {
        optionsBuilder.UseSqlServer(_connectionString);
        base.OnConfiguring(optionsBuilder);
    }
}
```

 For Entity Framework 6, replace the `Microsoft.`
`EntityFrameworkCore` namespace with `System.Data.Entity` and
call the base constructor of `DbContext` passing it the connection string.

3. Add the following connection string to the `appsettings.json` file:

```
{
  "Data": {
    "Blog": {
      "ConnectionString":"Server=(local)\\SQLEXPRESS;
      Database=Blog;
      Integrated Security=SSPI;MultipleActiveResultSets=true"
    }
  }
}
```

 With Entity Framework 6, we would add this connection string to the `Web.`
`config` file, under the `connectionStrings` section, with the name
`Blog`. Of course, change the connection string to match your system
settings, for example, the name of the SQL Server instance (`SQLEXPRESS`,
in this example).

4. In the `Controllers\BlogController.cs` file, modify the `Index` method with the following code:

```
using BusinessLogic;
using DataAccess;
using System.Linq;
using Microsoft.AspNetCore.Mvc;
using Microsoft.Extensions.Configuration;
namespace UI.Controllers
{
    public class BlogController : Controller
    {
        private readonly BlogContext _blogContext;
        public BlogController(IConfiguration config)
        {
            _blogContext = new
             BlogContext(config["Data:Blog:ConnectionString"]);
        }
        public IActionResult Index()
        {
            var blog = _blogContext.Blogs.First();
            return View(blog);
        }
    }
}
```

 For Entity Framework 6, remove the `config` parameter from the `HomeController` constructor, and initialize `BlogContext` with the `ConfigurationManager.ConnectionStrings["Blog"].ConnectionString` value.

5. Finally, in `Startup.cs`, we need to register the `IConfiguration` service so that it can be injected into the `HomeController` constructor. Please add the following lines to the `ConfigureServices` method:

```
public void ConfigureServices(IServiceCollection services)
{
    services.AddMvc();
    services.AddSingleton<IConfiguration>
     (_ => Configuration);
}
```

Prior to version 5, ASP.NET MVC does not include any built-in Inversion of Control containers, unlike ASP.NET Core. You will need to bring your own and register it with the `DependencyResolver.SetResolver` method, or rely on a third-party implementation.

How it works...

The blog entity is created but not mapped explicitly to a database structure. This takes advantage of convention over configuration, found in the code-first approach, wherein the properties are examined and then the table mappings are determined. This is obviously a time saver, but it is fairly limited if you have a non-standard database schema. The other big advantage of this approach is that the entity is *persistence-ignorant*. In other words, it has no knowledge of how it is to be stored in the database.

The `BlogContext` class has a few key elements to understand. The first is to understand the inheritance from `DbContext`. `DbContext` is the code-first context class, which encapsulates all connection pooling, entity change tracking, and database interactions. We added a constructor to take in the connection string, so that it knows where to connect to.

We used the standard built-in functionality for the connection string, storing it in a text (JSON) file, but this could easily be any application setting store; one such location would be the .NET Core secrets file. We pass the connection string on the construction of the `BlogContext`. It enables us to pass that connection string from anywhere so that we are not coupled. Because Entity Framework is agnostic when it comes to data sources—can use virtually any database server–we need to tell it to use the SQL Server provider, and to connect to it using the supplied connection string. That's what the `UseSqlServer` method does.

There's more...

Approaching the use of code-first development, we have several overarching themes and industry standards that we need to be aware of. Knowing about them will help us leverage the power of this tool without falling into the pit of using it without understanding.

Convention over configuration

This is a design paradigm that says that default rules dictate how an application will behave, but allows the developer to override any of the default rules with specific behavior, in case it is needed. This allows us, as programmers, to avoid using a lot of configuration files or code to specify how we intended something to be used or configured. In our case, Entity Framework allows the most common behaviors to use default conventions that remove the need for a majority of the configurations. When the behavior we wish to create is not supported by the convention, we can easily override the convention and add the required behavior to it without the need to get rid of it everywhere else. This leaves us with a flexible and extendable system to configure the database interaction.

Model-View-Controller

In our example, we use **Microsoft ASP.NET MVC**. We would use MVC 5 for Entity Framework 6 and .NET 4.x, and MVC Core 1 for Entity Framework Core 1 and .NET Core, and, in both cases, the Razor view engine for rendering the UI. We have provided some simple views that will allow us to focus on the solutions and the code without needing to deal with UI design and markup.

Single Responsibility Principle

One of the **SOLID** principles of development, the **Single Responsibility Principle** (**SRP**), states that every class should have only one reason to change. In this chapter, there are several examples of that in use, for example, the separation of model, view and controller, as prescribed by MVC.

Entities in code-first have the structure of data as their singular responsibility in memory. This means that we will only need to modify the entities if the structure needs to be changed. By contrast, the code automatically generated by the database-first tools of Entity Framework inherits your entities from base classes within the Entity Framework **Application Programming Interface** (**API**). The process of Microsoft making occasional updates to the base classes of Entity Framework is the one that introduces a second reason to change, thus violating our principle.

Provider Model

Entity Framework relies on providers for achieving different parts of its functionality. These are called providers, and the most important, for sure, is the one that supplies the connection to the underlying data store. Different providers exist for different data sources, from traditional relational databases such as SQL Server, to non-relational ones, such as **Redis** and **Azure Table Storage**. There's even one for abstracting a database purely in memory!

Testing

While we did not actively test this recipe, we layered in the abstractions to do so. All of the other recipes will be executed and presented using test-driven development, as we believe it leads to better software design and a much clearer representation of intent.

See also

In this chapter:

- ▸ *Unit testing and mocking*
- ▸ *Implementing the unit of work pattern*
- ▸ *Implementing the repository pattern*

Unit testing and mocking

Software development is not just writing code. We also need to test it, to confirm that it does what is expected. There are several kinds of tests, and unit tests are one of the most popular. In this chapter, we will set up the unit test framework that will accompany us throughout the book. Another important concept is that of mocking; by mocking a class (or interface), we can provide a *dummy* implementation of it that we can use instead of the *real thing*. This comes in handy in unit tests, because we do not always have access to real-life data and environments, and this way, we can pretend we do.

Getting ready

We will be using the NuGet Package Manager to install the Entity Framework Core 1 package, `Microsoft.EntityFrameworkCore`. We will be using a SQL Server database for storing the data, so we will also need `Microsoft.EntityFrameworkCore.SqlServer`.

To mock interfaces and base classes, we will use `Moq`.

Finally, `xunit` is the package we will be using for the unit tests and `dotnet-text-xunit` adds tooling support for Visual Studio. Note that the `UnitTests` project is a .NET Core App 1.0 (netcoreapp1.0), that `Microsoft.EntityFrameworkCore.Design` is configured as a build dependency, and `Microsoft.EntityFrameworkCore.Tools` is set as a tool.

Open **Using EF Core Solution** from the included source code examples.

Execute the database setup script from the code samples included for this recipe. This can be found in the `DataAccess` project within the `Database` folder.

How to do it...

1. Start by adding the required NuGet packages to the `UnitTests` project. We'll edit and add two dependencies, the main `xUnit` library and its runner for .NET Core, and then set the `runner` command.

2. Now, let's add a base class to the project; create a new C# class file and call it `BaseTests.cs`:

```
using Microsoft.Extensions.Configuration;
namespace UnitTests
{
    public abstract class BaseTest
    {
        protected BaseTest()
        {
            var builder = new ConfigurationBuilder()
                .AddJsonFile("appsettings.json");
```

```
                    Configuration = builder.Build();
                }
                protected IConfiguration Configuration
                    { get; private set; }
            }
        }
```

3. Now, for a quick test, add a new C# file, called `SimpleTest.cs`, to the project, with this content:

```csharp
using Moq;
using Xunit;
namespace UnitTests
{
    public class SimpleTest : BaseTest
    {
        [Fact]
        public void CanReadFromConfiguration()
        {
            var connectionString =
            Configuration["Data:Blog:ConnectionString"];
            Assert.NotNull(connectionString);
            Assert.NotEmpty(connectionString);
        }
        [Fact]
        public void CanMock()
        {
            var mock = new Mock<IConfiguration>();
            mock.Setup(x => x[It.IsNotNull<string>()])
              .Returns("Dummy Value");
            var configuration = mock.Object;
            var value = configuration["Dummy Key"];
            Assert.NotNull(value);
            Assert.NotEmpty(value);
        }
    }
}
```

4. If you want to have the **xUnit** runner running your unit tests automatically, you will need to set the test command as the profile to run in the project properties:

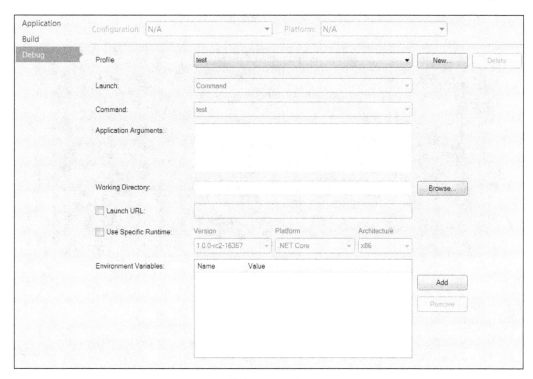

Project properties

How it works...

We have a unit tests base class that loads configuration from an external file, in pretty much the same way as the ASP.NET Core template does. Any unit tests that we will define later on should inherit from this one.

When the runner executes, it will discover all unit tests in the project—those public concrete methods marked with the `[Fact]` attribute. It will then try to execute them and evaluate any Assert calls within.

The **Moq** framework lets you define your own implementations for any abstract or interface methods that you wish to make testable. In this example, we are mocking the `IConfiguration` class, and saying that any attempt to retrieve a configuration value should have a dummy value as the result.

If you run this project, you will get the following output:

Running unit tests

There's more...

Testing to the edges of an application requires that we adhere to certain practices that allow us to shrink the untestable sections of the code. This will allow us to unit test more code, and make our integration tests far more specific.

One class under test

An important point to remember while performing unit testing is that we should only be testing a single class. The point of a unit test is to ensure that a single operation of this class performs the way we expect it to.

This is why simulating classes that are not under test is so important. We do not want the behavior of these supporting classes to affect the outcomes of unit tests for the class that is being tested.

Integration tests

Often, it is equally important to test the actual combination of your various classes to ensure they work properly together. These integration tests are valuable, but are almost always more brittle, require more setup, and are run slower than the unit tests. We certainly need integration tests on any project of a reasonable size, but we want unit tests first.

Arrange, Act, Assert

Most unit tests can be viewed as having three parts: **Arrange**, **Act**, and **Assert**. Arrange is where we prepare the environment to perform the test, for instance, mocking the `IDBContext` with dummy data with the expectation that Set will be called. Act is where we perform the action under test, and is most often a singular line of code. Assert is where we ensure that the proper result was reached. Note the comments in the preceding examples that call out these sections. We will use them throughout the book to make it clear what the test is trying to do.

Mocking

Mocking and stubbing—providing a pre-built implementation for methods to intercept—is a very interesting topic. There are numberless frameworks that can provide mocking capabilities for even the most challenging scenarios, such as static methods and properties. Mocking fits nicely with unit tests because we seldom have an environment that is identical to the one where we will be deploying, but we don't have "real" data. Also, data changes, and we need a way to be able to reproduce things consistently.

Creating databases from code

As we start down the code-first path, there are a couple of things that could be true. If we already have a database, then we will need to configure our objects to that schema, but what if we do not have one? That is the subject of this recipe: creating a database from the objects we declare.

Getting ready

We will be using the NuGet Package Manager to install the Entity Framework Core 1 package, `Microsoft.EntityFrameworkCore`. We will also be using a SQL Server database for storing the data, so we will also need `Microsoft.EntityFrameworkCore.SqlServer`.

To mock interfaces and base classes, we will use `Moq`.

Finally, `xunit` is the package we will be using for the unit tests and `dotnet-text-xunit` adds tooling support for Visual Studio. Note that the `UnitTests` project is a .NET Core App 1.0 (netcoreapp1.0), that `Microsoft.EntityFrameworkCore.Design` is configured as a build dependency, and `Microsoft.EntityFrameworkCore.Tools` is set as a tool.

Open **Using EF Core Solution** from the included source code examples.

Execute the database setup script from the code samples included for this recipe. This can be found in the `DataAccess` project within the `Database` folder.

How to do it...

1. First, we write a unit test with the following code in a new C# file called
   `DatabaseTest.cs`, in the `UnitTests` project:

```csharp
using BusinessLogic;
using Xunit;
using DataAccess;
namespace UnitTests
{
    public class DatabaseTest : BaseTest
    {
        [Fact]
        public void CanCreateDatabase()
        {
            //Arrange
            var connectionString =
             Configuration["Data:Blog:ConnectionString"];
            var context =
             new BlogContext(connectionString);
            //Act
            var created = context.Database.EnsureCreated();
            //Assert
            Assert.True(created);
        }
    }
}
```

2. We will need to add a connection string to the `UnitTests` project to our database;
   we do so by providing an identical `appSettings.json` file to the one introduced in
   the previous recipe:

```json
{
    "Data": {
        "Blog": {
            "ConnectionString":
            "Server=(local)\\SQLEXPRESS;Database=Blog;Integrated
             Security=SSPI;MultipleActiveResultSets=true"
        }
    }
}
```

 Change the connection string to match your specific
settings.

3. In the `DataAccess` project, we will use the C# `BlogContext` class that was introduced in the previous chapter:

```
using Microsoft.EntityFrameworkCore;
using BusinessLogic;
namespace DataAccess
{
    public class BlogContext : DbContext
    {
        private readonly string _connectionString;
        public BlogContext(string connectionString)
        {
            _connectionString = connectionString;
        }
        public DbSet<Blog> Blogs { get; set; }
        protected override void OnConfiguring(
            DbContextOptionsBuilder optionsBuilder)
        {
            optionsBuilder.UseSqlServer(_connectionString);
            base.OnConfiguring(optionsBuilder);
        }
    }
}
```

How it works...

Entity Framework will initialize itself by calling the `OnConfiguring` method whenever it needs to get data; after that, it knows about the database to use. The `EnsureCreated` method will make sure that the database either already exists or is created in the moment.

There's more...

When we start a green field project, we have that rush of happiness to be working in a problem domain that no one has touched before. This can be exhilarating and daunting at the same time. The objects we define and the structure of our program come naturally to a programmer, but most of us need to think differently to design the database schema. This is where the tools can help to translate our objects and intended structure into the database schema if we leverage some patterns. We can then take full advantage of being object-oriented programmers.

A word of caution: previous versions of Entity Framework offered mechanisms such as **database initializers**. These not only would create the database, but also rebuild it, in case the code-first model had changed, and even add some initial data. For better or worse, these mechanisms are now gone, and we will need to leverage Entity Framework Core Migrations for similar features. We will discuss Migrations in another recipe.

See also

In this chapter:

- ▸ *Unit testing and mocking*

Creating mock database connections

When working with Entity Framework in a test-driven manner, we need to be able to slip a layer between our last line of code and the framework. This allows us to simulate the database connection without actually hitting the database.

We will be using the NuGet Package Manager to install the Entity Framework Core 1 package, `Microsoft.EntityFrameworkCore`. We will also be using a SQL Server database for storing the data, so we will also need `Microsoft.EntityFrameworkCore.SqlServer`.

To mock interfaces and base classes, we will use `Moq`.

Finally, `xunit` is the package we will be using for the unit tests and `dotnet-text-xunit` adds tooling support for Visual Studio. Note that the `UnitTests` project is a .NET Core App 1.0 (netcoreapp1.0), that `Microsoft.EntityFrameworkCore.Design` is configured as a build dependency, and `Microsoft.EntityFrameworkCore.Tools` is set as a tool.

Open **Using EF Core Solution** from the included source code examples.

Execute the database setup script from the code samples included for this recipe. This can be found in the `DataAccess` project within the `Database` folder.

How to do it...

1. In the `DataAccess` project, add a new C# interface named `IDbContext` using the following code:

```
using System.Linq;
namespace DataAccess
{
    public interface IDbContext
    {
        IQueryable<T> Set<T>() where T : class;
    }
}
```

2. Add a new unit test in the `UnitTests` project to test so we can supply dummy results for fake database calls with the following code:

```
using System.Linq;
using DataAccess;
```

```
using BusinessLogic;
using Moq;
using Xunit;
namespace UnitTests
{
    public class MockTest : BaseTest
    {
        [Fact]
        public void CanMock()
        {
          //Arrange
            var data = new[] { new Blog { Id = 1, Title = "Title" },
              newBlog { Id = 2, Title = "No Title" }
                }.AsQueryable();
            var mock = new Mock<IDbContext>();
            mock.Setup(x => x.Set<Blog>()).Returns(data);
            //Act
            var context = mock.Object;
            var blogs = context.Set<Blog>();
            //Assert
            Assert.Equal(data, blogs);
        }
    }
}
```

3. In the `DataAccess` project, update the C# class named `BlogContext` with the following code:

```
using BusinessLogic;
using System.Linq;
using Microsoft.EntityFrameworkCore;
namespace DataAccess
{
    public class BlogContext : DbContext, IDbContext
    {
        private readonly string _connectionString;
        public BlogContext(string connectionString)
        {
            _connectionString = connectionString;
        }
        public DbSet<Blog> Blogs { get; set; }
        IQueryable<T> IDbContext.Set<T>()
        {
            return base.Set<T>();
        }
        protected override void OnConfiguring
          (DbContextOptionsBuilder optionsBuilder)
        {
```

```
                optionsBuilder.UseSqlServer(_connectionString);
                base.OnConfiguring(optionsBuilder);
        }
        public void Rollback()
        {
            ChangeTracker.Entries().ToList().ForEach(x =>
            {
                x.State = EntityState.Detached;
                var keys = GetEntityKey(x.Entity);
                Set(x.Entity.GetType(), keys);
            });
        }
    }
}
```

How it works...

We implemented a fake class —a mock—that mimics some of the functionality of our `IDbContext` interface that we wish to expose and make testable; in this case, it is just the retrieval of data. This allows us to keep our tests independent of the actual data in the database. Now that we have data available from our mock, we can test whether it acts exactly like we coded it to. Knowing the inputs of the data access code, we can test the outputs for validity. We made our existing `BlogContext` class implement the interface where we define the contract that we wish to mock, `IDbContext`, and we configured a mock class to return dummy data whenever its `Set` method was called.

This layering is accomplished by having a `Set` method as an abstraction between the public framework method of `Set<T>` and our code, so we can change the type to something constructible. By layering this method, we can now control every return from the database in the test scenarios.

This layering also provides a better separation of concerns, as the `DbSet<T>` in Entity Framework mingles multiple independent concerns, such as connection management and querying, into a single object, whereas `IQueryable<T>` is the standard .NET interface for performing queries against a data source (`DbSet<T>` implements `IQueryable<T>`). We will continue to separate these concerns in future recipes.

See also

In this chapter:

- ▶ *Unit testing and mocking*

Implementing the repository pattern

This recipe is an implementation of the **Repository Pattern**, which allows us to abstract the underlying data source and the queries used to obtain the data.

Getting ready

We will be using the NuGet Package Manager to install the Entity Framework Core 1 package, `Microsoft.EntityFrameworkCore`. We will also be using a SQL Server database for storing the data, so we will also need `Microsoft.EntityFrameworkCore.SqlServer`.

To mock interfaces and base classes, we will use `Moq`.

Finally, `xunit` is the package we will be using for the unit tests and `dotnet-text-xunit` adds tooling support for Visual Studio. Note that the `UnitTests` project is a .NET Core App 1.0 (netcoreapp1.0), that `Microsoft.EntityFrameworkCore.Design` is configured as a build dependency, and `Microsoft.EntityFrameworkCore.Tools` is set as a tool.

Open **Using EF Core Solution** from the included source code examples.

Execute the database setup script from the code samples included for this recipe. This can be found in the `DataAccess` project within the `Database` folder.

How to do it...

1. Create a new file in the `DataAccess` project, with this content:

    ```
    using System.Linq;
    namespace DataAccess
    {
        public interface IRepository<out T> where T : class
        {
            IQueryable<T> Set<T>() where T : class;
            void RollbackChanges();
            void SaveChanges();
        }
    }
    ```

2. In the `DataAccess` project, add a new C# interface named `IBlogRepository` with the following code:

    ```
    using System.Linq;
    namespace DataAccess
    {
        public interface IBlogRepository : IRepository<Blog>
        {
        }
    }
    ```

3. In the `DataAccess` project, create a new C# class named `BlogRepository` containing the following code:

```
using System.Data.Entity;
using System.Linq;
using BusinessLogic;
namespace DataAccess
{
    public class BlogRepository : IBlogRepository
    {
        private readonly IDbContext _context;
        public BlogRepository(IDbContext context)
        {
            _context = context;
        }
        public IQueryable<Blog> Set()
        {
            return _context.Set<Blog>();
        }
    }
}
```

4. We'll add a new unit test in the `UnitTests` project that defines a test for using the repository with the following code:

```
using System.Linq;
using BusinessLogic;
using DataAccess;
using Moq;
using Xunit;
namespace UnitTests
{
    public class RepositoryTest : BaseTest
    {
        [Fact]
        public void ShouldAllowGettingASetOfObjectsGenerically()
        {
            //Arrange
            var data = new[] { new Blog { Id = 1, Title = "Title" },
                newBlog { Id = 2, Title = "No Title" }
                  }.AsQueryable();
            var mock = new Mock<IDbContext>();
            mock.Setup(x => x.Set<Blog>()).Returns(data);
            var context = mock.Object;
            var repository = new BlogRepository(context);
```

```
//Act
var blogs = repository.Set();
//Assert
Assert.Equal(data, blogs);
                }
            }
        }
```

5. In the `BlogController` class of the `UI` project, update the usage of `BlogContext` so it uses `IBlogRepository` with the following code:

```
using BusinessLogic;
using DataAccess;
using System.Linq;
using Microsoft.AspNet.Mvc;
namespace UI.Controllers
{
    public class BlogController : Controller
    {
        private readonly IBlogRepository _repository;
        public BlogController(IBlogRepository repository)
        {
            _repository = repository;
        }
        public IActionResult Index()
        {
            var blog = _repository.Set().First();
            return View(blog);
        }
    }
}
```

6. Finally, we need to register the `IBlogRepository` service for dependency injection so that it can be passed automatically to the HomeController's constructor. We do that in the `Startup.cs` file in the `UI` project, in the `ConfigureServices` method:

```
public void ConfigureServices(IServiceCollection services)
{
    services.AddMvc();
    services.AddSingleton<IConfiguration>(_ =>
      Configuration);
    services.AddScoped<IDbContext>(_ => new
      BlogContext(Configuration["Data:Blog:ConnectionString"]));
    services.AddScoped<IBlogRepository>(_ => new
      BlogRepository(_.GetService<IDbContext>()));
}
```

How it works...

We start off with a test that defines what we hope to accomplish. We use mocking (or verifiable fake objects) to ensure that we get the behavior that we expect. The test states that any `BlogRepository` function will communicate with the context to connect for the data. This is what we are hoping to accomplish, as doing so allows us to layer tests and extension points into the domain.

The usage of the repository interface is a key part of this flexible implementation as it will allow us to leverage mocks, and test the business layer, while still maintaining an extensible solution. The interface to the context is a straightforward API for all database communication. In this example, we only need to read data from the database, so the interface is very simple.

Even in this simple implementation of the interface, we see that there are opportunities to increase reusability. We could have created a method or property that returned the list of blogs, but then we would have had to modify the context and interface for every new entity. Instead, we set up the `Set` method to take a generic type, which allows us to add entities to the usage of the interface without modifying the interface. We will only need to modify the implementation.

Notice that we constrained the `IRepository` interface to accept only the reference types for `T`, using the where `T : class` constraint. We did this because value types cannot be stored using Entity Framework; if you had a base class, you could use it here to constrain the usage of the generic even further. Importantly, not all reference types are valid for `T`, but the constraint is as close as we can get using C#. Interfaces are not valid because Entity Framework cannot construct them when it needs to create an entity. Instead, it will produce a runtime exception, as they are valid reference types and therefore the compiler won't complain.

Once we have the context, we need to wrap it with an abstraction. `IBlogRepository` will allow us to query the data without allowing direct control over the database connection. We can hide the details of the specific implementation, the actual context object, while surfacing a simplified API for gathering data. We can also introduce specific operations for the `Blog` entity here.

The other interface that we abstracted is the `IDbContext` interface. This abstraction allows us to intercept operations just before they are sent to the database. This makes the untestable part of the application as thin as possible. We can, and will, test right up to the point of database connection.

We had to register the two interfaces, `IDbContext` and `IBlogRepository`, in the ASP.NET dependency resolver. This is achieved at startup time, so that any code that requires these services can use them. You will notice that the registration for `IBlogRepository` makes use of the `IDbContext` registration. This is OK, because it is a requirement for the actual implementation of `BlogRepository` to rely on `IDbContext` to actually retrieve the data.

There's more...

Keeping the repository implementation clean requires us to leverage some principles and patterns that are at the core of object-oriented programming, but not specific to using Entity Framework. These principles will not only help us to write clean implementations of Entity Framework, but can also be leveraged by other areas of our code.

Dependency Inversion Principle

Dependency inversion is another SOLID principle. This states that all of the dependencies of an object should be clearly visible and passed in, or injected, to create the object. The benefit of this is twofold: the first is exposing all of the dependencies so the effects of using a piece of code are clear to those who will use the class. The second benefit is that by injecting these dependencies at construction, they allow us to unit test by passing in mocks of the dependent objects. Granular unit tests require the ability to abstract dependencies, so we can ensure only one object is under test.

Repository and caching

This repository pattern gives us the perfect area for implementing a complex or global caching mechanism. If we want to persist a value into the cache at the point of retrieval, and not retrieve it again, the `repository` class is the perfect location for such logic. This layer of abstraction allows us to move beyond simple implementations and start thinking about solving business problems quickly, and later extend to handle more complex scenarios as they are warranted by the requirements of the specific project. You can think of repository as a well-tested 80%+ solution. Put off anything more until the last responsible moment.

Mocking

The usage of mocks is commonplace in tests because mocks allow us to verify underlying behavior without having more than one object under test. This is a fundamental piece of the puzzle for test-driven development. When you test at a unit level, you want to make sure that the level directly following the one you are testing was called correctly while not actually executing the specific implementation. This is what mocking buys us.

Where generic constraint

There are times when we need to create complex sets of queries that will be used frequently, but only by one or two objects. When this situation occurs, we want to reuse that code without needing to duplicate it for each object. This is where the `where` constraint helps us. It allows us to limit generically defined behavior to an object or set of objects that share a common interface or base class. The extension possibilities are nearly limitless.

See also

In this chapter:

- ▶ *Implementing the unit of work pattern*
- ▶ *Creating mock database connections*

Implementing the unit of work pattern

In the next example, we present an implementation of the Unit of Work pattern. This pattern was introduced by Martin Fowler, and you can read about it at `http://martinfowler.com/eaaCatalog/unitOfWork.html`. Basically, this pattern states that we keep track of all entities that are affected by a business transaction and send them all at once to the database, sorting out the ordering of the changes to apply—inserts before updates, and so on.

Getting ready

We will be using the NuGet Package Manager to install the Entity Framework Core 1 package, `Microsoft.EntityFrameworkCore`. We will also be using a SQL Server database for storing the data, so we will also need `Microsoft.EntityFrameworkCore.SqlServer`.

To mock interfaces and base classes, we will use `Moq`.

Finally, `xunit` is the package we will be using for the unit tests and `dotnet-text-xunit` adds tooling support for Visual Studio. Note that the `UnitTests` project is a .NET Core App 1.0 (netcoreapp1.0), that `Microsoft.EntityFrameworkCore.Design` is configured as a build dependency, and `Microsoft.EntityFrameworkCore.Tools` is set as a tool.

Open **Using EF Core Solution** from the included source code examples.

Execute the database setup script from the code samples included for this recipe. This can be found in the `DataAccess` project within the `Database` folder.

How to do it...

1. First, we start by adding a new unit test in the `UnitTests` project to define the tests for using a unit of work pattern with the following code:

```
using System;
using System.Linq;
using BusinessLogic;
using DataAccess;
using Moq;
using Xunit;
namespace UnitTests
```

```
{
    public class UnitOfWorkTest : BaseTest
    {
        [Fact]
        public void ShouldReadToDatabaseOnRead()
        {
            //Arrange
            var findCalled = false;
            var mock = new Mock<IDbContext>();
            mock.Setup(x => x.Set<Blog>()).Callback
              (() => findCalled = true);
            var context = mock.Object;
            var unitOfWork = new UnitOfWork(context);
            var repository = new BlogRepository(context);
            //Act
            var blogs = repository.Set();
            //Assert
            Assert.True(findCalled);
        }
        [Fact]
        public void ShouldNotCommitToDatabaseOnDataChange()
        {
            //Arrange
            var saveChangesCalled = false;
            var data = new[] { new Blog() { Id = 1, Title = "Test" }
              }.AsQueryable();
            var mock = new Mock<IDbContext>();
            mock.Setup(x => x.Set<Blog>()).Returns(data);
            mock.Setup(x => x.SaveChanges()).Callback(() =>
            saveChangesCalled = true);
            var context = mock.Object;
            var unitOfWork = new UnitOfWork(context);
            var repository = new BlogRepository(context);
            //Act
            var blogs = repository.Set();
            blogs.First().Title = "Not Going to be Written";
            //Assert
            Assert.False(saveChangesCalled);
        }
        [Fact]
        public void ShouldPullDatabaseValuesOnARollBack()
        {
            //Arrange
            var saveChangesCalled = false;
```

```
        var rollbackCalled = false;
      var data = new[] { new Blog() { Id = 1, Title = "Test" }
        }.AsQueryable();
      var mock = new Mock<IDbContext>();
      mock.Setup(x => x.Set<Blog>()).Returns(data);
      mock.Setup(x => x.SaveChanges()).Callback(() =>
      saveChangesCalled = true);
      mock.Setup(x => x.Rollback()).Callback(() =>
        rollbackCalled = true);
      var context = mock.Object;
      var unitOfWork = new UnitOfWork(context);
      var repository = new BlogRepository(context);
      //Act
      var blogs = repository.Set();
      blogs.First().Title = "Not Going to be Written";
      repository.RollbackChanges();
      //Assert
      Assert.False(saveChangesCalled);
      Assert.True(rollbackCalled);
  }
  [Fact]
  public void ShouldCommitToDatabaseOnSaveCall()
  {
      //Arrange
      var saveChangesCalled = false;
      var data = new[] { new Blog() { Id = 1, Title = "Test" }
        }.AsQueryable();
      var mock = new Mock<IDbContext>();
      mock.Setup(x => x.Set<Blog>()).Returns(data);
        mock.Setup(x => x.SaveChanges()).Callback(() =>
      saveChangesCalled = true);
      var context = mock.Object;
      var unitOfWork = new UnitOfWork(context);
      var repository = new BlogRepository(context);
      //Act
      var blogs = repository.Set();
      blogs.First().Title = "Going to be Written";
      repository.SaveChanges();
      //Assert
      Assert.True(saveChangesCalled);
  }
  [Fact]
  public void ShouldNotCommitOnError()
```

```
        {
            //Arrange
            var rollbackCalled = false;
            var data = new[] { new Blog() { Id = 1, Title = "Test" }
              }.AsQueryable();
            var mock = new Mock<IDbContext>();
            mock.Setup(x => x.Set<Blog>()).Returns(data);
            mock.Setup(x => x.SaveChanges()).Throws(new
              Exception());
            mock.Setup(x => x.Rollback()).Callback(() =>
              rollbackCalled = true);
            var context = mock.Object;
            var unitOfWork = new UnitOfWork(context);
            var repository = new BlogRepository(context);
            //Act
            var blogs = repository.Set();
            blogs.First().Title = "Not Going to be
              Written";
            try
            {
                repository.SaveChanges();
            }
            catch
            {
            }
            //Assert
            Assert.True(rollbackCalled);
        }
    }
}
```

2. In the `DataAccess` project, create a new C# class named `BlogContext` with the following code:

```
using BusinessLogic;
using System.Linq;
using Microsoft.EntityFrameworkCore;
using Microsoft.Extensions.Configuration;
using Microsoft.EntityFrameworkCore.Metadata.Internal;
namespace DataAccess
{
    public class BlogContext : DbContext, IDbContext
    {
```

```
        private readonly string _connectionString;

        public BlogContext(string connectionString)
        {
            _connectionString = connectionString;
        }
        public DbSet<Blog> Blogs { get; set; }
        protected override void OnConfiguring
          (DbContextOptionsBuilder optionsBuilder)
        {
            optionsBuilder.UseSqlServer(_connectionString);
            base.OnConfiguring(optionsBuilder);
        }
        public void Rollback()
        {
            ChangeTracker.Entries().ToList().ForEach(x =>
            {
                x.State = EntityState.Detached;
                var keys = GetEntityKey(x.Entity);
                Set(x.Entity.GetType(), keys);
            });
        }

        public DbSet<T> Set<T>() where T : class
        {
            return Set<T>();
        }

        public object[] GetEntityKey<T>(T entity) where T : class
        {
            var state = Entry(entity);
            var metadata = state.Metadata;
            var key = metadata.FindPrimaryKey();
            var props = key.Properties.ToArray();
            return props.Select(x =>
            x.GetGetter().GetClrValue(entity)).ToArray();
        }
    }
}
```

3. In the `DataAccess` project, create a new C# interface called `IDbContext` with the following code:

```
using System.Linq;
using Microsoft.EntityFrameworkCore;
using Microsoft.EntityFrameworkCore.ChangeTracking;
namespace DataAccess
{
    public interface IDbContext
    {
```

```
        ChangeTracker ChangeTracker { get; }
        DbSet<T> Set<T>() where T : class;
        IQueryable<T> Set<T>() where T : class;
        EntityEntry<T> Entry<T>(T entity) where T : class;
        int SaveChanges();
        void Rollback();
    }
}
```

4. In the `DataAccess` project, create a new C# interface called `IUnitOfWork` with the following code:

```
namespace DataAccess
{
  public interface IUnitOfWork
  {
    void RegisterNew<T>(T entity) where T : class;
    void RegisterUnchanged<T>(T entity) where T : class;
    void RegisterChanged<T>(T entity) where T : class;
    void RegisterDeleted<T>(T entity) where T : class;
    void Refresh();
    void Commit();
    IDbContext Context { get; }
  }
}
```

5. In the `DataAccess` project, add a new C# class named `UnitOfWork` with the following code:

```
using Microsoft.EntityFrameworkCore;
namespace DataAccess
{
  public class UnitOfWork : IUnitOfWork
  {
    public IDbContext Context { get; private set; }
    public UnitOfWork(IDbContext context)
    {
      Context = context;
    }
    public void RegisterNew<T>(T entity) where T : class
    {
      Context.Set<T>().Add(entity);
    }
    public void RegisterUnchanged<T>(T entity) where T : class
    {
```

```
            Context.Entry(entity).State = EntityState.Unchanged;
        }
        public void RegisterChanged<T>(T entity) where T : class
        {
            Context.Entry(entity).State = EntityState.Modified;
        }
        public void RegisterDeleted<T>(T entity) where T : class
        {
            Context.Set<T>().Remove(entity);
        }
        public void Refresh()
        {
            Context.Rollback();
        }
        public void Commit()
        {
            Context.SaveChanges();
        }
    }
}
```

6. Create a new C# file in the `DataAccess` project with this content:

```
using System.Linq;
namespace DataAccess
{
    public interface IRepository<out T> where T : class
    {
        IQueryable<T> Set();
        void RollbackChanges();
        void SaveChanges();
    }
}
```

7. Also in the `DataAccess` project, add a new C# interface named `IBlogRepository` with the following code:

```
using System.Linq;
namespace DataAccess
{
    public interface IBlogRepository : IRepository<Blog>
    {
    }
}
```

8. In the `DataAccess` project, create a new C# class named `BlogRepository` containing the following code:

```csharp
using System.Linq;
using BusinessLogic;
namespace DataAccess
{
  public class BlogRepository : IBlogRepository
  {
    private readonly IUnitOfWork _unitOfWork;
    public BlogRepository(IUnitOfWork unitOfWork)
    {
      _unitOfWork = unitOfWork;
    }
    public IQueryable<Blog> Set
    {
      return _unitOfWork.Context.Set<Blog>();
    }
    public void RollbackChanges()
    {
      _unitOfWork.Refresh();
    }
    public void SaveChanges()
    {
      try
      {
        _unitOfWork.Commit();
      }
      catch (Exception)
      {
        _unitOfWork.Refresh();
        throw;
      }
    }
  }
}
```

9. In `BlogController`, update `BlogContext` to use `IBlogRepository` with the following code:

```csharp
using BusinessLogic;
using System.Linq;
using DataAccess;
using Microsoft.AspNet.Mvc;
using Microsoft.Extensions.Configuration;
namespace UI.Controllers
```

```
    {
      public class BlogController : Controller
      {
        private IBlogRepository _repository;
        public BlogController(IBlogRepository repository)
        {
          _repository = repository;
        }
        //
        // GET: /Blog/
        public IActionResult Index()
        {
          var blog = _repository.Set().First();
          return View(blog);
        }
      }
    }
```

10. Finally, register the `IUnitOfWork` interface in the `Startup.cs` file, in the `ConfigureServices` method:

```
public void ConfigureServices(IServiceCollection services)
{
    services.AddMvc();
        services.AddSingleton<IConfiguration>(_ => Configuration);
        services.AddScoped<IDbContext>(_ => new
         BlogContext(Configuration["Data:Blog:ConnectionString"]));
        services.AddScoped<IBlogRepository>(_ => new
         BlogRepository(_.GetService<IDbContext>()));
        services.AddScoped<IUnitOfWork>(_ => new
         UnitOfWork(_.GetService<IDbContext>()));
}
```

How it works...

The tests set up the scenarios in which we would want to use a unit of work pattern: reading, updating, rolling back, and committing. The key to this is that these are all separate actions, not dependent on anything before or after them. If the application is web-based, this gives you a powerful tool to tie to the HTTP request so any unfinished work is cleaned up, or to ensure that you do not need to call `SaveChanges`, since it can happen automatically.

The unit of work was originally created to track the changes made so they could be persisted, and it functions the same way now. We are using a more powerful, but less recognized, feature defining the scope of the unit of work. We gave the ability to control both scope and the changes that are committed in the database in this scenario. We have also put in some clean-up, which will ensure that even in the event of a failure, our unit of work will try to clean up after itself before throwing the error to be handled at a higher level. We do not want to ignore these errors, but we do want to make sure they do not destroy the integrity of our database.

In addition to this tight encapsulation of work against the database, pass in our unit of work to each repository. This enables us to couple multiple object interactions to a single unit of work. This will allow us to write code that's specific to the object, without giving up the shared feature set of the database context. This is an explicit unit of work, but Entity Framework, in the context, defines it to give you an implicit unit of work. If you want to tie this to the HTTP request, rollback on error, or tie multiple data connections together in new and interesting ways, then you will need to code in an explicit implementation such as this one.

This basic pattern will help to streamline data access, and resolve the concurrency issues caused by conflicts in the objects that are affected by a transaction.

There's more...

The unit of work is a concept that is deep at the heart of Entity Framework and adheres, out of the box, to the principles following it. Knowing these principles, and why they are leveraged, will help us use Entity Framework to its fullest without running into the walls built in the system on purpose.

Call per change

There is a cost for every connection to the database. If we were to make a call to keep the state in the database in sync with the state in the application, we would have thousands of calls, each with connection, security, and network overhead. Limiting the number of times that we hit the database not only allows us to control this overhead, but also allows the database software to handle the larger transactions for which it was built.

Interface Segregation Principle

Some might be inclined to ask why we should separate unit of work from the repository pattern. Unit of work is definitely a separate responsibility from repository, and as such it is important to not only define separate classes, but also to ensure that we keep small, clear interfaces. The `IDbContext` interface is specific in the area of dealing with database connections through an Entity Framework object context. This allows the mocking of a context to give us testability to the lowest possible level.

The `IUnitOfWork` interface deals with the segregation of work, and ensures that the database persistence happens only when we intend it to, ignorant of the layer under it that does the actual commands. The `IRepository` interface deals with selecting objects back from any type of storage, and allows us to remove all thoughts of how the database interaction happens from our dependent code base. These three objects, while related in layers, are separate concerns, and therefore need to be separate interfaces.

Refactoring

We have added `IUnitOfWork` to our layered approach to database communication, and if we have seen anything over the hours of coding, it is code changes. We change it for many reasons, but the bottom line is that code changes often, and we need to make it easy to change. The layers of abstraction that we have added to this solution with `IRepository`, `IUnitOfWork`, and `IDbContext`, have all given us a point at which the change would be minimally painful, and we can leverage the interfaces in the same way. This refactoring to add abstraction levels is a core tenet of clean, extensible code. Removing the concrete implementation details from related objects, and coding to an interface, forces us to encapsulate behavior and abstract our sections of code.

See also

In this chapter:

> ▶ *Implementing the repository pattern*

2
Mapping Entities

In this chapter, we will cover the following topics:

- ► Mapping non-public members
- ► Mapping interfaces
- ► Shadow properties
- ► Creating one-to-one maps
- ► Creating one-to-many maps
- ► Creating many-to-many maps
- ► Creating custom conventions
- ► Using sequence key generators
- ► Using GUIDs as keys
- ► Implementing inheritance–Table per class Hierarchy

Introduction

Object-relational mappers such as Entity Framework rely on mappings to translate Object-oriented concepts—classes, properties, references, inheritance – to the database world – composed of tables and columns – and vice versa. For example, a table normally translates to a .NET class, and its columns translate to the class properties.

Mapping entities and their properties is something that Entity Framework does automatically, and does generally well. There are some cases, however, in which we need to give it a hand. In this chapter, we will have a look at some special cases: it's going to be all about mappings.

Mapping non-public members

A well-encapsulated domain model does not contain just public members. The problem is that Entity Framework automatically maps public properties, but does not do so for non-public ones. In this recipe, we will see how we can map non-public properties of entities, so that Entity Framework recognizes them.

Getting ready

We will be using the NuGet Package Manager to install the Entity Framework Core 1 package, `Microsoft.EntityFrameworkCore`. We will also be using a SQL Server database to store the data, so we will also need `Microsoft.EntityFrameworkCore.SqlServer`.

Finally, `xunit` is the package we will be using for the unit tests, and `dotnet-text-xunit` adds tooling support for Visual Studio. Note that the `UnitTests` project is a .NET Core App 1.0 (netcoreapp1.0), that `Microsoft.EntityFrameworkCore.Design` is configured as a build dependency, and `Microsoft.EntityFrameworkCore.Tools` is set as a tool.

Open **Using EF Core Solution** from the included source code examples.

Execute the database setup script from the code samples included for this recipe. This can be found in the `DataAccess` project within the `Database` folder.

How to do it...

Let's get connected to the database using the following steps:

1. Add a new C# class named `Blog` with the following code to the `BusinessLogic` project (which should be empty):

```
using System;
namespace BusinessLogic
{
  public class Blog
  {
    public int Id { get; set; }
    public string Title { get; set; }
    private DateTime Timestamp { get; set; }
  }
}
```

2. Create a new C# class named `BlogContext` with the following code in the
   `DataAccess` project:

```csharp
using System;
using Microsoft.EntityFrameworkCore;
using BusinessLogic;
namespace DataAccess
{
  public class BlogContext : DbContext
  {
    private readonly string _connectionString;
    public BlogContext(string connectionString)
    {
      _connectionString = connectionString;
    }
    public DbSet<Blog> Blogs { get; set; }
    protected override void OnConfiguring(
    DbContextOptionsBuilder optionsBuilder)
    {
      optionsBuilder
      .UseSqlServer(_connectionString);
      base.OnConfiguring(optionsBuilder);
    }
    protected override void OnModelCreating(
    ModelBuilder modelBuilder)
    {
      modelBuilder.Entity<Blog>().Property(
      typeof (DateTime), "Timestamp").IsRequired();
      base.OnModelCreating(modelBuilder);
    }
  }
}
```

For Entity Framework 6, replace the `Microsoft.EntityFrameworkCore`
namespace with `System.Data.Entity` and call the base constructor
of `DbContext`, passing it the connection string. Finally, drop the
`OnConfiguring` method.

3. Add the following connection string to the `appsettings.json` file:

```
{
   "Data": {
     "Blog": {
       "ConnectionString":"Server=(local)\\SQLEXPRESS;
       Database=Blog;
       Integrated Security=SSPI;
       MultipleActiveResultSets=true"
     }
   }
}
```

> For Entity Framework 6, we would add this connection string to the `Web.config` file, under the `connectionStrings` section, with the name `Blog`. Of course, change the connection string to match your system settings, for example, the name of the SQL Server instance (`SQLEXPRESS`, in this example).

How it works...

Entity Framework offers two method overloads for explicitly mapping or modifying the mapping of a property: one that is strongly typed, and another that isn't. We can't use the strongly typed one, because since we are doing it from a different class, we wouldn't have access to the private properties, so we use the one that takes a .NET type and a property name. Entity Framework will accept the property even if it is not public. The way to explicitly register a property is in the `OnModelCreating` method of `DbContext`. This is an infrastructure method that gets called automatically when the model is being built into memory.

There's more...

As we register our private properties, we can also change their mappings, such as whether maximum length is required or not, and so on.

Please also take into account that you shouldn't define private properties for references to other entities (one-to-one, many-to-one, one-to-many, many-to-many) because doing so will prevent the usage of lazy loading for it. The actual mechanism is beyond the scope of this book, but be warned.

> Although Entity Framework Core 1.0 does not support lazy loading, future versions will, and so it is recommended that you take it in consideration.

See also

In this chapter:

- ▸ *Shadow properties*
- ▸ *Mapping interfaces*

The official documentation for Entity Framework Core is located at `https://docs.efproject.net/en/latest/`.

Mapping interfaces

Other than mapping whole classes, it is also possible to define attributes of properties that are, for example, defined in interfaces. This kind of mapping could apply to several classes, all those that implement the given interface.

Getting ready

We will be using the NuGet Package Manager to install the Entity Framework Core 1 package, `Microsoft.EntityFrameworkCore`. We will also be using a SQL Server database to store the data, so we will also need `Microsoft.EntityFrameworkCore.SqlServer`.

Finally, `xunit` is the package we will be using for the unit tests, and `dotnet-text-xunit` adds tooling support for Visual Studio. Note that the `UnitTests` project is a .NET Core App 1.0 (netcoreapp1.0), that `Microsoft.EntityFrameworkCore.Design` is configured as a build dependency, and `Microsoft.EntityFrameworkCore.Tools` is set as a tool.

Open **Using EF Core Solution** from the included source code examples.

Execute the database setup script from the code samples included for this recipe. This can be found in the `DataAccess` project within the `Database` folder.

How to do it...

Let's get connected to the database using the following steps:

1. Add a C# marker interface called `IAuditable` to the blank `BusinessLogic` project:

```
namespace BusinessLogic
{
    public interface IAuditable { }
}
```

2. Add a new C# class named `Blog` with the following code to the `BusinessLogic` project:

```
using System;
namespace BusinessLogic
{
  public class Blog : IAuditable
  {
    public int Id { get; set; }
    public string Title { get; set; }
  }
}
```

3. Now we define the `BlogContext` class, in a file of the same name, in the `DataAccess` project:

```
using Microsoft.EntityFrameworkCore;
using BusinessLogic;
using System;
using System.Reflection;
namespace DataAccess
{
  public class BlogContext : DbContext
  {
    private readonly string _connectionString;
    public BlogContext(string connectionString)
    {
      _connectionString = connectionString;
    }
    public DbSet<Blog> Blogs { get; set; }
    protected override void OnConfiguring
      (DbContextOptionsBuilder optionsBuilder)
    {
      optionsBuilder.UseSqlServer(_connectionString);
      base.OnConfiguring(optionsBuilder);
    }
    protected override void OnModelCreating(ModelBuilder
      modelBuilder)
    {
      modelBuilder.Entity<Blog>().Property(typeof(DateTime),
        "Timestamp").IsRequired();
      foreach (var entityType in modelBuilder.Model.
        GetEntityTypes())
      {
        if (typeof(IAuditable).IsAssignableFrom(entityType.
          ClrType))
        {
          modelBuilder.Entity(entityType.ClrType)
            .Property(typeof(string),
              "CreatedBy").HasMaxLength(50).IsRequired();
```

```
            modelBuilder.Entity(entityType.ClrType)
                .Property(typeof(string),
                "UpdatedBy").HasMaxLength(50).IsRequired();
            modelBuilder.Entity(entityType.ClrType)
                .Property(typeof(DateTime),
                "CreatedOn").IsRequired();
            modelBuilder.Entity(entityType.ClrType)
                .Property(typeof(DateTime),
                "UpdatedOn").IsRequired();
        }
    }
    base.OnModelCreating(modelBuilder);
    }
  }
}
```

 For Entity Framework 6, replace the `Microsoft.EntityFrameworkCore` namespace with `System.Data.Entity` and call the base constructor of `DbContext`, passing it the connection string. Finally, drop the `OnConfiguring` method.

4. Add the following connection string to the `appsettings.json` file:

```
{
    "Data": {
        "Blog": {
            "ConnectionString":"Server=(local)\\SQLEXPRESS;
            Database=Blog;
            Integrated Security=SSPI; MultipleActiveResultSets=true"
        }
    }
}
```

 For Entity Framework 6, we would add this connection string to the `Web.config` file, in the `connectionStrings` section, with the name `Blog`. Of course, change the connection string to match your system settings, for example, the name of the SQL Server instance (`SQLEXPRESS`, in this example).

How it works...

The OnModelCreating method is called by Entity Framework to give developers a chance to change the model for the entities that it will be managing. In it, we look for entities that implement the IAuditable interface and we set some attributes for its properties (maximum length, required). This doesn't prevent us from explicitly setting additional attributes for specific entities implementing IAuditable (such as Blog), but for those, the problem is already solved. Following is the diagram showing IAuditable interface and Blog class:

Auditable class and interface

See also

In this chapter:

- *Mapping shadow properties*
- *Mapping interfaces*

Shadow properties

Going one step further from private properties, in a well-defined model, it may make sense to hide certain properties from the developers so that they do not make unwanted changes to them, consciously or not.

Historically, Entity Framework, like most ORMs, has three models:

- **POCO model**: This represents the .NET classes and their properties and references
- **Database model**: This represents the tables, views, and columns (in the case of relational data stores) where data is actually stored
- **Mapping model**: This model binds the two preceding models; this is where we say that the MyEntity class is to be stored in the MY_ENTITY table and the Id property goes into the MY_ENTITY_ID column

Entity Framework used to call these models *Conceptual Model*, *Storage Model*, and *Mapping Model*. If you are curious, refer to the following link: `https://msdn.microsoft.com/en-us/data/jj650889`.

So, what we are looking for is a way to have a backing data store for entities and properties that does not reflect in the POCO classes. Enter shadow properties.

A shadow property is not reflected in a class, so, it is virtually impossible – unless you know what you are doing and where to look for it – to set or change the values for it. A typical use case could be auditing properties: `CreatedBy`, `CreatedOn`, `UpdatedBy`, and `UpdatedOn`; we want these to always be controlled by the infrastructure, not the developers.

Getting ready

We will be using the NuGet Package Manager to install the Entity Framework Core 1 package, `Microsoft.EntityFrameworkCore`. We will also be using a SQL Server database to store the data, so we will also need `Microsoft.EntityFrameworkCore.SqlServer`.

Finally, `xunit` is the package we will be using for the unit tests, and `dotnet-text-xunit` adds tooling support for Visual Studio. Note that the `UnitTests` project is a .NET Core App 1.0 (netcoreapp1.0), that `Microsoft.EntityFrameworkCore.Design` is configured as a build dependency, and `Microsoft.EntityFrameworkCore.Tools` is set as a tool.

Open **Using EF Core Solution** from the included source code examples.

Execute the database setup script from the code samples included for this recipe. This can be found in the `DataAccess` project within the `Database` folder.

How to do it...

Let's get connected to the database using the following steps:

1. Add a C# marker interface called `IAuditable` to the `BusinessLogic` project, which should initially be empty:

    ```
    namespace BusinessLogic
    {
      public interface IAuditable { }
    }
    ```

2. Add a new C# class named `Blog` with the following code to the `BusinessLogic` project:

```csharp
namespace BusinessLogic
{
  public class Blog : IAuditable
  {
    public int Id { get; set; }
    public string Title { get; set; }
  }
}
```

3. Create a new C# class named `BlogContext` with the following code in the `DataAccess` project:

```csharp
using Microsoft.EntityFrameworkCore;
using BusinessLogic;
using System;
using System.Linq;
using System.Reflection;
using System.Security.Principal;

namespace DataAccess
{
  public class BlogContext : DbContext
  {
    private readonly string _connectionString;
    public BlogContext(string connectionString)
    {
      _connectionString = connectionString;
    }
    public Func<string> GetCurrentUser { get; set; } =
      () => WindowsIdentity.GetCurrent().Name;
    public Func<DateTime> GetCurrentTimestamp
      { get; set; } = () => DateTime.UtcNow;
    public DbSet<Blog> Blogs { get; set; }
    public override int SaveChanges()
    {
      foreach (var entry in ChangeTracker.Entries()
        .Where(e => (e.Entity is IAuditable) &&
        (e.State == EntityState.Added) ||
        (e.State == EntityState.Modified)))
      {
        entry.Property(Auditable.UpdatedBy)
          .CurrentValue = GetCurrentUser();
        entry.Property(Auditable.UpdatedOn)
          .CurrentValue = GetCurrentTimestamp();
        if (entry.State == EntityState.Added)
        {
          entry.Property(Auditable.CreatedBy)
```

```
        .CurrentValue = GetCurrentUser();
      entry.Property(Auditable.CreatedOn)
        .CurrentValue = GetCurrentTimestamp();
    }
  }
  return base.SaveChanges();
}
protected override void OnConfiguring
  (DbContextOptionsBuilder optionsBuilder)
{
  optionsBuilder.UseSqlServer(_connectionString);
  base.OnConfiguring(optionsBuilder);
}
protected override void OnModelCreating(ModelBuilder
  modelBuilder)
{
  modelBuilder.Entity<Blog>().Property(
    typeof(DateTime), "Timestamp").IsRequired();
  foreach (var entityType in modelBuilder.Model.
    GetEntityTypes())
  {
    if (typeof(IAuditable).IsAssignableFrom(
      entityType.ClrType))
    {
      modelBuilder.Entity(entityType.ClrType)
        .Property(typeof(string),
        Auditable.CreatedBy).HasMaxLength(50).IsRequired();
      modelBuilder.Entity(entityType.ClrType)
        .Property(typeof(string),
        Auditable.UpdatedBy).HasMaxLength(50).IsRequired();
      modelBuilder.Entity(entityType.ClrType)
        .Property(typeof(DateTime),
        Auditable.CreatedOn).IsRequired();
      modelBuilder.Entity(entityType.ClrType)
        .Property(typeof(DateTime),
        Auditable.UpdatedOn).IsRequired();
    }
  }
  base.OnModelCreating(modelBuilder);
}
  }
}
```

For Entity Framework 6, replace the `Microsoft.EntityFrameworkCore` namespace with `System.Data.Entity` and call the base constructor of `DbContext`, passing it the connection string. Finally, drop the `OnConfiguring` method.

4. Add the following connection string to the `appsettings.json` file:

```
{
  "Data": {
    "Blog": {
      "ConnectionString":"Server=(local)\\SQLEXPRESS;
      Database=Blog;
      Integrated Security=SSPI; MultipleActiveResultSets=true"
    }
  }
}
```

 For Entity Framework 6, we would add this connection string to the `Web.config` file, under the `connectionStrings` section, with the name `Blog`. Of course, change the connection string to match your system settings, for example, the name of the SQL Server instance (`SQLEXPRESS`, in this example).

How it works...

Remember that the `OnModelCreating` method is called the first time the `DbContext` is used to connect to the data store. It offers a chance to revise or update the model that Entity Framework will use. In this case, we are iterating through all of the mapped entities, sorting out those that implement `IAuditable`, and, for those, we are registering a bunch of audit properties. Note that these properties are not reflected in the `IAuditable` interface, but we know they are there: the `SaveChanges` method, again, iterates through all the entity instances waiting to be persisted (added or modified) and sets the auditing values explicitly. There are two properties, `GetCurrentUser` and `GetCurrentTimestamp`, that are used to return the current user and the current timestamp: out of the box, these return the Windows account running the code and the current date and time in UTC format, respectively. The values returned from these properties are used to fill the properties in the `IAuditable` implementation. For querying shadow properties, the syntax is somewhat cumbersome, as we need to use the `EF` static class, which isn't exactly intuitive. There's no other way, though, since there are no backing properties that we can use. Following is the diagram showing `IAuditable` interface being implemented by the `Blog` class:

Blog class implementing the IAuditable interface

See also

In this chapter:

- ▸ *Mapping non-public members*
- ▸ *Mapping interfaces*

You can read more about shadow properties on the official Entity Framework Core documentation site: `https://docs.efproject.net/en/latest/modeling/shadow-properties.html`.

Creating one-to-one maps

Entities can be related to each other in different ways. A one-to-one relation is one where each individual entity may be related to another, and this other one, if it exists, is directly related to the first. Examples include the following:

- ▸ A relation from a person to their address, assuming that no two people share the same address
- ▸ Additional details for an order
- ▸ A person and their pet
- ▸ A country and its head of state

A one-to-one relation is easy to represent in domain model terms: each of the entities has a reference to the other. Only one side can be made required; otherwise, we would have a problem: which one comes first? Let's see how we can map this kind of relation in Entity Framework Core.

Getting ready

We will be using the NuGet Package Manager to install the Entity Framework Core 1 package, `Microsoft.EntityFrameworkCore`. We will also be using a SQL Server database to store the data, so we will also need `Microsoft.EntityFrameworkCore.SqlServer`.

Finally, `xunit` is the package we will be using for the unit tests, and `dotnet-text-xunit` adds tooling support for Visual Studio. Note that the `UnitTests` project is a .NET Core App 1.0 (netcoreapp1.0), that `Microsoft.EntityFrameworkCore.Design` is configured as a build dependency, and `Microsoft.EntityFrameworkCore.Tools` is set as a tool.

Open **Using EF Core Solution** from the included source code examples.

Execute the database setup script from the code samples included for this recipe. This can be found in the `DataAccess` project within the `Database` folder.

How to do it...

Let's create a one-to-one relation by following these easy steps:

1. Add a class named `Blog` to the `BusinessLogic` project:

    ```
    namespace BusinessLogic
    {
      public class Blog
      {
        public int BlogId { get; set; }
        public string Title { get; set; }
        public BlogDetail Detail { get; set; }
      }
    }
    ```

2. Add another class, this time, `BlogDetail`, to the same project:

    ```
    using System;
    namespace BusinessLogic
    {
      public class BlogDetail
      {
        public int BlogId { get; set; }
        public Blog Blog { get; set; }
        public DateTime CreatedOn { get; set; }
        public string Description { get; set; }
        public string Url { get; set; }
      }
    }
    ```

3. Now, we need to add the mapping logic. Add a class called `BlogContext` to the `DataAccess` project:

```
using Microsoft.EntityFrameworkCore;
using BusinessLogic;
using System;
using System.Linq;
using System.Reflection;
using Microsoft.EntityFrameworkCore.Metadata;

namespace DataAccess
{
  public class BlogContext : DbContext
  {
    private readonly string _connectionString;
    public BlogContext(string connectionString)
    {
      _connectionString = connectionString;
    }
    public DbSet<Blog> Blogs { get; set; }
    protected override void OnConfiguring(
      DbContextOptionsBuilder optionsBuilder)
    {
      optionsBuilder.UseSqlServer(_connectionString);
      base.OnConfiguring(optionsBuilder);
    }
    protected override void OnModelCreating(
      ModelBuilder modelBuilder)
    {
      modelBuilder
        .Entity<BlogDetail>()
        .HasKey(b => b.BlogId);
      modelBuilder.Entity<BlogDetail>()
        .HasOne(b => b.Blog)
        .WithOne(b => b.Detail)
        .IsRequired();
      modelBuilder
        .Entity<Blog>()
        .HasOne(b => b.Detail)
        .WithOne(d => d.Blog).OnDelete
          (DeleteBehavior.Cascade);
      base.OnModelCreating(modelBuilder);
    }
  }
}
```

For Entity Framework 6, replace the `Microsoft.EntityFrameworkCore` namespace with `System.Data.Entity` and call the base constructor of `DbContext`, passing it the connection string. Finally, drop the `OnConfiguring` method.

4. Add the following connection string to the `appsettings.json` file:

```
{
  "Data": {
    "Blog": {
      "ConnectionString":"Server=(local)\\SQLEXPRESS;
      Database=Blog;
      Integrated Security=SSPI; MultipleActiveResultSets=true"
    }
  }
}
```

 For Entity Framework 6, we would add this connection string to the `Web.config` file, under the `connectionStrings` section, with the name `Blog`. Of course, change the connection string to match your system settings, for example, the name of the SQL Server instance (`SQLEXPRESS`, in this example).

How it works...

We explicitly tell our `BlogContext` via fluent mapping that the `Blog` entity has a one-to-one relation with `BlogDetail`; that is done in the `OnModelCreating` infrastructure method. We say that `BlogDetail` shares the same key as `Blog` (`BlogId`), and that when a `Blog` is deleted, it will cascade to its `Detail` (`WillCascadeOnDelete`). This cascading is very important, because `BlogDetail` doesn't make sense without `Blog`. On the `BlogDetail` entity, the `Blog` property is mandatory. The following diagram shows a one-to-one relation between `Blog` and `BlogDetail`:

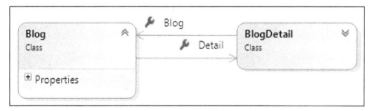

One-to-one relation

There's more...

Cascade deletes are something that we cannot configure using attributes; we always have to use fluent mapping.

See also

In this chapter:

- *Creating one-to-many maps*
- *Creating many-to-many maps*

Relationships are described in the official documentation: `https://docs.efproject.net/en/latest/modeling/relationships.html`. Cascade deletes are there too: `https://docs.efproject.net/en/latest/saving/cascade-delete.html`.

Creating one-to-many maps

When an entity can be associated with one or more entities of another type, and each of these entities is associated with at most one entity of the first type, we call that one-to-many. It is one of the more basic kinds of relation, and, if looked at from the other endpoint, it becomes a many-to-one relation. Some examples of this include the following:

- A blog and its posts
- A parent and their children
- A folder and its sub-folders
- An order and its details (items included)

You may notice that there is one difference: in some of these relations, the *many* side cannot exist without the *one*—for example, a child without a parent–while in others, it can—there can be a folder without a parent folder.

This is easy to represent in the domain model; the *one* side holds a collection of entities of the *many* side, and the *many* side holds a reference to an entity on the *one* side. Pretty simple.

Getting ready

We will be using the NuGet Package Manager to install the Entity Framework Core 1 package, `Microsoft.EntityFrameworkCore`. We will also be using a SQL Server database to store the data, so we will also need `Microsoft.EntityFrameworkCore.SqlServer`.

Finally, `xunit` is the package we will be using for the unit tests, and `dotnet-text-xunit` adds tooling support for Visual Studio. Note that the `UnitTests` project is a .NET Core App 1.0 (netcoreapp1.0), that `Microsoft.EntityFrameworkCore.Design` is configured as a build dependency, and `Microsoft.EntityFrameworkCore.Tools` is set as a tool.

Open **Using EF Core Solution** from the included source code examples.

Execute the database setup script from the code samples included for this recipe. This can be found in the `DataAccess` project within the `Database` folder.

How to do it...

Let's create a one-to-one relation by following these easy steps:

1. Add a class named `Blog` to the `BusinessLogic` project:

```
using System.Collections.Generic;
namespace BusinessLogic
{
  public class Blog
  {
    public int BlogId { get; set; }
    public string Title { get; set; }
    public ICollection<Post> Posts { get; private set; } = new
      HashSet<Post>();
  }
}
```

2. Add another class, `Post`, to the same project, in a new file:

```
using System;
namespace BusinessLogic
{
  public class Post
  {
    public int PostId { get; set; }
    public string Title { get; set; }
    public DateTime Timestamp { get; set; }
    public string Body { get; set; }
    public Blog Blog { get; set; }
  }
}
```

3. Now, we need to add the context. Add a class called `BlogContext` to the `DataAccess` project:

```
using Microsoft.EntityFrameworkCore;
using BusinessLogic;
```

```
namespace DataAccess
{
  public class BlogContext : DbContext
  {
    private readonly string _connectionString;
    public BlogContext(string connectionString)
    {
      _connectionString = connectionString;
    }
    public DbSet<Blog> Blogs { get; set; }
    protected override void OnConfiguring(
    DbContextOptionsBuilder optionsBuilder)
    {
      optionsBuilder
      .UseSqlServer(_connectionString);
      base.OnConfiguring(optionsBuilder);
    }
    protected override void OnModelCreating(
    ModelBuilder modelBuilder)
    {
      modelBuilder
        .Entity<Post>()
        .HasOne(p => p.Blog)
        .WithMany(b => b.Posts)
        .Is Required();
        base.OnModelCreating(modelBuilder);
    }
  }
}
```

 For Entity Framework 6, replace the `Microsoft.
EntityFrameworkCore` namespace with `System.Data.Entity` and
call the base constructor of `DbContext`, passing it the connection string.
Finally, drop the `OnConfiguring` method.

4. Add the following connection string to the `appsettings.json` file:

```
{
  "Data":{
    "Blog":{
      "ConnectionString":"Server=(local)\\SQLEXPRESS;
      Database=Blog;
      Integrated Security=SSPI; MultipleActiveResultSets=true"
    }
  }
}
```

For Entity Framework 6, we would add this connection string to the `Web.config` file, under the `connectionStrings` section, with the name `Blog`. Of course, change the connection string to match your system settings, for example, the name of the SQL Server instance (`SQLEXPRESS`, in this example).

How it works...

We explicitly tell our `BlogContext` via fluent mapping, that the entity `Blog` has a one-to-one relation with `BlogDetail`; that is done in the infrastructure method `OnModelCreating`. We say that `BlogDetail` shares the same key as `Blog` (`BlogId`), and that when a `Blog` is deleted, it will cascade to its `Detail` (`WillCascadeOnDelete`). This is very important, because the `BlogDetail` entity doesn't make sense without the `Blog` property. On the `BlogDetail` entity, I marked the `Blog` property as mandatory (`Required`), but that really depends on the use case. Remember, a folder may not necessarily have a parent – the root folder – but a child needs a parent. Depending on your use case, you may or not need to mark the *one* side as required. Related to that is `WillCascadeOnDelete`; it doesn't make sense to cascade deletes if the *many* side can live without the *one*. In summary, `Required` and `WillCascadeOnDelete` go together; if you do not need one, you shouldn't need the other. The following diagram shows a one-to-many relation between `Blog` and `Post`:

One-to-many relationship

There's more...

We can use attributes to indicate to Entity Framework that one side of the relationship is required:

```
using System;
namespace BusinessLogic
{
  public class Post
  {
    public int PostId { get; set; }
    public string Title { get; set; }
    public DateTime Timestamp { get; set; }
    public string Body { get; set; }
```

```
        [Required]
        public Blog Blog { get; set; }
    }
}
```

Also, notice the `Posts` property in the `Blog` class using a weird syntax. Basically, I defined a private setter and I am initializing it as `HashSet`. This is because it rarely makes sense to replace the collection altogether, just adding items to it is easier. `HashSet` ensures there is no duplication of items, and I initialize it beforehand so that it can be immediately used – it comes as a consequence of having the private setter.

 The initialization syntax for automatic properties was introduced in C# 6.

See also

In this chapter:

- *Creating one-to-many maps*
- *Creating many-to-many maps*

Creating many-to-many maps

A many-to-many relation is another of those "canonical" ones. Essentially, each entity on one of the sides can be associated with many entities on the other side, and this goes the other way too. Just think of these use cases:

- A post and its tags, where a tag can have multiple posts and a post multiple tags
- Books and authors
- Projects and developers

Usually, a many-to-many relation is easy to represent in classes: each side holds a collection of entities of the other side. In Entity Framework Core, however, things are not so simple. I'm sorry to break this to you, but as it happens, many-to-many relations are not supported! Do not be alarmed, though, there's still something we can do about it! This was a change from previous versions (Entity Framework 6.x) and one that will certainly be fixed. In the meantime, let's get it working.

 In Entity Framework Core, many-to-many relations are simulated with a middle entity. This even allows you to have additional attributes in it.

Getting ready

We will be using the NuGet Package Manager to install the Entity Framework Core 1 package, `Microsoft.EntityFrameworkCore`. We will also be using a SQL Server database to store the data, so we will also need `Microsoft.EntityFrameworkCore.SqlServer`.

Finally, `xunit` is the package we will be using for the unit tests, and `dotnet-text-xunit` adds tooling support for Visual Studio. Note that the `UnitTests` project is a .NET Core App 1.0 (netcoreapp1.0), that `Microsoft.EntityFrameworkCore.Design` is configured as a build dependency, and `Microsoft.EntityFrameworkCore.Tools` is set as a tool.

Open **Using EF Core Solution** from the included source code examples.

Execute the database setup script from the code samples included for this recipe. This can be found in the `DataAccess` project within the `Database` folder.

How to do it...

Let's represent a many-to-many relation of posts and tags:

1. Add a class named `Blog` to the `BusinessLogic` project:

```csharp
using System.Collections.Generic;
namespace BusinessLogic
{
  public class Blog
  {
    public int BlogId { get; set; }
    public string Title { get; set; }
    public ICollection<Post> Posts { get; private set; } = new
      HashSet<Post>();
  }
}
```

2. Add another class, `Post`, to the same project, in a new file:

```csharp
using System;
using System.Collections.Generic;
namespace BusinessLogic
{
  public class Post
  {
    public int PostId { get; set; }
    public string Title { get; set; }
    public DateTime Timestamp { get; set; }
    public string Body { get; set; }
    public Blog Blog { get; set; }
```

```
        public ICollection<PostTag> Tags { get; private set; } = new
          HashSet<PostTag>();
    }
}
```

3. Now let's add the `Tag` class, again in the `BusinessLogic` project:

```
using System.Collections.Generic;
namespace BusinessLogic
{
  public class Tag
  {
    public int TagId { get; set; }
    public string Name { get; set; }
    public ICollection<PostTag> Tags { get; private set; } = new
      HashSet<PostTag>();
  }
}
```

4. Finally, add the mapping class, `PostTag`:

```
namespace BusinessLogic
{
  public class PostTag
  {
    public int PostId { get; set; }
    public Post Post { get; set; }
    public int TagId { get; set; }
    public Tag Tag { get; set; }
  }
}
```

5. Now, we need to add the context and tie everything together. Add a class called `BlogContext`, this time to the `DataAccess` project:

```
using Microsoft.EntityFrameworkCore;
using BusinessLogic;
namespace DataAccess
{
  public class BlogContext : DbContext
  {
    private readonly string _connectionString;
    public BlogContext(string connectionString)
    {
      _connectionString = connectionString;
    }
    public DbSet<Blog> Blogs { get; set; }
    protected override void OnConfiguring(
```

```
DbContextOptionsBuilder optionsBuilder)
{
  optionsBuilder
  .UseSqlServer(_connectionString);
  base.OnConfiguring(optionsBuilder);
}
protected override void OnModelCreating(
ModelBuilder modelBuilder)
{
  modelBuilder
    .Entity<Tag>();
  modelBuilder
    .Entity<PostTag>()
    .HasKey(x => new { x.PostId, x.TagId });
  modelBuilder
    .Entity<Post>()
    .HasMany(p => p.Tags)
    .WithOne(t => t.Post)
    .OnDelete(DeleteBehavior.Cascade)
    .IsRequired();
  modelBuilder
    .Entity<Tag>()
    .HasMany(t => t.Tags)
    .WithOne(p => p.Tag)
    .OnDelete(DeleteBehavior.Cascade)
    .IsRequired();
  base.OnModelCreating(modelBuilder);
}
  }
}
```

 For Entity Framework 6, replace the `Microsoft.EntityFrameworkCore` namespace with `System.Data.Entity` and call the base constructor of `DbContext`, passing it the connection string. Finally, drop the `OnConfiguring` method.

6. Add the following connection string to the `appsettings.json` file:

```
{
  "Data": {
    "Blog": {
      "ConnectionString":"Server=(local)\\SQLEXPRESS;
      Database=Blog;
      Integrated Security=SSPI; MultipleActiveResultSets=true"
    }
  }
}
```

For Entity Framework 6, we would add this connection string to the `Web.config` file, under the `connectionStrings` section, with the name `Blog`. Of course, change the connection string to match your system settings, for example, the name of the SQL Server instance (`SQLEXPRESS`, in this example).

How it works...

Entity Framework Core does not support many-to-many relations, period. To get around this limitation, we need to replace our many-to-many with two many-to-ones, and have an entity in the middle (the "one") that continues the relation to the other end. In essence, we are bringing to the domain model exactly the same configuration we have in the database model. Remember that a many-to-many relation always needs a middle or mapping table in between the related tables. That's exactly the point of the `PostTag` class. Arguably, with this approach, we have a benefit: we can add some payload to the "mapping" entity (`PostTag`), such as some attributes that enrich this relation. `PostTag` has a composite primary key, which consists of both the `PostId` and the `TagId` attributes. Cascade mapping is required in this case, because we don't want to have "orphaned" `PostTag` entities. We need to explicitly tell Entity Framework to map the `Tag` class, because, since it isn't a root aggregate, there is no collection for it in the `BlogContext` class, and therefore Entity Framework knows nothing about it. The following diagram shows the many-to-many relation between `Tag`, `PostTag` and `Post`:

Many-to-many relationship with a middle entity

There's more...

You may like to know that Entity Framework Core automatically detects one-to-many relations so there is no mapping configuration required: all it takes is to have, on one side, a collection of entities, and on this other entity, a reference to the entity on the other side.

See also

In this chapter:

- *Creating one-to-one maps*
- *Creating one-to-many maps*

Creating custom conventions

Entity Framework Code First (4.1) introduced mapping conventions. Basically, Entity Framework would figure out certain patterns from the domain model and would configure things appropriately. In subsequent versions, these conventions were made customizable, meaning one could define and apply bespoke ones for our specific use cases. This is very useful, because it prevents us from writing the same code over and over. Some examples of custom conventions might include the following:

- ▸ Defining the maximum length for string properties
- ▸ Showing whether certain properties are mandatory or not
- ▸ Automatically setting cascading behaviors

Unfortunately, version 1.0 of Entity Framework Core dropped this; fortunately, it is still possible to achieve with some extra work.

Getting ready

We will be using the NuGet Package Manager to install the Entity Framework Core 1 package, `Microsoft.EntityFrameworkCore`. We will also be using a SQL Server database to store the data, so we will also need `Microsoft.EntityFrameworkCore.SqlServer`.

Finally, `xunit` is the package we will be using for the unit tests, and `dotnet-text-xunit` adds tooling support for Visual Studio. Note that the `UnitTests` project is a .NET Core App 1.0 (netcoreapp1.0), that `Microsoft.EntityFrameworkCore.Design` is configured as a build dependency, and `Microsoft.EntityFrameworkCore.Tools` is set as a tool.

Open **Using EF Core Solution** from the included source code examples.

Execute the database setup script from the code samples included for this recipe. This can be found in the `DataAccess` project within the `Database` folder.

How to do it...

Let's represent a many-to-many relation of posts and tags:

1. Add a class named `Blog` to the `BusinessLogic` project:

```
using System.Collections.Generic;
namespace BusinessLogic
{
  public class Blog
  {
    public int BlogId { get; set; }
    public string Title { get; set; }
```

```
    public ICollection<Post> Posts { get; private set; } = new
      HashSet<Post>();
  }
}
```

2. Add another class, `Post`, to the same project, in a new file:

```
namespace BusinessLogic
{
  public class Post
  {
    public int PostId { get; set; }
    public string Title { get; set; }
    public DateTime Timestamp { get; set; }
    public string Body { get; set; }
    public Blog Blog { get; set; }
  }
}
```

3. Let's now define our convention interface. Add a file named `IConvention.cs` to the `DataAccess` project with the following content:

```
using Microsoft.EntityFrameworkCore;
namespace DataAccess.Conventions
{
  public interface IConvention
  {
    void Apply(ModelBuilder modelBuilder);
  }
}
```

4. We'll also create a custom convention, for defining the maximum length of string properties. Add a `StringLengthConvention` class to `DataAccess`:

```
using System.Linq;
using Microsoft.EntityFrameworkCore;
namespace DataAccess.Conventions
{
  public sealed class StringLengthConvention : IConvention
  {
    internal const string MaxLengthAnnotation = "MaxLength";
    internal const int DefaultStringLength = 50;
    public static readonly IConvention Instance = new
      StringLengthConvention();
    public void Apply(ModelBuilder modelBuilder)
    {
      foreach (var entity in modelBuilder.Model.GetEntityTypes())
      {
```

```
            foreach (var property in entity.GetProperties().Where(p =>
             p.ClrType == typeof(string)))
            {
              var maxLength = property
              .FindAnnotation(MaxLengthAnnotation);
              if (maxLength == null)
              {
                maxLength = property
                .AddAnnotation
                (MaxLengthAnnotation,
                DefaultStringLength);
              }
            }
          }
        }
      }
    }
}
```

5. Now, we need to add the context and use this convention. Add a class called `BlogContext` to the `DataAccess` project:

```
using System.Collections.Generic;
using Microsoft.EntityFrameworkCore;
using BusinessLogic;
using BusinessLogic.Conventions;
namespace DataAccess
{
  public class BlogContext : DbContext, IDbContextConventions
  {
    private readonly string _connectionString;
    public BlogContext(string connectionString)
    {
      _connectionString = connectionString;
      Conventions
      .Add(StringLengthConvention.Instance);
    }
    public ISet<IConvention> Conventions { get; private set; } =
      new HashSet<IConvention>();
    public DbSet<Blog> Blogs { get; set; }
    protected override void OnConfiguring(
    DbContextOptionsBuilder optionsBuilder)
    {
      optionsBuilder
      .UseSqlServer(_connectionString);
      base.OnConfiguring(optionsBuilder);
    }
```

```
      protected void ApplyConventions(
      ModelBuilder modelBuilder)
      {
        foreach (var convention in Conventions)
        {
          convention.Apply(modelBuilder);
        }
      }
      protected override void OnModelCreating(
      ModelBuilder modelBuilder)
      {
        ApplyConventions(modelBuilder);
        base.OnModelCreating(modelBuilder);
      }
    }
  }
```

 For Entity Framework 6, replace the `Microsoft.`
`EntityFrameworkCore` namespace with `System.Data.Entity`
and call the base constructor of `DbContext`, passing it the connection
string. Finally, drop the `OnConfiguring` method.

6. The final piece is the `IDbContextConventions` interface; add it to a new file in
   `DataAccess`:

```
using System.Collections.Generic;
namespace DataAccess.Conventions
{
  public interface IDbContextConventions
  {
    ISet<IConvention> Conventions { get; }
  }
}
```

7. Add the following connection string to the `appsettings.json` file:

```
{
  "Data": {
    "Blog": {
      "ConnectionString":"Server=(local)\\SQLEXPRESS;
      Database=Blog;
      Integrated Security=SSPI; MultipleActiveResultSets=true"
    }
  }
}
```

For Entity Framework 6, we would add this connection string to the `Web.config` file, under the `connectionStrings` section, with the name `Blog`. Of course, change the connection string to match your system settings, for example, the name of the SQL Server instance (`SQLEXPRESS`, in this example).

How it works...

The point where we can define the mapping is in the `OnModelCreating` infrastructure method; here, we have a reference to the `ModelBuilder` class, which is the place where all of it goes, and allows us to check what we already have configured. We define an interface, `IConvention`, with a single method that takes a `ModelBuilder` instance as a parameter, so that we can do in it the same way we would in `OnModelCreating`. We have a class, `StringLengthConvention`, that checks, by looking at annotations, if all string properties are missing a maximum length setting, and in that case, it adds one. Then, the `BlogContext` is set to have a collection of conventions, which it applies one by one in `OnModelCreating`; because we add a `StringLengthConvention` instance in the `BlogContext` constructor, it will always be applied. The `IDbContextConventions` interface is somewhat unnecessary, but I still see value in having it to signal that the context applies conventions. Finally, in case you are wondering, I created a public static field in `StringLengthConvention` because there really is no need – although it is harmless – to have multiple instances of this class, since it holds no state. The following diagram shows convention classes and interfaces:

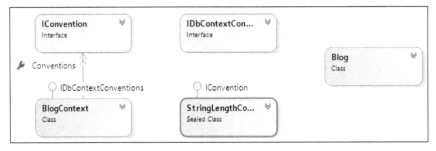

Convention classes and interfaces

There's more...

All of the mapping code that we added in the previous chapter can be easily turned into conventions, but you should refrain from doing so for specific cases: for example, in my view, it makes no sense to tie `Posts` to `Tags`, because these are specific to the model, but it might make sense to look for properties implementing specific interfaces or inheriting from a well-known base class. `ModelBuilder` exposes the model Entity Framework knows about in its `Model` property.

Finally, with the approach outlined here, we have the choice of having DbContext-derived classes adding their own, default conventions, or adding these from the outside.

See also

In this chapter:

- *Creating shadow properties*
- *Mapping interfaces*
- *Creating one-to-one maps*
- *Creating one-to-many maps*
- *Creating many-to-many maps*

Using sequence key generators

Historically, Entity Framework offered two ways to handle primary key generation:

- Using the SQL Server IDENTITY mechanism
- Manually setting the key

There are several problems with this approach. One is that the IDENTITY mechanism really only works in SQL Server, although similar features exist in other RDBMs, such as the MySQL AUTOINCREMENT. Another one is that the ORM, because it doesn't know the key to be inserted beforehand, needs to get into some trouble to figure it out after a record is inserted. Finally, there are far more efficient and flexible mechanisms that do not rely on a specific database engine, such as the **High-Low algorithm**.

Knowing this, Microsoft took a step forward and introduced an implementation of High-Low in Entity Framework Core 1. The downside to it is that, for now at least, it requires SQL Server 2012: the way it was implemented is dependent on sequences that were only introduced in SQL Server 2012. So we're still stuck.

Getting ready

We will be using the NuGet Package Manager to install the Entity Framework Core 1 package, Microsoft.EntityFrameworkCore. We will also be using a SQL Server database to store the data, so we will also need Microsoft.EntityFrameworkCore.SqlServer.

Finally, xunit is the package we will be using for the unit tests, and dotnet-text-xunit adds tooling support for Visual Studio. Note that the UnitTests project is a .NET Core App 1.0 (netcoreapp1.0), that Microsoft.EntityFrameworkCore.Design is configured as a build dependency, and Microsoft.EntityFrameworkCore.Tools is set as a tool.

Open **Using EF Core Solution** from the included source code examples.

We will also be using a SQL Server 2012 database to store the data. The reason for this is that only SQL Server 2012 supports sequences.

Execute the database setup script from the code samples included for this recipe. This can be found in the `DataAccess` project within the `Database` folder.

How to do it...

Let's create a simple domain model that uses sequences as the backing key-generation strategy:

1. First, add a `Blog` class to the `BusinessLogic` project:

```
using System.Collections.Generic;
namespace BusinessLogic
{
  public class Blog
  {
    public int BlogId { get; set; }
    public string Title { get; set; }
    public ICollection<Post> Posts { get; private set; } = new
      HashSet<Post>();
  }
}
```

2. Now, let's add `Post` as well:

```
using System;
namespace BusinessLogic
{
  public class Post
  {
    public int PostId { get; set; }
    public string Title { get; set; }
    public DateTime Timestamp { get; set; }
    public string Body { get; set; }
    public Blog Blog { get; set; }
  }
}
```

3. Next comes `BlogContext`, this time in the `DataAccess` project:

```
using Microsoft.EntityFrameworkCore;
using BusinessLogic;
using BusinessLogic.Conventions;
namespace DataAccess
{
  public class BlogContext : DbContext
```

```
  {
    private readonly string _connectionString;
    public BlogContext(string connectionString)
    {
      _connectionString = connectionString;
    }
    public DbSet<Blog> Blogs { get; set; }
    protected override void OnConfiguring(
    DbContextOptionsBuilder optionsBuilder)
    {
      optionsBuilder
      .UseSqlServer(_connectionString);
      base.OnConfiguring(optionsBuilder);
    }
    protected override void OnModelCreating(
    ModelBuilder modelBuilder)
    {
      modelBuilder.ForSqlServerUseSequenceHiLo();
      base.OnModelCreating(modelBuilder);
    }
  }
}
```

 For Entity Framework 6, replace the `Microsoft.`
`EntityFrameworkCore` namespace with `System.Data.Entity` and
call the base constructor of `DbContext`, passing it the connection string.
Finally, drop the `OnConfiguring` method.

4. Add the following connection string to the `appsettings.json` file:

```
{
  "Data": {
    "Blog": {
      "ConnectionString":"Server=(local)\\SQLEXPRESS;
      Database=Blog;
      Integrated Security=SSPI; MultipleActiveResultSets=true"
    }
  }
}
```

For Entity Framework 6, we would add this connection string to the `Web.config` file, under the `connectionStrings` section, with the name `Blog`. Of course, change the connection string to match your system settings, for example, the name of the SQL Server instance (`SQLEXPRESS`, in this example).

How it works...

The key here is the call to the `ForSqlServerUseSequenceHiLo` extension method in `OnModelCreating`: it tells Entity Framework Core to use the new sequence-based High-Low key generation algorithm instead of the default one based on SQL Server's `IDENTITY`. Everything will work smoothly, and there's no need to do anything else. Behind the covers, what happens is Entity Framework creates a sequence in SQL Server. Before it inserts any records in the database, it increments this sequence and reserves a range of integer values, which it will use to feed any new records it has to insert. After this range is exhausted, Entity Framework reserves another one, and so on. Do keep in mind that this will only work in SQL Server 2012 or newer, because older versions have no knowledge of sequences.

There's more...

The example shown sets sequences as the global generation pattern. It is also possible, however, to just use sequences for some entities and use `IDENTITY` for the rest:

```
protected override void OnModelCreating(ModelBuilder modelBuilder)
{
  modelBuilder
    .Entity<Blog>()
    .Property(b => b.BlogId)
    .ForSqlServerUseSequenceHiLo();
  base.OnModelCreating(modelBuilder);
}
```

The only configurable properties of a sequence are its name and schema. To change them, we just need to provide values to the default parameters of `ForSqlServerUseSequenceHiLo`: `modelBuilder.ForSqlServerUseSequenceHiLo("dbo", "MyOwnSequence")`.

See also

In this chapter:

- ▸ *Using GUIDs as keys*

See more about the High-Low algorithm at `https://www.quora.com/What-is-the-Hi-Lo-algorithm-and-when-is-it-useful`.

Using GUIDs as keys

We know that Entity Framework can generates keys using either the IDENTITY or SEQUENCE (SQL Server 2012) features. It is also possible, however, to leverage GUIDs to generate keys on either the client or the server side.

Client-side generated GUID keys should work equally well in any database that supports GUIDs: SQL Server has the UNIQUEIDENTIFIER type, Oracle has RAW(16), MySQL and PostgreSQL have UUID, and so on.

Getting ready

We will be using the NuGet Package Manager to install the Entity Framework Core 1 package, Microsoft.EntityFrameworkCore. We will also be using a SQL Server database to store the data, so we will also need Microsoft.EntityFrameworkCore.SqlServer.

Finally, xunit is the package we will be using for the unit tests, and dotnet-text-xunit adds tooling support for Visual Studio. Note that the UnitTests project is a .NET Core App 1.0 (netcoreapp1.0), that Microsoft.EntityFrameworkCore.Design is configured as a build dependency, and Microsoft.EntityFrameworkCore.Tools is set as a tool.

Open **Using EF Core Solution** from the included source code examples.

Execute the database setup script from the code samples included for this recipe. This can be found in the DataAccess project within the Database folder.

How to do it...

Let's create a simple domain model that uses sequences as the backing key generation strategy:

1. First, add a Blog class to the BusinessLogic project:

```
using System;
using System.Collections.Generic;
namespace BusinessLogic
{
  public class Blog
  {
    public Guid BlogId { get; set; }
    public string Title { get; set; }
    public ICollection<Post> Posts { get; private set; } = new
     HashSet<Post>();
  }
}
```

2. Let's add a `Post` class as well, in the `BusinessLogic` project:

```csharp
using System;
namespace BusinessLogic
{
  public class Post
  {
    public Guid PostId { get; set; }
    public string Title { get; set; }
    public DateTime Timestamp { get; set; }
    public string Body { get; set; }
    public Blog Blog { get; set; }
  }
}
```

3. Next comes `BlogContext`, this time in the `DataAccess` project:

```csharp
using Microsoft.EntityFrameworkCore;
using BusinessLogic;
using BusinessLogic.Conventions;
namespace DataAccess
{
  public class BlogContext : DbContext
  {
    private readonly string _connectionString;
    public BlogContext(string connectionString)
    {
      _connectionString = connectionString;
    }
    public DbSet<Blog> Blogs { get; set; }
    protected override void OnConfiguring(
    DbContextOptionsBuilder optionsBuilder)
    {
      optionsBuilder
      .UseSqlServer(_connectionString);
      base.OnConfiguring(optionsBuilder);
    }
  }
}
```

 For Entity Framework 6, replace the `Microsoft.EntityFrameworkCore` namespace with `System.Data.Entity` and call the base constructor of `DbContext`, passing it the connection string. Finally, drop the `OnConfiguring` method.

4. Add the following connection string to the `appsettings.json` file:

```
{
  "Data": {
    "Blog": {
      "ConnectionString":"Server=(local)\\SQLEXPRESS;
      Database=Blog;
      Integrated Security=SSPI; MultipleActiveResultSets=true"
    }
  }
}
```

 For Entity Framework 6, we would add this connection string to the `Web.config` file, under the `connectionStrings` section, with the name `Blog`. Of course, change the connection string to match your system settings, for example, the name of the SQL Server instance (`SQLEXPRESS`, in this example).

How it works...

GUID primary keys are treated specially by Entity Framework: when it finds one, it just uses the value it has (if any), or, it assigns it one using a GUID-generation algorithm. Note that we didn't have to do anything in order to configure its usage, it just works out of the box. In the initialization for the ID properties we are assigning it a new GUID, and that's all Entity Framework needs.

There's more...

In SQL Server, you can also have server-generated GUIDs. The best option for that is to have a default value in the table. We can achieve it with the following code:

```
protected override void OnModelCreating(
ModelBuilder modelBuilder)
{
  modelBuilder
    .Entity<Blog>()
    .Property(b => b.BlogId)
    .HasDefaultValueSql("NEWSEQUENTIALID()");
  modelBuilder
    .Entity<Post>()
    .Property(b => b.PostId)
    .HasDefaultValueSql("NEWSEQUENTIALID()");
  base.OnModelCreating(modelBuilder);
}
```

This uses SQL Server's `NEWSEQUENTIALID()` function, which has some advantages over `NEWID()`, namely, the values it returns are sequential and therefore more suitable for use in a clustered index, such as the one typically used by SQL Server primary keys.

 For a good overview of the problems associated with having GUID primary keys, have a look at `http://www.informit.com/articles/article.aspx?p=25862`. This article predates the `NEWSEQUENTIALID()` function, however, which solves the ordering problem.

See also

In this chapter:

▶ *Using sequence key generators*

Implementing inheritance – Table per Class hierarchy

The relational and the object-oriented world, although similar, are in fact quite different. In the object-oriented world, we have classes and inheritance, references to other classes, virtual and static members, and different visibilities, which all make our life as developers easier. Relational databases are very simple: all we have are tables (and views) and foreign keys. So, an object-relational mapper such as Entity Framework faces a difficult task translating from one to the other where there is no 1:1 correspondence of concepts: this is called the object-relational impedance mismatch.

In this topic, we will focus on inheritance. Tables do not have inheritance, but there are some patterns that help us mimic it:

▶ **Table per hierarchy/Single table inheritance**: A single table is used for a class hierarchy; all base and derived table's properties are mapped to columns of this table; a special column, called discriminator, is used to tell to which class each record corresponds

▶ **Table per type/Class table inheritance**: The base class is mapped to a table that contains columns for each property defined in it, and each concrete class is mapped to a specific table, which only contains columns for the concrete class, and holds a foreign key to the base table

▶ **Table per concrete type/Concrete table inheritance**: In this pattern, each concrete class gets its own table, which contains columns for all of the properties of the class: the inherited and the specific

In the past, Entity Framework offered support for each of these mapping patterns, but, as of Entity Framework Core 1, only Table per hierarchy is supported (it is likely to change in subsequent versions, though). Let's see how we can implement it.

Getting ready

We will be using the NuGet Package Manager to install the Entity Framework Core 1 package, `Microsoft.EntityFrameworkCore`. We will also be using a SQL Server database to store the data, so we will also need `Microsoft.EntityFrameworkCore.SqlServer`.

Finally, `xunit` is the package we will be using for the unit tests, and `dotnet-text-xunit` adds tooling support for Visual Studio. Note that the `UnitTests` project is a .NET Core App 1.0 (netcoreapp1.0), that `Microsoft.EntityFrameworkCore.Design` is configured as a build dependency, and `Microsoft.EntityFrameworkCore.Tools` is set as a tool.

Open **Using EF Core Solution** from the included source code examples.

Execute the database setup script from the code samples included for this recipe. This can be found in the `DataAccess` project within the `Database` folder.

How to do it...

We will be creating a class hierarchy that will be interpreted by Entity Framework and persisted in a relational database:

1. First, add a `Blog` class to the `BusinessLogic` project:

```
using System.Collections.Generic;
namespace BusinessLogic
{
  public class Blog
  {
    public int BlogId { get; set; }
    public string Title { get; set; }
    public ICollection<BlogContent> Contents { get; private set; }
      = new HashSet<BlogContent>();
  }
}
```

2. Now we add the base class for the blog's contents, `BlogContent`, in a new file in the `BusinessLogic` project:

```
using System.Collections.Generic;
namespace BusinessLogic
{
  public abstract class BlogContent
```

```
  {
    public int BlogContent Id { get; set; }
    public string Title { get; set; }
    public DateTime Timestamp { get; set; }
    public Blog Blog { get; set; }
  }
}
```

3. Let's add a `PostContent` class as well, in the `BusinessLogic` project inheriting from `BlogContent`:

```
namespace BusinessLogic
{
  public class PostContent : BlogContent
  {
    public string Body { get; set; }
  }
}
```

4. Now we create another class inheriting from `BlogContent`, and we call it `FileContent`:

```
namespace BusinessLogic
{
  public class FileContent : BlogContent
  {
    public string ContentType { get; set; }
    public int ? Size { get; set; }
    public byte [] Contents { get; set; }
  }
}
```

5. Next comes the `BlogContext`, this time in the `DataAccess` project:

```
using Microsoft.EntityFrameworkCore;
using BusinessLogic;
using BusinessLogic.Conventions;
namespace DataAccess
{
  public class BlogContext : DbContext
  {
    private readonly string _connectionString;
    public BlogContext(string connectionString)
    {
      _connectionString = connectionString;
    }
    public DbSet<BlogContent> Contents { get; set; }
    protected override void OnConfiguring(
```

```
      DbContextOptionsBuilder optionsBuilder)
      {
        optionsBuilder
        .UseSqlServer(_connectionString);
        base.OnConfiguring(optionsBuilder);
      }
      protected override void OnModelCreating(
      ModelBuilder modelBuilder)
      {
        modelBuilder
          .Entity<BlogContent>()
          .HasKey(p => p.BlogContentId);
        modelBuilder
          .Entity<BlogContent>()
          .HasOne(p => p.Blog)
          .WithMany(b => b.Contents)
          .IsRequired();
        modelBuilder
          .Entity<FileContent>()
          .HasBaseType<BlogContent>();
        modelBuilder
          .Entity<Post Content >()
          .HasBaseType<BlogContent>();
        base.OnModelCreating(modelBuilder);
      }
    }
  }
```

 For Entity Framework 6, replace the Microsoft.EntityFrameworkCore namespace with System.Data.Entity and call the base constructor of DbContext, passing it the connection string. Finally, drop the OnConfiguring method.

6. Add the following connection string to the appsettings.json file:

```
{
  "Data": {
    "Blog": {
      "ConnectionString":"Server=(local)\\SQLEXPRESS;
      Database=Blog;
      Integrated Security=SSPI; MultipleActiveResultSets=true"
    }
  }
}
```

For Entity Framework 6, we would add this connection string to the `Web.config` file, under the `connectionStrings` section, with the name `Blog`. Of course, change the connection string to match your system settings, for example, the name of the SQL Server instance (`SQLEXPRESS`, in this example).

How it works...

We have an abstract base class, `BlogContents`, that describes the common properties of all the contents to be stored in a blog. Of that, we have two special cases: posts and files, each with its own specific properties. Note that all of the properties in the `Post` and `File` classes are nullable: the `Size` property was made so by making it a nullable integer. This is very important, just think of it: because all the properties of all the derived classes must fit in it, not all the columns will be appropriate for all classes. The following screenshot shows different Data tools in Visual Studio:

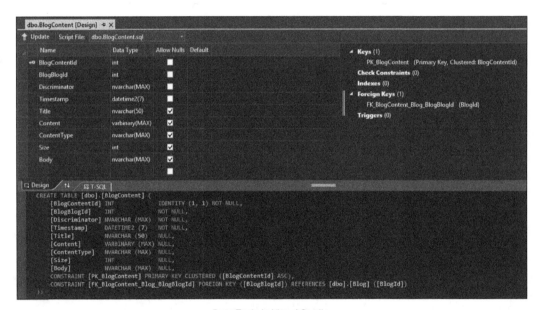

Data Tools in Visual Studio

The `BlogContext` class exposes a property, `Contents`, of the `BlogContent` type, as shown in the following diagram:

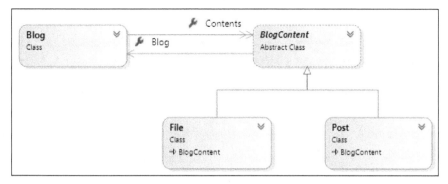

Classes with inheritance

There's more...

You can query for a specific type in a number of ways:

- ▶ Directly on the `Contents` property, by adding an `is` clause:

```
from content in ctx.Contents where content is Post select content
```

- ▶ By calling the `Set` method of `DbContext` with a generic parameter of the desired type: `ctx.Set<File>()`.

- ▶ Another option is to get all `BlogContents` and then iterate through the collection:

```
var contents = ctx.Contents.ToList();
foreach (var content in contents)
{
  if (content is Post)
  {
    //…
  }
  else if (content is File)
  {
    //…
  }
}
```

It's best if you choose a strategy that filters data in the database so that not everything needs to come to the client, saving precious time and resources.

3
Validation and Changes

In this chapter, we will cover the following topics:

- ▶ Validating simple properties
- ▶ Validating the whole entity
- ▶ Validating groups of entities
- ▶ Intercepting saving changes
- ▶ Intercepting property changes
- ▶ Setting the state of an entity
- ▶ Improving MVC UI with Entity Framework validation
- ▶ Inserting, updating, and deleting entities with stored procedures
- ▶ Updating the database from model changes
- ▶ Dumping the SQL script for the database creation

Introduction

In this chapter, we will be looking at how we can make Entity Framework validate our entities for us. Of course, we don't want to be inserting bad data into the database, and Entity Framework can help us with that by intercepting data before it is sent to the database.

After that, we will see how we can manipulate the state of entities being tracked, how we can intercept changes being made to them, and use custom SQL to retrieve, update, and delete entities.

At the very end of the chapter, we will have a look at the migrations functionality that allows us to evolve our model and have the database reflect those changes.

Validating simple properties

Let's see how we can use attributes to validate properties.

Getting ready

We will be using NuGet Package Manager to install the Entity Framework Core 1 package, `Microsoft.EntityFrameworkCore`. We will also be using a SQL Server database for storing the data, so we will also need `Microsoft.EntityFrameworkCore.SqlServer`.

Finally, `xunit` is the package we will be using for the unit tests and `dotnet-text-xunit` adds tooling support for Visual Studio. Note that the `UnitTests` project is a .NET Core App 1.0 (netcoreapp1.0), where `Microsoft.EntityFrameworkCore.Design` is configured as a build dependency and `Microsoft.EntityFrameworkCore.Tools` is set as a tool.

Open **Using EF Core Solution** from the included source code examples.

Execute the database setup script from the code samples included with this recipe. This can be found in the `DataAccess` project within the `Database` folder.

How to do it...

Let's create a sample entity and a validation attribute, and modify our context to take advantage of it:

1. Add a new C# class named `Blog` with the following code to the `BusinessLogic` project, which should initially be empty:

    ```
    using System;
    namespace BusinessLogic
    {
      public class Blog
      {
        public int BlogId { get; set; }
        public string Name { get; set; }
        [PastDate]
        public DateTime CreationDate { get; set; }
        public string Url { get; set; }
      }
    }
    ```

2. Now, create a validation attribute that won't let us use a date later than today. Place the following code in a file named `PastDateAttribute.cs` in the `BusinessLogic` project:

    ```
    using System;
    using System.ComponentModel.DataAnnotations;
    ```

```csharp
namespace BusinessLogic
{
  [AttributeUsage(AttributeTargets.Property, AllowMultiple =
    false, Inherited = true)]
  public class PastDateAttribute : ValidationAttribute
  {
    protected override ValidationResult IsValid(object value,
     ValidationContext validationContext)
    {
      if (!(value is DateTime))
      {
        return ValidationResult.Success;
      }
      var date = (DateTime) value;
      var now = DateTime.UtcNow;
      if (date.Date > now.Date)
      {
        return new ValidationResult("Cannot insert a future
          date");
      }
      return ValidationResult.Success;
    }
  }
}
```

3. Create a new C# class named BlogContext with the following code in the DataAccess project:

```csharp
using System;
using System.Collections.Generic;
using System.ComponentModel.DataAnnotations;
using System.Linq;
using Microsoft.EntityFrameworkCore;
using Microsoft.EntityFrameworkCore.Infrastructure;
using BusinessLogic;
namespace DataAccess
{
  public class BlogContext : DbContext
  {
    private readonly string _connectionString;
    public BlogContext(string connectionString)
    {
      _connectionString = connectionString;
    }
    public DbSet<Blog> Blogs { get; set; }
    protected void ValidateDirtyEntries()
    {
      var serviceProvider = GetService<IServiceProvider>();
```

```
          var items = new Dictionary<object, object>();
          foreach (var entry in ChangeTracker.Entries()
        .Where(e => (e.State == EntityState.Added) || (e.State ==
          EntityState.Modified)))
          {
            var entity = entry.Entity;
            var context = new ValidationContext(entity,
              serviceProvider, items);
            var results = new List<ValidationResult>();
            if (Validator.TryValidateObject(entity, context, results,
              true) ==
             false)
            {
              foreach (var result in results)
              {
                if (result != ValidationResult.Success)
                {
                   throw new ValidationException(
                   result.ErrorMessage);
                }
              }
            }
          }
        }
        protected override void OnConfiguring(DbContextOptionsBuilder
         optionsBuilder)
        {
          optionsBuilder
          .UseSqlServer(_connectionString);
          base.OnConfiguring(optionsBuilder);
        }
        public override int SaveChanges()
        {
          ValidateDirtyEntries();
          return base.SaveChanges();
        }
      }
    }
```

 For Entity Framework 6, replace the namespace `Microsoft.EntityFrameworkCore` for `System.Data.Entity` and call the base constructor of `DbContext`, passing it the connection string. Finally, drop the `OnConfiguring` method.

4. Now, let's add a unit test, this time, in the `UnitTests` project, in a file called `ValidationTests.cs`:

```
using Xunit;
using BusinessLogic;
using DataAccess;
using System;
using System.ComponentModel.DataAnnotations;
using Microsoft.Extensions.Configuration;
namespace UnitTests
{
  public class ValidationTests : BaseTests
  {
    [Fact]
    public void CanValidateAttributes()
    {
      //Arrange
      using (var ctx = new
       BlogContext(Configuration["Data:Blog:ConnectionString"]))
      {
        var blog = new Blog { CreationDate = DateTime.Now.
          AddDays(1) };
        //Assert
        Assert.ThrowsAny<ValidationException>(() =>
        {
          ctx.Blogs.Add(blog);
          //Act
          ctx.SaveChanges();
        });
      }
    }
  }
}
```

5. Of course, we will need the base class `BaseTests`, which should also go in the `UnitTests` project:

```
using Microsoft.Extensions.Configuration;
namespace UnitTests
{
  public abstract class BaseTests
  {
    protected BaseTests()
    {
      var configurationBuilder = new ConfigurationBuilder();
      configurationBuilder
      .AddJsonFile("appSettings.json");
      Configuration = configurationBuilder.Build();
```

```
        }
        protected IConfiguration Configuration { get; set; }
    }
}
```

6. Finally, add the following connection string to the `appsettings.json` file:

```
{
    "Data": {
        "Blog": {
            "ConnectionString":"Server=(local)\\SQLEXPRESS;
            Database=Blog;
            Integrated Security=SSPI; MultipleActiveResultSets=true"
        }
    }
}
```

> For Entity Framework 6, we would add this connection string to the `Web.config` file, under the `connectionStrings` section, with the name `Blog`. Of course, do change the connection string to match your system settings, for example, the name of the SQL Server instance (`SQLEXPRESS`, in this example).

How it works...

The "old" `System.ComponentModel.DataAnnotations` namespace defines the `ValidationAttribute` class; this is a base class for attributes that perform validation on the item they are located, be it a property or a whole class. Here we define a custom validation attribute, `PastDateAttribute`, that, when invoked, will check if the target value is a `DateTime`, and if so, if this value is previous to today; if the date is later than today, it will return an error; otherwise, it will return the well-known success value, `ValidationResult.Success`. Of course, if the value is not a `DateTime` at first, it will yield success too. We decorate the `CreationDate` property in the `Blog` class with it.

The previous versions of Entity Framework used to validate `ValidationAttribute` derived attributes automatically, but that is no longer the case. Because of that, we need to override the `SavingChanges DbContext` method and hook our own validation behavior. Luckily, the static `Validator` class does take care of that, and more, as we will see later on.

The missing piece is figuring out what entities need to be validated; for that, we look at the `ChangeTracker` contained entities with states `Added` or `Modified` – these are the entities that we either told Entity Framework to persist or modify after loading them from the store.

There's more...

Multiple `ValidationAttribute` derived attributes can be added to the same or different properties of a class, or even to the class itself. We will see this and more in the next chapter.

One thing that you need to keep in mind is, because the `ValidationAttribute` attributes are generic, their target values will always be prototyped as an object. Because of that, you always have to check if the actual target matches what you expect – in this example, it was the `DateTime` type.

By the way, there are several out-of-the-box validation attributes included in `System.ComponentModel.DataAnnotations`:

- `CompareAttribute`: This compares for equality of the values of two properties
- `CreditCardAttribute`: This checks if a string value matches a credit card
- `CustomValidationAttribute`: This performs custom validation by calling a named method in a given type; the validation result will come from this method
- `DataTypeAttribute`: This checks if a value matches a given type (date, date and time, time, duration, phone number (US format), currency, single line text, HTML, multiline text, e-mail address, password, URL, image URL, credit card, postal code, or uploaded file); some of the other attributes are shortcuts to some of these types
- `EmailAddressAttribute`: This checks if a string value is a valid e-mail address
- `EnumDataTypeAttribute`: This checks that a given value is a valid member of an enumerated type
- `FileExtensionsAttribute`: This checks that a file name has a valid extension, according to a defined set
- `MaxLengthAttribute`: This checks the maximum string length of a value
- `MinLengthAttribute`: This checks a string value for a required minimum length
- `PhoneAttribute`: This checks if a string value represents a valid phone number (beware: US format only)
- `RangeAttribute`: This checks that a numeric value is contained within a given threshold (minimum and maximum values)
- `RegularExpressionAttribute`: This checks that a string value matches a given regular expression
- `RequiredAttribute`: This checks that a value is present (not null)
- `StringLengthAttribute`: This validates the maximum and minimum required lengths of a string value; equivalent to applying a `MaxLengthAttribute` and a `MinLengthAttribute` attribute together
- `UrlAttribute`: This checks that a value is a valid URL

See also

In this chapter:

- ▸ *Validating the whole entity*
- ▸ *Validating groups of entities*

To learn more about `DataAnnotations` validations refer to the following link:

`https://msdn.microsoft.com/en-us/library/ee256141(VS.100).aspx`.

Validating the whole entity

In the previous recipe, we saw how we can validate simple, decoupled properties. In real life, though, there is usually the need to validate properties against each other, or perform some validation that even uses values from outside the validating entity. We will have a look at two different ways to achieve this.

Getting ready

We will be using NuGet Package Manager to install the Entity Framework Core 1 package, `Microsoft.EntityFrameworkCore`. We will also be using a SQL Server database for storing the data, so we will also need `Microsoft.EntityFrameworkCore.SqlServer`.

Finally, `xunit` is the package we will be using for the unit tests and `dotnet-text-xunit` adds tooling support for Visual Studio. Note that the `UnitTests` project is a .NET Core App 1.0 (netcoreapp1.0), where `Microsoft.EntityFrameworkCore.Design` is configured as a build dependency and `Microsoft.EntityFrameworkCore.Tools` is set as a tool.

Open **Using EF Core Solution** from the included source code examples.

Execute the database setup script from the code samples included with this recipe. This can be found in the `DataAccess` project within the `Database` folder.

How to do it...

In this recipe, we'll play a bit with the various forms by which we can validate entities and their properties:

1. Add a new C# class named `Blog` with the following code to the `BusinessLogic` project:

   ```
   using System.Collections.Generic;
   using System.ComponentModel.DataAnnotations;
   namespace BusinessLogic
   ```

```
{
  [BlogValidation]
  public class Blog : IValidatableObject
  {
    public int BlogId { get; set; }
    [CustomValidation(typeof(ForbiddenWordsValidator),
     "IsValid")]
    public string Name { get; set; }
    public DateTime CreationDate { get; set; }
    public string Url { get; set; }
    public IEnumerable<ValidationResult>
     Validate(ValidationContext validationContext)
    {
      yield return ForbiddenWordsValidator.IsValid(Name);
    }
  }
}
```

2. Now we will create a validation attribute that will validate the whole entity: create a file named `BlogValidationAttribute.cs` in the `BusinessLogic` project:

```
using System;
using System.ComponentModel.DataAnnotations;
namespace BusinessLogic
{
  [AttributeUsage(AttributeTargets.Class,
   AllowMultiple = false, Inherited = true)]
  public class BlogValidationAttribute :
  ValidationAttribute
  {
    protected override ValidationResult IsValid(object
     value, ValidationContext validationContext)
    {
      if (!(value is Blog))
      {
        return ValidationResult.Success;
      }
      var blog = (Blog) value;
      //TODO: check the blog for invalid values
      //for now, let's assume something is wrong
        with the name
      yield return new ValidationResult("Invalid name",
       new [] { "Name" });
      //yield return ValidationResult.Success;
    }
  }
}
```

3. Next, the `ForbiddenWordsValidator` class, also in `BusinessLogic` project:

```
using System;
using System.ComponentModel.DataAnnotations;
namespace BusinessLogic
{
  public static class ForbiddenWordsValidator
  {
    public static ValidationResult IsValid(string word)
    {
      //TODO: check if the word is valid, maybe using a dictionary
      //for now, let's assume it isn't valid
      return new ValidationResult("Bad word detected");
      //if the word is ok, just return success
      //return ValidationResult.Success;
    }
  }
}
```

4. Finally, create a new C# class named `BlogContext` with the following code in the `DataAccess` project:

```
using System;
using System.ComponentModel.DataAnnotations;
using Microsoft.EntityFrameworkCore;
using Microsoft.EntityFrameworkCore.Infrastructure;
using BusinessLogic;
namespace DataAccess
{
  public class BlogContext : DbContext
  {
    private readonly string _connectionString;
    public BlogContext(string connectionString)
    {
      _connectionString = connectionString;
    }
    public DbSet<Blog> Blogs { get; set; }
    protected void ValidateDirtyEntries()
    {
      var serviceProvider = (this as IAccessor<IServiceProvider>).
        Service;
      var items = new Dictionary<object, object>();
      foreach (var entry in ChangeTracker.Entries()
      .Where(e =>
      (e.State == EntityState.Added) ||
        (e.State == EntityState.Modified)))
```

```
      {
        var entity = entry.Entity;
        var context = new ValidationContext(entity,
          serviceProvider, items);
        var results = new List<ValidationResult>();
        if (Validator.TryValidateObject(entity, context, results,
          true) == false)
        {
          foreach (var result in results)
          {
            if (result != ValidationResult.Success)
            {
              throw new ValidationException(
                result.ErrorMessage);
            }
          }
        }
      }
    }
    protected override void OnConfiguring(
    DbContextOptionsBuilder optionsBuilder)
    {
      optionsBuilder
      .UseSqlServer(_connectionString);
      base.OnConfiguring(optionsBuilder);
    }
    public override int SaveChanges()
    {
      ValidateDirtyEntries();
      return base.SaveChanges();
    }
  }
}
```

 For Entity Framework 6, replace the namespace `Microsoft.EntityFrameworkCore` for `System.Data.Entity` and call the base constructor of `DbContext`, passing it the connection string. Finally, drop the `OnConfiguring` method.

5. We'll add a unit test in the `UnitTests` project, in a file called `ValidationTests.cs`:

```
using Xunit;
using BusinessLogic;
using DataAccess;
namespace UnitTests
{
  public class ValidationTests : BaseTests
  {
    [Fact]
    public void CanValidateAll()
    {
      //Arrange
      using (var ctx = new BlogContext(
      Configuration["Data:Blog:ConnectionString"]))
      {
        var blog = new Blog { Name = "A Bad Word" };
        //Assert
        Assert.ThrowsAny<ValidationException>(() =>
        {
          ctx.Blogs.Add(blog);
          //Act
          ctx.SaveChanges();
        });
      }
    }
  }
}
```

6. We'll also add the base class `BaseTests`, also in the `UnitTests` project:

```
using Microsoft.Extensions.Configuration;
namespace UnitTests
{
  public abstract class BaseTests
  {
    protected BaseTests()
    {
      var configurationBuilder = new ConfigurationBuilder();
      configurationBuilder
      .AddJsonFile("appSettings.json");
      Configuration = configurationBuilder.Build();
    }
    protected IConfiguration Configuration { get; set; }
  }
}
```

7. Add the following connection string to the `appsettings.json` file:

```
{
  "Data": {
    "Blog": {
      "ConnectionString":"Server=(local)\\SQLEXPRESS;
      Database=Blog;
       Integrated Security=SSPI;
       MultipleActiveResultSets=true"
    }
  }
}
```

> For Entity Framework 6, we would add this connection string to the `Web.config` file, under the `connectionStrings` section, with the name `Blog`. Of course, do change the connection string to match your system settings, for example, the name of the SQL Server instance (`SQLEXPRESS`, in this example).

How it works...

What we have here are three different validation options:

- The `BlogValidationAttribute`, when applied to the `Blog` class, will perform some custom validation of it (here you have just its skeleton); it has access to all of the public members of the class, and can even change the values, although it is not recommended

- The implementation of `IValidatableObject`, an interface also coming from `System.ComponentModel.DataAnnotations`, allows a class to validate itself

- The `CustomValidationAttribute`, in this example applied to the `Name` property of the `Blog` class, will trigger a call to a public static method in the supplied class (`ForbiddenWordsValidator`, whose actual implementation is left as an exercise)

Let's analyze each of these options.

The first one, a class-level validation attribute, is capable of validating the class as a whole. The problem is that it needs to have knowledge of the class it is pointed to, so that it can look at the appropriate properties. Of course, it can rely on abstract base classes or interfaces, but it still needs to know about them.

Having the class validate itself is interesting – after all, who knows it best? – except from a reusability point of view: the logic will be inside the class and not really useful outside of it.

The third option, a generic validation attribute, is useful because we can have a collection of validation methods and reuse them in different places. In this example, the validation attribute is declared on a string property and hence the validation method only knows about strings, but the attribute can also be declared at the class level; in this case, of course, the validation method's argument must be of the right type.

Note that both the `ValidationAttribute` derived classes as the `IValidatableObject` and the generic validation method, all return results as `ValidationResult`, where `ValidationResult.Success` always means *is valid*. The `Validator` class knows how to handle all of these scenarios, which is quite helpful.

Try to implement the content of `BlogValidationAttribute` and `ForbiddenWordsValidator` and see if you can provide your own validations!

See also

In this chapter:

- ▶ *Validating simple properties*
- ▶ *Validating groups of entities*

Validating groups of entities

We've seen how we can validate single properties or entities, but what if we need to validate several entities at the same time? This may be because we cannot allow duplicate values, or for any other reason. Let's look at a possible solution.

We will be using NuGet Package Manager to install the Entity Framework Core 1 package, `Microsoft.EntityFrameworkCore`. We will also be using a SQL Server database for storing the data, so we will also need `Microsoft.EntityFrameworkCore.SqlServer`.

Finally, `xunit` is the package we will be using for the unit tests and `dotnet-text-xunit` adds tooling support for Visual Studio. Note that the `UnitTests` project is a .NET Core App 1.0 (netcoreapp1.0), where `Microsoft.EntityFrameworkCore.Design` is configured as a build dependency and `Microsoft.EntityFrameworkCore.Tools` is set as a tool.

Open **Using EF Core Solution** from the included source code examples.

Execute the database setup script from the code samples included with this recipe. This can be found in the `DataAccess` project within the `Database` folder.

How to do it...

Let's see how we can validate groups of entities of the same type and state (added, modified) before they are actually stored:

1. Add a new C# class named `Blog` with the following code to the `BusinessLogic` project:

```
using System.Collections.Generic;
using System.ComponentModel.DataAnnotations;
namespace BusinessLogic
{
  public class Blog : IGroupValidatable
  {
    public int BlogId { get; set; }
    public string Name { get; set; }
    public DateTime CreationDate { get; set; }
    public string Url { get; set; }
  }
}
```

2. The `IGroupValidatable` marker interface also goes to the `BusinessLogic` project:

```
namespace BusinessLogic
{
  public interface IGroupValidatable { }
}
```

3. Let's now create a `BlogContext` with the following code in the `DataAccess` project:

```
using System;
using System.ComponentModel.DataAnnotations;
using Microsoft.EntityFrameworkCore;
using Microsoft.EntityFrameworkCore.Infrastructure;
using BusinessLogic;
namespace DataAccess
{
  public class BlogContext : DbContext
  {
    private readonly string _connectionString;
    public BlogContext(string connectionString)
    {
      _connectionString = connectionString;
    }
    public DbSet<Blog> Blogs { get; set; }
```

```
protected void ValidateEntries(Type type, IEnumerable<object>
  entities,
 EntityState state)
{
  if (type == typeof(Blog))
  {
    var count = entities.Count();
    var countDistinctNames = entities
    .OfType<Blog>()
    .Select(b => b.Name.ToLowerInvariant())
    .Distinct()
    .Count();
    if (count != countDistinctNames)
    {
      throw new ValidationException("Duplicate blog names
          detected");
    }
  }
}
protected void ValidateDirtyEntries()
{
  var addedEntries = ChangeTracker.Entries()
  .Where(e => (e.Entity is IGroupValidatable) && (e.State ==
  EntityState.Added))
  .Select(e => e.Entity)
  .GroupBy(e => e.GetType())
  .Select(g => new { Type = g.Key, Entities = g.ToList() });
  var modifiedEntries = ChangeTracker.Entries()
  .Where(e => (e.Entity is IGroupValidatable) && (e.State ==
  EntityState.Modified))
  .Select(e => e.Entity)
  .GroupBy(e => e.GetType())
  .Select(g => new { Type = g.Key, Entities = g.ToList() });
  foreach (var g in addedEntries)
  {
    ValidateEntries(g.Type, g.Entities,
      EntityState.Added);
  }
  foreach (var g in modifiedEntries)
  {
    ValidateEntries(g.Type, g.Entities,
    EntityState.Modified);
  }
}
protected override void OnConfiguring(
```

```
        DbContextOptionsBuilder optionsBuilder)
        {
          optionsBuilder
          .UseSqlServer(_connectionString);
          base.OnConfiguring(optionsBuilder);
        }
        public override int SaveChanges()
        {
          ValidateDirtyEntries();
          return base.SaveChanges();
        }
      }
    }
```

 For Entity Framework 6, replace the namespace `Microsoft.EntityFrameworkCore` for `System.Data.Entity` and call the base constructor of `DbContext`, passing it the connection string. Finally, drop the `OnConfiguring` method.

4. Now let's add a unit test, appropriately, in the `UnitTests` project, in a file called `ValidationTests.cs`:

```
using Xunit;
using BusinessLogic;
using DataAccess;
namespace UnitTests
{
  public class ValidationTests : BaseTests
  {
    [Fact]
    public void CanValidateDuplicates()
    {
      //Arrange
      using (var ctx = new BlogContext(
      Configuration["Data:Blog:ConnectionString"]))
      {
        var blog1 = new Blog { Name = "A Blog Name" };
        var blog2 = new Blog { Name = "A Blog Name" };
        //Assert
        Assert.ThrowsAny<ValidationException>(() =>
        {
          ctx.Blogs.Add(blog1);
          ctx.Blogs.Add(blog2);
          //Act
```

```
            ctx.SaveChanges();
        });
    }
  }
 }
}
```

5. Let's also add the base class `BaseTests`, in the `UnitTests` project:

```
using Microsoft.Extensions.Configuration;
namespace UnitTests
{
  public abstract class BaseTests
  {
    protected BaseTests()
    {
      var configurationBuilder = new ConfigurationBuilder();
      configurationBuilder
      .AddJsonFile("appSettings.json");
      Configuration = configurationBuilder.Build();
    }
    protected IConfiguration Configuration { get; set; }
  }
}
```

6. Add the following connection string to the `appsettings.json` file:

```
{
  "Data": {
    "Blog": {
      "ConnectionString":"Server=(local)\\SQLEXPRESS;
      Database=Blog;
      Integrated Security=SSPI; MultipleActiveResultSets=true"
    }
  }
}
```

For Entity Framework 6, we would add this connection string to the `Web. config` file, under the `connectionStrings` section, with the name `Blog`. Of course, do change the connection string to match your system settings, for example, the name of the SQL Server instance (`SQLEXPRESS`, in this example).

How it works...

We know that the `SaveChanges` infrastructure method is called by Entity Framework when it is about to persist the entities it is tracking to the data store. We also know that the `ChangeTracker` member is responsible for keeping track of these entities. By looking at the added and modified entities that are waiting to be stored, we can filter them by a certain interface (`IGroupValidatable`) and group them by their concrete entity. Then we just need to pass them to a method that does the appropriate validation, in this case, detecting duplicate blog names. This is a case where, if individual property or entity validation does not help, we need to look at the whole set.

See also

In this chapter:

▸ *Validating simple properties*

▸ *Validating the whole entity*

Intercepting saving changes

The .NET framework makes heavy use of a well-known design pattern called Observer. This pattern enables an interested party to register for notifications about a target object. In .NET parlance, this is called events. In this recipe, we will see how we can use events to receive notifications when an entity is about to be saved, and act upon it, including canceling the changes. Let's see how to do it.

Getting ready

We will be using NuGet Package Manager to install the Entity Framework Core 1 package, `Microsoft.EntityFrameworkCore`. We will also be using a SQL Server database for storing the data, so we will also need `Microsoft.EntityFrameworkCore.SqlServer`.

Finally, `xunit` is the package we will be using for the unit tests and `dotnet-text-xunit` adds tooling support for Visual Studio. Note that the `UnitTests` project is a .NET Core App 1.0 (netcoreapp1.0), where `Microsoft.EntityFrameworkCore.Design` is configured as a build dependency and `Microsoft.EntityFrameworkCore.Tools` is set as a tool.

Open **Using EF Core Solution** from the included source code examples.

Execute the database setup script from the code samples included with this recipe. This can be found in the `DataAccess` project within the `Database` folder.

How to do it...

We want to be notified for each entity that is about to be persisted (added, updated, or deleted) and possibly act upon it:

1. Add a new C# class named `Blog` with the following code to the `BusinessLogic` project:

```
using System;
using System.Collections.Generic;
using System.ComponentModel.DataAnnotations;
namespace BusinessLogic
{
  public class Blog
  {
    public int BlogId { get; set; }
    public string Name { get; set; }
    public DateTime CreationDate { get; set; }
    public string Url { get; set; }
  }
}
```

2. Let's now create a `BlogContext` with the following code in the `DataAccess` project:

```
using System;
using System.ComponentModel.DataAnnotations;
using Microsoft.EntityFrameworkCore;
using Microsoft.EntityFrameworkCore.Infrastructure;
using BusinessLogic;
namespace DataAccess
{
  public class BlogContext : DbContext
  {
    private readonly string _connectionString;
    public BlogContext(string connectionString)
    {
      _connectionString = connectionString;
    }
    public DbSet<Blog> Blogs { get; set; }
    public event EventHandler<EntityEventArgs> SavingChanges;
    protected void OnSavingChanges(EntityEventArgs e)
    {
      var handler = SavingChanges;
      if (handler != null)
      {
        handler(this, e);
      }
    }
```

```
      if (e.Cancel == true)
      {
        if (e.State == EntityState.Added)
        {
          Entry(e.Entity).State = EntityState.Detached;
        }
        else
        {
          Entry(e.Entity).State = EntityState.Unchanged;
        }
      }
    }
    protected override void OnConfiguring(
     DbContextOptionsBuilder optionsBuilder)
    {
      optionsBuilder
      .UseSqlServer(_connectionString);
      base.OnConfiguring(optionsBuilder);
    }
    public override int SaveChanges()
    {
      foreach (var entry in ChangeTracker.Entries().Where(e =>
        e.State !=
       EntityState.Unchanged))
      {
        var args = new EntityEventArgs(entry.Entity, entry.State);
        OnSavingChanges(args);
      }
      return base.SaveChanges();
    }
  }
}
```

For Entity Framework 6, replace the namespace `Microsoft.EntityFrameworkCore` for `System.Data.Entity` and call the base constructor of `DbContext`, passing it the connection string. Finally, drop the `OnConfiguring` method.

3. We need to create the event class in its own file, `EntityEventArgs.cs`, also in project `DataAccess`:

```
using Microsoft.EntityFrameworkCore;
using System.ComponentModel;
namespace DataAccess
{
```

```csharp
      public sealed class EntityEventArgs : CancelEventArgs
      {
        public EntityEventArgs(object entity, EntityState state)
        {
          Entity = entity;
          State = state;
        }
        public EntityState State { get; private set; }
        public object Entity { get; private set; }
      }
    }
```

4. Now, let's add a unit test to a file called `EventTests.cs` in the `UnitTests` project:

```csharp
using Xunit;
using BusinessLogic;
using DataAccess;
using System;
namespace UnitTests
{
  public class EventTests : BaseTests
  {
    [Fact]
    public void CanPreventChanges()
    {
      //Arrange
      using (var ctx = new BlogContext(
      Configuration["Data:Blog:ConnectionString"]))
      {
        ctx.SavingChanges += (sender, e) =>
        {
          e.Cancel = true;
        };
        var blog = new Blog { Name = "A Blog Name",
         CreationDate = DateTime.UtcNow };
        //Act
        ctx.Blogs.Add(blog);
        //Assert
        Assert.True(ctx.SaveChanges() == 0);
      }
    }
    [Fact]
    public void CanSetValues()
    {
      //Arrange
      using (var ctx = new BlogContext(
```

```
      Configuration["Data:Blog:ConnectionString"]))
      {
        ctx.SavingChanges += (sender, e) =>
        {
          ((Blog) e.Entity).CreationDate = DateTime.UtcNow;
        };
        var blog = new Blog { Name = "A Blog Name",
        Url = "http://some.blog" };
        //Act
        ctx.Blogs.Add(blog);
        //Assert
        Assert.True(ctx.SaveChanges() == 1);
      }
    }
  }
}
```

5. Let's also add the base class `BaseTests`, in the `UnitTests` project:

```
using Microsoft.Extensions.Configuration;
namespace UnitTests
{
  public abstract class BaseTests
  {
    protected BaseTests()
    {
      var configurationBuilder = new ConfigurationBuilder();
      configurationBuilder
      .AddJsonFile("appSettings.json");
      Configuration = configurationBuilder.Build();
    }
    protected IConfiguration Configuration { get; set; }
  }
}
```

6. Add the following connection string to the `appsettings.json` file:

```
{
  "Data": {
    "Blog": {
      "ConnectionString":"Server=(local)\\SQLEXPRESS;
      Database=Blog;
      Integrated Security=SSPI; MultipleActiveResultSets=true"
    }
  }
}
```

For Entity Framework 6, we would add this connection string to the `Web.config` file, under the `connectionStrings` section, with the name `Blog`. Of course, do change the connection string to match your system settings, for example, the name of the SQL Server instance (`SQLEXPRESS`, in this example).

How it works...

The infrastructure method `SavingChanges` is called whenever Entity Framework "feels" it needs to persist any changes it knows about. What we do here is iterate through all of the entities being tracked – held inside the `ChangeTracker` instance – and, for each one that requires handling (is not unchanged), call another method, `OnSavingChanges`, passing it an argument which includes the entity itself and its perceived state. This method raises an event (if it has any event handlers subscribed) and checks if any of the handlers has canceled it. If it has, it acts accordingly: if the entity was added, discard it, and if it was marked as changed or deleted, set it to unchanged. The event mechanism allows for decoupled code; the actual logic to either change the entity or cancel its persistence can be elsewhere, not in the context.

See also

In this chapter:

▸ *Setting the state of an entity*

▸ *Intercepting property changes*

Intercepting property changes

This time, we will be looking at individual property value changes. If a modified value is not what we want, we veto it, therefore returning to the original one.

Getting ready

We will be using NuGet Package Manager to install the Entity Framework Core 1 package, `Microsoft.EntityFrameworkCore`. We will also be using a SQL Server database for storing the data, so we will also need `Microsoft.EntityFrameworkCore.SqlServer`.

Finally, `xunit` is the package we will be using for the unit tests and `dotnet-text-xunit` adds tooling support for Visual Studio. Note that the `UnitTests` project is a .NET Core App 1.0 (netcoreapp1.0), where `Microsoft.EntityFrameworkCore.Design` is configured as a build dependency and `Microsoft.EntityFrameworkCore.Tools` is set as a tool.

Open **Using EF Core Solution** from the included source code examples.

Execute the database setup script from the code samples included with this recipe. This can be found in the `DataAccess` project within the `Database` folder.

How to do it...

We will have a close look at each modified property of each modified entity that is currently being tracked by Entity Framework:

1. Add a new C# class named `Blog` with the following code to the `BusinessLogic` project:

```csharp
using System.Collections.Generic;
using System.ComponentModel.DataAnnotations;
namespace BusinessLogic
{
  public class Blog
  {
    public int BlogId { get; set; }
    public string Name { get; set; }
    public DateTime CreationDate { get; set; }
    public string Url { get; set; }
  }
}
```

2. Let's now create a `BlogContext` with the following code in the `DataAccess` project:

```csharp
using System;
using System.ComponentModel.DataAnnotations;
using Microsoft.EntityFrameworkCore;
using Microsoft.EntityFrameworkCore.Infrastructure;
using BusinessLogic;
namespace DataAccess
{
  public class BlogContext : DbContext
  {
    private readonly string _connectionString;
    public BlogContext(string connectionString)
    {
      _connectionString = connectionString;
    }
    public DbSet<Blog> Blogs { get; set; }
    protected override void OnConfiguring(
    DbContextOptionsBuilder optionsBuilder)
    {
      optionsBuilder
      .UseSqlServer(_connectionString);
```

```
    base.OnConfiguring(optionsBuilder);
}
protected bool ValidateProperty(object entity, string
  propertyName,
 object originalValue, object currentValue)
{
  if (entity is Blog)
  {
    if (propertyName == "CreationDate")
    {
      var originalDate = (DateTime) originalValue;
      var currentDate = (DateTime) currentValue;
      if (currentValue.Date > originalValue.Date)
      {
        return false;
      }
    }
  }
  return true;
}
protected void ValidateModifiedProperties()
{
  ChangeTracker.DetectChanges();
  foreach (var entry in ChangeTracker.Entries()
  .Where(e => e.State == EntityState.Modified))
  {
    foreach (var propName in entry.Metadata.GetProperties()
    .Select(p => p.Name))
    {
      var prop = entry.Property(propName);
      if (prop.IsModified == true)
      {
        if (ValidateProperty(entry.Entity,
        propName, prop.OriginalValue,
        prop.CurrentValue) == false)
        {
          prop.CurrentValue = prop.OriginalValue;
        }
      }
    }
  }
  ChangeTracker.DetectChanges();
}
public override int SaveChanges()
```

```
    {
      ValidateModifiedProperties();
      return base.SaveChanges();
    }
  }
}
```

 For Entity Framework 6, replace the namespace `Microsoft.EntityFrameworkCore` for `System.Data.Entity` and call the base constructor of `DbContext`, passing it the connection string. Finally, drop the `OnConfiguring` method.

3. Now, let's add a unit test to a file called `ValidationTests.cs` in the `UnitTests` project:

```
using Xunit;
using BusinessLogic;
using DataAccess;
namespace UnitTests
{
  public class ValidationTests : BaseTests
  {
    [Fact]
    public void CanPreventChanges()
    {
      //Arrange
      using (var ctx = new BlogContext(
      Configuration["Data:Blog:ConnectionString"]))
      {
        var blog = new Blog { Name = "A Blog Name", CreationDate =
         DateTime.UtcNow };
        //Act
        ctx.Blogs.Add(blog);
        ctx.SaveChanges();
        blog.CreationDate = DateTime.UtcNow.AddDays(1);
        //Assert
        Assert.True(ctx.SaveChanges() == 0);
      }
    }
  }
}
```

4. Let's also add the base class `BaseTests`, in the `UnitTests` project:

```
using Microsoft.Extensions.Configuration;
namespace UnitTests
{
  public abstract class BaseTests
  {
    protected BaseTests()
    {
      var configurationBuilder = new ConfigurationBuilder();
      configurationBuilder
      .AddJsonFile("appSettings.json");
      Configuration = configurationBuilder.Build();
    }
    protected IConfiguration Configuration { get; set; }
  }
}
```

5. Add the following connection string to the `appsettings.json` file:

```
{
  "Data": {
    "Blog": {
      "ConnectionString":"Server=(local)\\SQLEXPRESS;
      Database=Blog;
      Integrated Security=SSPI; MultipleActiveResultSets=true"
    }
  }
}
```

For Entity Framework 6, we would add this connection string to the `Web.config` file, under the `connectionStrings` section, with the name `Blog`. Of course, do change the connection string to match your system settings, for example, the name of the SQL Server instance (`SQLEXPRESS`, in this example).

How it works...

The change tracking mechanism in Entity Framework means that whenever a change is made to an entity being tracked, Entity Framework eventually finds about it. For each entity that was either attached to a context or loaded from the data store, Entity Framework knows the original values for each mapped property, and, of course, it also knows the current ones.

What we do here is, we loop through all the modified entities, and for each entity, we look at its properties marked as modified by the change tracking implementation. We just pass these properties to a custom method to give it a chance to veto the modification. If it does, the original property value is restored. In this case, we are not throwing an exception, but we are silently restoring the original value. We call the `DetectChanges` method before and after the entities loop, first, to be sure that the dirty properties are detected and, second, to have Entity Framework correctly mark the entities as not modified if all of its modified properties had their original values restored.

See also

In this chapter:

▸ *Intercepting saving changes*

▸ *Setting the state of an entity*

Setting the state of an entity

Normally, Entity Framework knows two kinds of entities:

▸ Those that have been loaded through it, such as the result of a LINQ query

▸ Those that have been added to it

However, things can get more complicated; imagine, for a second, that you loaded one or more entities from a context in an ASP.NET web application and you stored them in the ASP. NET session. Because your `DbContext` normally only lives for the duration of an HTTP request, in the next request, you will get another one, which knows nothing about these entities. Another example would be if you loaded an entity from a query and accidentally made changes to it that you don't want to persist.

The solution for both these cases is to change the Entity Framework's perceived state of the entity (or entities). Let's see how this can be done.

Getting ready

We will be using NuGet Package Manager to install the Entity Framework Core 1 package, `Microsoft.EntityFrameworkCore`. We will also be using a SQL Server database for storing the data, so we will also need `Microsoft.EntityFrameworkCore.SqlServer`.

Finally, `xunit` is the package we will be using for the unit tests and `dotnet-text-xunit` adds tooling support for Visual Studio. Note that the `UnitTests` project is a .NET Core App 1.0 (netcoreapp1.0), where `Microsoft.EntityFrameworkCore.Design` is configured as a build dependency and `Microsoft.EntityFrameworkCore.Tools` is set as a tool.

Open **Using EF Core Solution** from the included source code examples.

Execute the database setup script from the code samples included with this recipe. This can be found in the `DataAccess` project within the `Database` folder.

How to do it...

For this example, we won't be implementing anything new, just a simple Blog-Post model and its associated context:

1. Add a new C# class named `Blog` with the following code to the `BusinessLogic` project:

    ```
    using System;
    using System.Collections.Generic;
    using System.ComponentModel.DataAnnotations;
    namespace BusinessLogic
    {
      public class Blog
      {
        public int BlogId { get; set; }
        public string Name { get; set; }
        public DateTime CreationDate { get; set; }
        public string Url { get; set; }
        public ICollection<Post> Posts { get; set; } = new
          HashSet<Post>();
      }
    }
    ```

> The weird syntax for initializing the `Posts` collection is specific to C# 5. In older versions, you have to instantiate the collection in a constructor.

2. Similar to `Blog` is the `Post` class:

    ```
    using System;
    using System.Collections.Generic;
    using System.ComponentModel.DataAnnotations;
    namespace BusinessLogic
    {
      public class Post
      {
        public int PostId { get; set; }
        public string Title { get; set; }
        public DateTime Timestamp { get; set; }
        public string Body { get; set; }
        public Blog Blog { get; set; }
      }
    }
    ```

3. Let's now create a `BlogContext` class with the following code in the `DataAccess` project:

```
using System.ComponentModel.DataAnnotations;
using Microsoft.EntityFrameworkCore;
using Microsoft.EntityFrameworkCore.Infrastructure;
using BusinessLogic;
namespace DataAccess
{
  public class BlogContext : DbContext
  {
    private readonly string _connectionString;
    public BlogContext(string connectionString)
    {
      _connectionString = connectionString;
    }
    public DbSet<Blog> Blogs { get; set; }
    protected override void OnConfiguring(
    DbContextOptionsBuilder optionsBuilder)
    {
      optionsBuilder
      .UseSqlServer(_connectionString);
      base.OnConfiguring(optionsBuilder);
    }
  }
}
```

 For Entity Framework 6, replace the namespace `Microsoft.EntityFrameworkCore` for `System.Data.Entity` and call the base constructor of `DbContext`, passing it the connection string. Finally, drop the `OnConfiguring` method.

4. Now, let's add a unit test to a file called `StateTests.cs` in the `UnitTests` project:

```
using Xunit;
using Microsoft.EntityFrameworkCore;
using System.Linq;
using BusinessLogic;
using DataAccess;
namespace UnitTests
{
  public class StateTests : BaseTests
  {
    [Fact]
```

```
      public void CanSetState()
      {
        //Arrange
        Blog blog = null;
        using (var ctx = new BlogContext(
        Configuration["Data:Blog:ConnectionString"]))
        {
          blog = ctx.Blogs.First();
        }
        using (var ctx = new BlogContext(
        Configuration["Data:Blog:ConnectionString"]))
        {
          //Assert
          Assert.Equal(EntityState.Detached,
           ctx.Entry(blog).State);
          ctx.Entry(blog).State = EntityState.Modified;
          //Act
          var changes = ctx.SaveChanges();
          //Assert
          Assert.True(changes == 1);
        }
      }
    }
  }
```

5. Let's also add the base class `BaseTests`, in the `UnitTests` project:

```
using Microsoft.Extensions.Configuration;
namespace UnitTests
{
  public abstract class BaseTests
  {
    protected BaseTests()
    {
      var configurationBuilder = new ConfigurationBuilder();
      configurationBuilder
      .AddJsonFile("appSettings.json");
      Configuration = configurationBuilder.Build();
    }
    protected IConfiguration Configuration { get; set; }
  }
}
```

6. Add the following connection string to the `appsettings.json` file:

```
{
  "Data": {
    "Blog": {
      "ConnectionString":"Server=(local)\\SQLEXPRESS;
      Database=Blog;
        Integrated Security=SSPI; MultipleActiveResultSets=true"
    }
  }
}
```

 For Entity Framework 6, we would add this connection string to the `Web.config` file, under the `connectionStrings` section, with the name `Blog`. Of course, do change the connection string to match your system settings, for example, the name of the SQL Server instance (`SQLEXPRESS`, in this example).

How it works...

The `Entry` method returns the Entity Framework entry for a given mapped entity. This entry holds the underlying entity's state, which can be one of the following values:

▶ `EntityState.Unchanged`: This entity is known from the Entity Framework context and is considered unchanged

▶ `EntityState.Modified`: This entity is known from the context and is considered modified

▶ `EntityState.Added`: This entity has just been added to the context and hasn't been persisted yet

▶ `EntityState.Deleted`: This entity is known by the context and has recently been asked for deletion, but hasn't yet been deleted from the store

▶ `EntityState.Detached`: This entity is not being tracked by the context, it knows nothing about it

We can manipulate the Entity Framework's known state of the entity by setting the `State` property. This way we can fool Entity Framework by making it think that the entity is in a state different than what would be expected. The two most obvious cases are attaching an entity to a new context (`EntityState.Unchanged`), having the context forget about it (`EntityState.Detached`). For all other cases, you have methods that know how to handle them (`Add`, `Delete`, and so on).

There's more...

An entity may have several other entities associated with it: just think, for once, of a blog and all of its posts. When you explicitly set an entity's state, you do the same for all of its related entities. The problem is, imagine some of these entities are in a different state: for example, the root entity is new, but it is associated with entities that already exist in the database. For this scenario, Entity Framework lets you traverse through all of an entity's associated entities and set each state individually. This is done using the `TrackGraph` method of the `ChangeTracker` member of `DbContext`:

```
ChangeTracker.TrackGraph(rootEntity, node =>
{
  if (node.Entry.Entity is Blog)
  {
    if ((node.Entry.Entity as Blog).BlogId != 0)
    {
      node.Entry.State = EntityState.Unchanged;
    }
    else
    {
      node.Entry.State = EntityState.Added;
    }
  }
  else if (node.Entry.Entity is Post)
  {
    if ((node.Entry.Entity as Post).PostId == 0)
    {
      node.Entry.State = EntityState.Added;
    }
    else
    {
      node.Entry.State = EntityState.Unchanged;
    }
  }
});
```

This code relies on a simple – but effective, in most cases – algorithm for finding out if an object is new or not. If it has its numeric identifier set to non-zero, then it is not new; otherwise, it is. If you call `TrackGraph` on a `Blog` instance, it will go through each of its Posts and give you a chance to set their state too.

See also

In this chapter:

> ▸ *Intercepting property changes*

Improving MVC UI with entity framework validation

In this recipe, we will leverage the data annotations to provide real-time feedback to the user, while those same annotations will validate objects before allowing them to be saved to the database. Because the UI uses the model properties to display errors, it is important that any validation exception thrown includes the property that caused it, so that the UI can reflect it.

Getting ready

We will be using NuGet Package Manager to install the Entity Framework Core 1 package, `Microsoft.EntityFrameworkCore`. We will also be using a SQL Server database for storing the data, so we will also need `Microsoft.EntityFrameworkCore.SqlServer`.

Finally, `xunit` is the package we will be using for the unit tests and `dotnet-text-xunit` adds tooling support for Visual Studio. Note that the `UnitTests` project is a .NET Core App 1.0 (netcoreapp1.0), where `Microsoft.EntityFrameworkCore.Design` is configured as a build dependency and `Microsoft.EntityFrameworkCore.Tools` is set as a tool.

Open **Using EF Core Solution** from the included source code examples.

Execute the database setup script from the code samples included with this recipe. This can be found in the `DataAccess` project within the `Database` folder.

How to do it...

Let's check if errors are thrown by following these steps:

1. Create a class named `Blog` in a file likewise named `Blog.cs`, in the `BusinessLogic` project:

```
using System;
using System.ComponentModel.DataAnnotations;
namespace BusinessLogic
{
  public class Blog
  {
    public int BlogId { get; set; }
    [Required]
```

```
        public string Name { get; set; }
        public DateTime CreationDate { get; set; }
        [MaxLength(50)]
        public string Url { get; set; }
    }
}
```

2. Add a context to the `DataAccess` project:

```
using System;
using System.ComponentModel.DataAnnotations;
using Microsoft.EntityFrameworkCore;
using Microsoft.EntityFrameworkCore.Infrastructure;
using BusinessLogic;
namespace DataAccess
{
  public class BlogContext : DbContext
  {
    private readonly string _connectionString;
    public BlogContext(string connectionString)
    {
      _connectionString = connectionString;
    }
    public DbSet<Blog> Blogs { get; set; }
    protected override void OnConfiguring(
    DbContextOptionsBuilder optionsBuilder)
    {
      optionsBuilder
      .UseSqlServer(_connectionString);
      base.OnConfiguring(optionsBuilder);
    }
  }
}
```

 For Entity Framework 6, replace the namespace `Microsoft.EntityFrameworkCore` for `System.Data.Entity` and call the base constructor of `DbContext`, passing it the connection string. Finally, drop the `OnConfiguring` method.

3. In the UI project, add a `BlogController` class under the `Controllers` folder, with the following code:

```
using System;
using System.Linq;
using System.Web.Mvc;
```

```csharp
using Microsoft.Extensions.Configuration;
using BusinessLogic;
using DataAccess;
namespace UI.Controllers
{
  public class BlogController : Controller
  {
    private readonly BlogContext _context;
    public BlogController(IConfiguration configuration)
    {
      _context = new BlogContext(
      configuration["Data:Blog:ConnectionString"]);
    }
    // GET: /Blog/
    public IActionResult Index()
    {
      var blog = _context.Set<Blog>().First();
      return View(blog);
    }
    // GET: /Blog/Create
    public IActionResult Create()
    {
      return View(new Blog());
    }
    //POST: /Blog/Save
    [HttpPost]
    public IActionResult Save(Blog blog)
    {
      if (!ModelState.IsValid)
      {
        return View();
      }
      return RedirectToAction("Index");
    }
  }
}
```

 For Entity Framework 6 and MVC 5, we would be returning `ActionResult` instead of `IActionResult`; the latter was only introduced in MVC 6.

4. Also in UI, add the following Razor view to the `Views\Blog` folder, in a file called `Index.cshtml`:

```
@model BusinessLogic.Blog
<h2>Display</h2>
@using (Html.BeginForm())
{
    <h4>Blog</h4>
    <hr/>
    @Html.ValidationSummary(true)
    <div>
        <label>@Html.LabelFor(model => model.Name)</label>
        @Html.EditorFor(model => model.Name)
        @Html.ValidationMessageFor(model => model.Name)
    </div>
    <div>
        <label>@Html.LabelFor(model => model.Url)</label>
        @Html.EditorFor(model => model.Url)
        @Html.ValidationMessageFor(model => model.Url)
    </div>
    <div>
        <label>@Html.LabelFor(model => model.CreationDate)</label>
        @Html.EditorFor(model => model.CreationDate)
        @Html.ValidationMessageFor(model => model.CreationDate)
    </div>
    <input type="submit" value="Save" />
}
```

5. This is a recipe that deals specifically with the UI interaction, and therefore cannot be easily wrapped in testing. However, we can verify that the UI responds manually to the same responses that we get programmatically. So, we add the following test in the `UnitTests` project:

```
using Xunit;
using System;
using System.Collections.Generic;
using System.Linq;
using System.Text;
using BusinessLogic;
using DataAccess;
using Microsoft.EntityFrameworkCore;
namespace UnitTests
{
    public class ValidationTest : BaseTests
    {
        [Fact]
        public void ShouldErrorOnNameTooLong()
```

```csharp
    {
      //Arrange
      using (var ctx = new BlogContext(
      Configuration["Data:Blog:ConnectionString"]))
      {
        var builder = new StringBuilder();
        for (var i = 0; i < 20; i++)
        {
          builder.Append("Repeat this");
        }
        var blog = new Blog()
        {
          CreationDate = DateTime.UtcNow,
          Name = builder.ToString(),
          Url = "http://Some.url"
        };
        //Act
        ctx.Set<Blog>().Add(blog);
        //Assert
        Assert.ThrowsAny<ValidationException>(() =>
        ctx.SaveChanges());
      }
    }
    [Fact]
    public void ShouldErrorOnUrlRequired()
    {
      using (var ctx = new BlogContext(
       Configuration["Data:Blog:ConnectionString"]))
      {
        //Arrange
        var blog = new Blog()
        {
          CreationDate = DateTime.UtcNow,
          Name = "A Blog"
        };
        //Act
        ctx.Set<Blog>().Add(blog);
        //Assert
        Assert.ThrowsAny<ValidationException>(() =>
         ctx.SaveChanges());
      }
    }
  }
 }
}
```

6. Now we need to add the base unit tests class, `BaseTests`:

```
using Microsoft.Extensions.Configuration;
namespace UnitTests
{
  public abstract class BaseTests
  {
    protected BaseTests()
    {
      var configurationBuilder = new ConfigurationBuilder();
      configurationBuilder
      .AddJsonFile("appSettings.json");
      Configuration = configurationBuilder.Build();
    }
    protected IConfiguration Configuration { get; set; }
  }
}
```

7. The connection string should go in the `appsettings.json` file:

```
{
  "Data": {
    "Blog": {
      "ConnectionString":"Server=(local)\\SQLEXPRESS;
      Database=Blog;
      Integrated Security=SSPI; MultipleActiveResultSets=true"
    }
  }
}
```

For Entity Framework 6, we would add this connection string to the `Web.config` file, under the `connectionStrings` section, with the name `Blog`. Of course, do change the connection string to match your system settings, for example, the name of the SQL Server instance (`SQLEXPRESS`, in this example).

8. Run the application, and we should get some verification on the UI from the same validation that executes from the unit test side, provided no data is entered for the `Url` property and too long data is entered for `Name`.

How it works...

We start off by specifying a test that will validate the data annotations on the database side. In this example, we will also have to validate the client-side feedback manually to ensure that we have met our intent. The `Blog` object is restricted with several simple validations (the `Required` and `MaxLength` attributes) that will give some error messages to the MVC view when the user changes inputs and the validation runs. The details of these restrictions, for our example, are not drastically important, but they give us a framework to test against. In the Razor UI, the MVC framework will use the validation attributes to put messages on the screen, close to the properties that caused the validation errors, as an instant feedback to the user.

There's more...

Validations like these are generated amazingly simply in an MVC user experience, but we need to understand how that is accomplished.

Understanding the HTML helper

The HTML helper that enables our validation message to be displayed for a property, must be used to display the message from our attribute. The editor for the helper will not display on its own. This also requires sending the business objects to the UI in strongly-typed views. One of the key features of Code First is that we can use the objects throughout our code base, because they are not tied to our database structure.

See also

In this chapter:

- *Validating simple properties*
- *Validating the whole entity*
- *Validating groups of entities*

Inserting, updating, and deleting entities with stored procedures

What if we do not want to rely on the EF automatically generated SQL to retrieve, create, update, or delete our entities? This can be because we have specific needs, such as logging whatever changes we make, or checking for the right permissions. In this case, the best alternative is to provide our own SQL, particularly if we want to use stored procedures for that purpose. The previous versions of Entity Framework allowed us to do that very easily; however, version 1.0 of Entity Framework Core doesn't (yet) include this capability. Let's see how we can get over it.

Getting ready

We will be using NuGet Package Manager to install the Entity Framework Core 1 package, `Microsoft.EntityFrameworkCore`. We will also be using a SQL Server database for storing the data, so we will also need `Microsoft.EntityFrameworkCore.SqlServer`.

Finally, `xunit` is the package we will be using for the unit tests and `dotnet-text-xunit` adds tooling support for Visual Studio. Note that the `UnitTests` project is a .NET Core App 1.0 (netcoreapp1.0), where `Microsoft.EntityFrameworkCore.Design` is configured as a build dependency and `Microsoft.EntityFrameworkCore.Tools` is set as a tool.

Open **Using EF Core Solution** from the included source code examples.

Execute the database setup script from the code samples included with this recipe. This can be found in the `DataAccess` project within the `Database` folder.

How to do it...

Let's look at inserting, updating, and deleting entities with stored procedures with the help of following steps:

1. Create a class named `Blog` in a file likewise named `Blog.cs`, in project `BusinessLogic` project:

```
using System;
using System.ComponentModel.DataAnnotations;
namespace BusinessLogic
{
  public class Blog
  {
    public int BlogId { get; set; }
    public string Name { get; set; }
    public DateTime CreationDate { get; set; }
    public string Url { get; set; }
  }
}
```

2. Add a context to the `DataAccess` project:

```
using System;
using System.ComponentModel.DataAnnotations;
using System.Data;
using Microsoft.EntityFrameworkCore;
using Microsoft.EntityFrameworkCore.Infrastructure;
using BusinessLogic;
namespace DataAccess
{
```

```csharp
public class BlogContext : DbContext
{
  private readonly string _connectionString;
  public BlogContext(string connectionString)
  {
    _connectionString = connectionString;
  }
  public DbSet<Blog> Blogs { get; set; }
  public override int SaveChanges()
  {
    var changes = 0;
    foreach (var in ChangeTracker.Entries()
    .Where(e => (e.State != EntityState.Unchanged) &&
     (e.Entity is Blog)))
    {
      var blog = e.Entity as Blog;
      switch (e.State)
      {
        case EntityState.Added:
        var con = Database.GetDbConnection();
        using (var cmd = con.CreateCommand())
        {
          con.Open();
          var name = cmd.CreateParameter();
          name.ParameterName = "p0";
          name.Value = blog.Name;
          var url = cmd.CreateParameter();
          url.ParameterName = "p1";
          url.Value = blog.Url;
          var creationDate = cmd.CreateParameter();
          creationDate.ParameterName = "p2";
          creationDate.Value = blog.CreationDate;
          var blogid = cmd.CreateParameter();
          blogid.ParameterName = "blogid";
          blogid.DbType = DbType.Int32;
          blogid.Direction = ParameterDirection.Output;
          cmd.CommandText = "EXEC @blogid = dbo.InsertBlog @Name
             = @p0, @Url = @p1, @CreationDate = @p2";
          cmd.Parameters.AddRange(new[] { name, url,
           creationDate, blogid });
          cmd.ExecuteNonQuery();
          blog.BlogId = (int) blogid.Value;
          con.Close();
```

```
      }
      break;
      case EntityState.Modified:
        Database.ExecuteSqlCommand("EXEC dbo.UpdateBlog @
          BlogId = @p0, @Name = @p1,
          @Url = @p2, @CreationDate = @p3", blog.BlogId,
        blog.Name, blog.Url, blog.CreationDate);
      break;
      case EntityState.Deleted:
        Database.ExecuteSqlCommand("EXEC dbo.DeleteBlog @
          BlogId = @p0", blog.BlogId);
      break;
    }
    e.State = EntityState.Unchanged;
    ++changes;
  }
  return changes + base.SaveChanges();
}
protected override void OnConfiguring(
DbContextOptionsBuilder optionsBuilder)
{
  optionsBuilder
  .UseSqlServer(_connectionString);
  base.OnConfiguring(optionsBuilder);
}
}
}
```

For Entity Framework 6, replace the namespace `Microsoft.EntityFrameworkCore` for `System.Data.Entity` and call the base constructor of `DbContext`, passing it the connection string. Finally, drop the `OnConfiguring` method.

3. Now we need to create the stored procedures in SQL Server; execute the following SQL in a SQL editor, such as Management Studio:

```
USE [Blog]
GO
CREATE PROCEDURE [dbo].[GetBlog]
(
  @BlogID INT = NULL
)
AS
```

```
BEGIN
  SET NOCOUNT ON
    SELECT BlogId, Name, Url, CreationDate
    FROM [dbo].[Blog]
    WHERE BlogId = ISNULL(@BlogId, BlogId)
    ORDER BY BlogId
    RETURN @@ROWCOUNT
END
CREATE PROCEDURE [dbo].[InsertBlog]
(
  @CreationDate DATETIME = NULL,
  Url NVARCHAR(50),
  @Name NVARCHAR(50)
)
AS
BEGIN
  SET NOCOUNT ON
  SET @CreationDate = ISNULL(@CreationDate, GETUTCDATE())
  INSERT INTO dbo.Blog (CreationDate, Url, Name)
  VALUES (@CreationDate, @Url, @Name)
  RETURN SCOPE_IDENTITY()
END
CREATE procedure [dbo].[UpdateBlog]
(
  @BlogId INT,
  @Name VARCHAR(50),
  @Url VARCHAR(50),
  @CreationDate DATETIME = NULL
)
AS
BEGIN
  SET NOCOUNT ON
  UPDATE dbo.Blog
  SET Name = ISNULL(@Name, Name), Url = ISNULL(@Url, URL),
CreationDate =
    ISNULL(@CreationDate, GETUTCDATE())
  WHERE BlogId = @BlogId
  RETURN @@ROWCOUNT
END
CREATE PROCEDURE [dbo].[DeleteBlog]
(
  @BlogId INT
)
AS
```

```
BEGIN
  SET NOCOUNT ON
  DELETE FROM dbo.Blog
  WHERE BlogId = @BlogId
  RETURN @@ROWCOUNT
END
```

4. Let's add some tests, so that we can see if it's working; add the following code to a file called `StoredProcedureTests.cs`, in project `UnitTests`:

```csharp
using Xunit;
using System;
using System.Linq;
using BusinessLogic;
using DataAccess;
using Microsoft.EntityFrameworkCore;
namespace UnitTests
{
  public class ValidationTest : BaseTests
  {
    [Fact]
    public void CanInsertBlog()
    {
      using (var ctx = new BlogContext(
      Configuration["Data:Blog:ConnectionString"]))
      {
        //Arrange
        var blog = new Blog()
        {
          CreationDate = DateTime.UtcNow,
          Name = "A Blog",
          Url = "http://Some.url"
        };
        //Act
        ctx.Set<Blog>().Add(blog);
        //Assert
        Assert.True(ctx.SaveChanges() == 1);
      }
    }
    [Fact]
    public void CanDeleteBlog()
    {
      using (var ctx = new BlogContext(
      Configuration["Data:Blog:ConnectionString"]))
      {
```

```
      //Arrange
      var blog = new Blog()
      {
        CreationDate = DateTime.UtcNow,
        Name = "A Blog",
        Url = "http://Some.url"
      };
      //Act
      ctx.Set<Blog>().Add(blog);
      ctx.SaveChanges();
      ctx.Set<Blog>().Remove(blog);
      //Assert
      Assert.True(ctx.SaveChanges() == 1);
    }
  }
  [Fact]
  public void CanUpdateBlog()
  {
    using (var ctx = new BlogContext(
    Configuration["Data:Blog:ConnectionString"]))
    {
      //Arrange
      var blog = new Blog()
      {
        CreationDate = DateTime.UtcNow,
        Name = "A Blog",
        Url = "http://Some.url"
      };
      //Act
      ctx.Set<Blog>().Add(blog);
      ctx.SaveChanges();
      blog.Name + " - Updated";
      //Assert
      Assert.True(ctx.SaveChanges() == 1);
    }
  }
}
}
```

5. Now we need to add the base unit tests class, `BaseTests`:

```
using Microsoft.Extensions.Configuration;
namespace UnitTests
{
  public abstract class BaseTests
  {
    protected BaseTests()
    {
      var configurationBuilder = new ConfigurationBuilder();
      configurationBuilder
      .AddJsonFile("appSettings.json");
      Configuration = configurationBuilder.Build();
    }
    protected IConfiguration Configuration { get; set; }
  }
}
```

6. The connection string should go in the `appsettings.json` file:

```
{
  "Data": {
    "Blog": {
      "ConnectionString":"Server=(local)\\SQLEXPRESS;
      Database=Blog;
      Integrated Security=SSPI; MultipleActiveResultSets=true"
    }
  }
}
```

For Entity Framework 6, we would add this connection string to the `Web.config` file, under the `connectionStrings` section, with the name `Blog`. Of course, do change the connection string to match your system settings, for example, the name of the SQL Server instance (`SQLEXPRESS`, in this example).

How it works...

We start off by creating stored procedures for the so-called CUD (short for create, update, and delete) operations. These are appropriately called `InsertBlog`, `UpdateBlog`, and `DeleteBlog`, and do nothing really special. The trick here is swapping Entity Framework's default handling of the persistence for the `Blog` entity and handle the three cases (new entities, modified entities, and deleted entities). We get the list of these from the `ChangeTracker`.

You will notice that the code for adding blog instances is considerably more complex. This is because we need to retrieve the generated primary key for the `BlogId` property and assign it to the class instance. The extension method `ExecuteSqlCommand` doesn't allow us to do that, because we can't inspect the returned value, so we have to do it "by hand". As for the other states, modified and deleted, we just call the stored procedures using `ExecuteSqlCommand`, because we don't need any result. In any case, we are incrementing the number of changes handled by ourselves, because we will want to return them as the result of `SaveChanges`, together with whatever the default implementation returns for any other entity class. We mark the entities we processed as unchanged, so that they are not processed again by the default EF implementation.

There's more...

This solution won't work, at least in some particular cases:

- ▶ **Cascade deletes**: In this, each stored procedure expects to return a single change (insert, update, or delete)
- ▶ **Optimistic concurrency checks**: In this, code does not take into account optimistic concurrency, namely, for deletes; if we need it, we will need to pass additional class properties to the stored procedure that will perform the delete

It is expected that future versions of Entity Framework will provide a more robust solution, similar to the one that existed in previous (pre-Core) versions.

See also

In this chapter:

- ▶ *Validating simple properties*

Updating the database from model changes

Entity Framework includes a migrations API since its Code First (4.1) version. What it does is, allows us to have named schemas for our code first model, that is, for the current state of the POCO model – the classes that compose it and their properties – we can create a named "bookmark". As we improve our model, we can create additional migrations, and keep "bookmarking" them. Whenever we want, we can ask the migrations API to apply them to the database.

Getting ready

We will be using NuGet Package Manager to install the Entity Framework Core 1 package, `Microsoft.EntityFrameworkCore`. We will also be using a SQL Server database for storing the data, so we will also need `Microsoft.EntityFrameworkCore.SqlServer`.

Finally, `xunit` is the package we will be using for the unit tests and `dotnet-text-xunit` adds tooling support for Visual Studio. Note that the `UnitTests` project is a .NET Core App 1.0 (netcoreapp1.0), where `Microsoft.EntityFrameworkCore.Design` is configured as a build dependency and `Microsoft.EntityFrameworkCore.Tools` is set as a tool.

Open **Using EF Core Solution** from the included source code examples.

Execute the database setup script from the code samples included with this recipe. This can be found in the `DataAccess` project within the `Database` folder.

How to do it...

Let's create a simple model from which we will create an initial migration, and then make some changes and create another one:

1. Add a new C# class named `Blog` with the following code to the `BusinessLogic` project:

```csharp
namespace BusinessLogic
{
  public class Blog
  {
    public int BlogId { get; set; }
    public string Name { get; set; }
    public DateTime CreationDate { get; set; }
  }
}
```

2. Create a new context named `BlogContext` with the following code in the `DataAccess` project:

```csharp
using System;
using System.ComponentModel.DataAnnotations;
using Microsoft.EntityFrameworkCore;
using Microsoft.EntityFrameworkCore.Infrastructure;
using Microsoft.Extensions.Configuration;
using BusinessLogic;
namespace DataAccess
{
  public class BlogContext : DbContext
  {
```

```
        private readonly string _connectionString;
        public BlogContext()
        {
          var configurationBuilder = new ConfigurationBuilder();
          configurationBuilder.AddJsonFile("appSettings.json");
          var configuration = configurationBuilder.Build();
          _connectionString = configuration["Data:Blog:ConnectionString"];
        }
        public DbSet<Blog> Blogs { get; set; }
        protected override void OnConfiguring(
        DbContextOptionsBuilder optionsBuilder)
        {
          optionsBuilder
          .UseSqlServer(_connectionString);
          base.OnConfiguring(optionsBuilder);
        }
      }
    }
```

 For Entity Framework 6, replace the namespace `Microsoft.EntityFrameworkCore` for `System.Data.Entity` and call the base constructor of `DbContext`, passing it the connection string. Finally, drop the `OnConfiguring` method.

3. Finally, add the following connection string to the `appsettings.json` file:

```
{
  "Data": {
    "Blog": {
      "ConnectionString":"Server=(local)\\SQLEXPRESS;
      Database=Blog;
      Integrated Security=SSPI; MultipleActiveResultSets=true"
    }
  }
}
```

 For Entity Framework 6, we would add this connection string to the `Web.config` file, under the `connectionStrings` section, with the name `Blog`. Of course, do change the connection string to match your system settings, for example, the name of the SQL Server instance (SQLEXPRESS, in this example).

4.   Now, let's execute the following command in a Command Prompt console, in the `DataAccess` project folder:

`dnx ef migrations add "Initial Version"`

You should see a success message.

5.   Let's add the following in the same console:

`dnx ef migrations list`

You should now get a single item `Initial Version`:

`20160515170259_Initial Version`

6.   Now, returning to the `Blog` class, let's add a `Url` property to it:

```
namespace BusinessLogic
{
  public class Blog
  {
    public int BlogId { get; set; }
    public string Name { get; set; }
    public DateTime CreationDate { get; set; }
    public string Url { get; set; }
  }
}
```

7.   And now, we create a new migration for the model changes:

`dnx ef migrations add "Added Url property"`

8.   Now ask for the current list:

`dnx ef migrations list`

You will get the two migrations, `Initial Version` and `Added Url property`, as follows:

`20160515170259_Initial Version`

`20160516180240_Added Url property`

9.   We will now apply our migrations to the database:

`dnx ef database update`

If you look at the database, you should see that the `Blog` table already contains a `Url` column.

10. If we want to return to a previous version, enter the following:

`dnx ef database update "Initial Version"`

The `Url` column should now have been dropped from the `Blog` table, since it didn't exist in the initial migration.

How it works...

The migrations API requires a context with a public parameterless constructor, so that it can instantiate it. It will introspect the model it contains and generate, for the configured data store (mind you, this will only work for relational data sources), a set of .NET classes that represent the database schema creation and dropping. When we create a new migration, it inspects the current model and tries to find out the changes it has, and then generates a new migration class.

There's more...

It is also possible to apply migrations in code, from within `DbContext`, by calling the `Migrate` method, with or without a migration name parameter. In the latter case, it will apply the latest migration: `Database.Migrate()`.

See also

In this chapter:

> ▸ *Dumping the SQL script for the database creation*

Dumping the SQL script for the database creation

The migrations API, part of Entity Framework since version 4.1 (Code First) knows how to update the database from the POCO model. Of course, it also knows how to dump the SQL script that it will then execute for that purpose. Sometimes it is important to have a look at that SQL script, and we will see how we can do that.

Getting ready

We will be using NuGet Package Manager to install the Entity Framework Core 1 package, `Microsoft.EntityFrameworkCore`. We will also be using a SQL Server database for storing the data, so we will also need `Microsoft.EntityFrameworkCore.SqlServer`.

Finally, `xunit` is the package we will be using for the unit tests and `dotnet-text-xunit` adds tooling support for Visual Studio. Note that the `UnitTests` project is a .NET Core App 1.0 (netcoreapp1.0), where `Microsoft.EntityFrameworkCore.Design` is configured as a build dependency and `Microsoft.EntityFrameworkCore.Tools` is set as a tool.

Open **Using EF Core Solution** from the included source code examples.

Execute the database setup script from the code samples included with this recipe. This can be found in the `DataAccess` project within the `Database` folder.

How to do it...

Let's create a simple model from which we will create a migration, and then export its script:

1. Add a new C# class named `Blog` with the following code to the `BusinessLogic` project:

```
namespace BusinessLogic
{
  public class Blog
  {
    public int BlogId { get; set; }
    public string Name { get; set; }
    public DateTime CreationDate { get; set; }
    public string Url { get; set; }
  }
}
```

2. Create a new context named `BlogContext` with the following code in the `DataAccess` project:

```
using System;
using System.ComponentModel.DataAnnotations;
using Microsoft.EntityFrameworkCore;
using Microsoft.EntityFrameworkCore.Infrastructure;
using Microsoft.Extensions.Configuration;
using BusinessLogic;
namespace DataAccess
{
  public class BlogContext : DbContext
  {
    private readonly string _connectionString;
    public BlogContext()
    {
      var configurationBuilder = new
      ConfigurationBuilder();
      configurationBuilder
      .AddJsonFile("appSettings.json");
      var configuration = configurationBuilder.Build();
      _connectionString = configuration["Data:Blog:ConnectionString"];
    }
    public DbSet<Blog> Blogs { get; set; }
```

```
    protected override void OnConfiguring(
    DbContextOptionsBuilder optionsBuilder)
    {
        optionsBuilder
        .UseSqlServer(_connectionString);
        base.OnConfiguring(optionsBuilder);
    }
  }
}
```

 For Entity Framework 6, replace the namespace `Microsoft.EntityFrameworkCore` for `System.Data.Entity` and call the base constructor of `DbContext`, passing it the connection string. Finally, drop the `OnConfiguring` method.

3. Finally, add the following connection string to the `appsettings.json` file:

```
{
    "Data": {
      "Blog": {
        "ConnectionString":"Server=(local)\\SQLEXPRESS;
        Database=Blog;
        Integrated Security=SSPI; MultipleActiveResultSets=true"
      }
    }
}
```

 For Entity Framework 6, we would add this connection string to the `Web.config` file, under the `connectionStrings` section, with the name `Blog`. Of course, do change the connection string to match your system settings, for example, the name of the SQL Server instance (`SQLEXPRESS`, in this example).

4. Now, let's execute the following command in a Command Prompt console, in the `DataAccess` project folder:

```
dnx ef migrations script
```

You should see the SQL script that Entity Framework generated for your model. You can now inspect it, modify it, or store it in your source control tool, by redirecting the output to a file.

Beware, if you make any changes to the SQL file, you may need to change your POCO model to reflect them.

How it works...

The migrations API instantiates your context class – you need to have a public parameterless constructor, don't forget that – and then generates the SQL that would be necessary to create the model in your relational database of choice (our example uses SQL Server).

There's more...

The migrations API will know what the current migration name is and will dump the appropriate SQL script for it. If you want, you can ask for the delta from one version to another, for example, assuming you have two migrations called Initial Version and Second Version:

dnx ef migrations script "Initial Version" "Second version"

See also

In this chapter:

> *Updating the database from model changes*

4

Transactions and Concurrency Control

In this chapter, we will cover the following topics:

- ▸ Using explicit transactions
- ▸ Using transactions in custom SQL operations
- ▸ Implementing optimistic concurrency in SQL Server
- ▸ Implementing optimistic concurrency in a database-agnostic way

Introduction

In this chapter, we will see how Entity Framework Core deals with concurrency, that is, multiple simultaneous (or almost) changes to the same database object. In particular, we will see the two most common ways to handle concurrency: optimistic concurrency control and pessimistic concurrency control, also known as transactions.

Using explicit transactions

Transactions define a boundary: anything (and everything) inside a transaction is either guaranteed to fail or succeed. Imagine a bank transfer from one bank to another. If you think of the steps involved, they are as follows:

1. Some amount is withdrawn from a bank account.
2. The same amount is deposited in another bank account.

One cannot exist without the other: both actions must either occur or neither of them can occur in isolation.

Transactions have what is commonly referred to as the **ACID** properties. This acronym is explained in the following sections.

Atomic

The execution of any transaction should either have the full intended effect or no effect at all. The results should be either complete (`commit`), or nothing should happen (`roll back`).

Consistent

Any transaction is a transition of state in an application, and therefore should preserve a consistent version of the application. For example, when updating a many-to-many relationship, both the foreign key and the reference table relationship should be updated.

Isolation

Each transaction should be isolated from all other incomplete transactions. Due to the transactions being in the state of transition, they are not consistent, and therefore should be removed from affecting the transaction that is currently executing.

Durability

System failures should not cause a committed transaction that fails to persist its effects. If we rename something, but the SQL database crashes in the middle of the `commit` operation, on recovery the transaction should still be fully committed (this normally involves another call to the database to execute the `commit` operation again).

It is outside the scope of this book to explain transactions in depth as there are lots of good references on that. Instead, we will see how we can make use of explicit transactions in Entity Framework Core.

Getting ready

We will be using the NuGet Package Manager to install Entity Framework Core 1 package, `Microsoft.EntityFrameworkCore`. We will also be using a SQL Server database for storing the data, so we will also need `Microsoft.EntityFrameworkCore.SqlServer`.

Finally, `xunit` is the package we will be using for the unit tests and `dotnet-text-xunit` adds tooling support for Visual Studio. Notice that the `UnitTests` project is a .NET Core App 1.0 (netcoreapp1.0), that `Microsoft.EntityFrameworkCore.Design` is configured as a build dependency and `Microsoft.EntityFrameworkCore.Tools` is set as a tool.

Open **Using EF Core Solution** from the included source code examples.

Execute the database setup script from the code samples included for this recipe. This can be found in the `DataAccess` project within the `Database` folder.

How to do it...

By default, Entity Framework creates an implicit transaction when it is saving its changes—the `SaveChanges` method is called. This is required for the **Unit of Work** pattern implementation, which states that all changes are either applied or none at all. In most cases, this is what you want, but you may also want to have more control over the process, for example, if you are to execute SQL outside of the context and you also want it to be inside the transaction:

1. Create a unit test class file called `Blog` in a `Blog.cs` file in the `BusinessLogic` project:

```
using System;
namespace BusinessLogic
{
    public class Blog
    {
        public int BlogId { get; set; }
        public string Name { get; set; }
        public DateTime CreationDate { get; set; }
        public string Url { get; set; }
    }
}
```

2. Now, create a C# data context class, call it `BlogContext`, and put it in the `DataAccess` project:

```
using System;
using Microsoft.Data.Entity;
using Microsoft.Data.Entity.Infrastructure;
using BusinessLogic;
namespace DataAccess
{
    public class BlogContext : DbContext
    {
        private readonly string _connectionString;
        public BlogContext(string connectionString)
        {
            _connectionString = connectionString;
        }
        public DbSet<Blog> Blogs { get; set; }
        protected override void OnConfiguring(
            DbContextOptionsBuilder optionsBuilder)
        {
            optionsBuilder
              .UseSqlServer(_connectionString);
            base.OnConfiguring(optionsBuilder);
        }
    }
}
```

 For Entity Framework 6, replace the `Microsoft.EntityFrameworkCore` namespaces with `System.Data.Entity` and call the base constructor of `DbContext` passing it the connection string. Finally, drop the `OnConfiguring` method.

3. Now, let's add a unit test in the `UnitTests` project, in a file called `TransactionTests.cs`:

```
using Xunit;
using BusinessLogic;
using DataAccess;
using System;
using System.Data;
using Microsoft.EntityFrameworkCore;
namespace UnitTests
{
    public class TransactionTests : BaseTests
    {
```

```
[Fact]
public void CanUseExplicitTransactions()
{
    //Arrange
    using (var ctx = new
      BlogContext(Configuration
        ["Data:Blog:ConnectionString"]))
    using (var tx =
      ctx.Database.BeginTransaction
        (IsolationLevel.Serializable))
    {
        var blog1 = new Blog { Name = "Blog 1",
            CreationDate = DateTime.Today };
        var blog2 = new Blog { Name = "Blog 2",
            CreationDate = DateTime.Today };
        ctx.AddRange(blog1, blog2);
        try
        {
            //Act
            ctx.SaveChanges();
            tx.Commit();
        }
        catch
        {
            tx.Rollback();
        }
        //Assert
        Assert.True(true);
    }
}
```

Note that the `BeginTransaction` method is an extension method coming from the `Microsoft.EntityFrameworkCore` namespace, and it differs from the `DatabaseFacade.BeginTransaction` method in that it takes a parameter. You can only call this method if you know for sure that Entity Framework is using a relational database—all of the examples in this book do.

4. We will need the base class for the unit tests, `BaseTests`, which should also go in the `UnitTests` project:

```
using Microsoft.Extensions.Configuration;
namespace UnitTests
{
    public abstract class BaseTests
    {
        protected BaseTests()
        {
            var configurationBuilder = new
                ConfigurationBuilder();
            configurationBuilder
                .AddJsonFile("appSettings.json");
            Configuration =
                configurationBuilder.Build();
        }
        protected IConfiguration Configuration { get;
            set;}
    }
}
```

5. Finally, add the following connection string to the `appsettings.json` file:

```
{
  "Data": {
    "Blog": {
      ConnectionString":"Server=(local)\\SQLEXPRESS;
      Database=Blog; Integrated Security=SSPI;
      MultipleActiveResultSets=true"
      }
  }
}
```

For Entity Framework 6, we would add this connection string to the `Web.config` file, under the `connectionStrings` section, with the name `Blog`. Of course, do change the connection string to match your system settings, for example, the name of the SQL Server instance (SQLEXPRESS, in this example).

How it works...

The `Database` property (appropriately, of type `DatabaseFacade`) in the `DbContext` exposes a few methods for managing transactions:

- `BeginTransaction/BeginTransactionAsync`: This starts a new database transaction, either synchronously or asynchronously

- `CommitTransaction`: This commits the current database transaction

- `RollbackTransaction`: This rolls back the current database transaction

There are also some extension methods related with transactions:

- `BeginTransaction/BeginTransactionAsync`: This version takes a single parameter of type `IsolationLevel`, by which we can tell Entity Framework to start a database transaction with an explicit isolation level.

- `UseTransaction`: This uses an ADO.NET transaction started explicitly. There's more on this later on.

When we create a transaction, we are therefore responsible for either committing it (therefore making the changes permanent) or rolling it back (aborting all changes made inside the transaction). That's what we do by either calling `Commit` or `Rollback`. The transaction object itself is disposable, meant to be used in a using block, which, in this case, means that if the transaction wasn't committed or rolled back, .NET will automatically call `Rollback` when the transaction is disposed of.

 .NET Core and, therefore, Entity Framework Core, do not support ambient transactions like those provided by the `System.Transactions` namespace that is available in .NET full.

See also

In this chapter:

- *Using transactions in custom SQL operations*

Using transactions in custom SQL operations

If we are using Entity Framework, we most likely want it to handle database operations for us. However, there may be cases where we need to leverage SQL directly, in order to achieve something that Entity Framework does not support, such as a complex SQL query or running stored procedures. For that, Entity Framework Core lets us use the underlying ADO.NET connection directly. If, however, we plan to make use of transactions created explicitly, we need to tell it to use the created transaction.

Getting ready

We will be using the NuGet Package Manager to install Entity Framework Core 1 package, `Microsoft.EntityFrameworkCore`. We will also be using a SQL Server database for storing the data, so we will also need `Microsoft.EntityFrameworkCore.SqlServer`.

Finally, `xunit` is the package we will be using for the unit tests and `dotnet-text-xunit` adds tooling support for Visual Studio. Notice that the `UnitTests` project is a .NET Core App 1.0 (netcoreapp1.0), that `Microsoft.EntityFrameworkCore.Design` is configured as a build dependency and `Microsoft.EntityFrameworkCore.Tools` is set as a tool.

Open **Using EF Core Solution** from the included source code examples.

Execute the database setup script from the code samples included for this recipe. This can be found in the `DataAccess` project within the `Database` folder.

How to do it...

Let's create an explicit transaction and then use it in a command:

1. We need a context to go in the `DataAccess` project, in a `BlogContext.cs` file:

```
using System;
using Microsoft.Data.Entity;
using Microsoft.Data.Entity.Infrastructure;
using BusinessLogic;
namespace DataAccess
{
    public class BlogContext : DbContext
    {
        private readonly string _connectionString;
```

```
        public BlogContext(string connectionString)
        {
            _connectionString = connectionString;
        }
        protected override void OnConfiguring(
            DbContextOptionsBuilder optionsBuilder)
        {
            optionsBuilder
              .UseSqlServer(_connectionString);
            base.OnConfiguring(optionsBuilder);
        }
    }
}
```

 For Entity Framework 6, replace the Microsoft.
EntityFrameworkCore namespaces with System.Data.
Entity and call the base constructor of DbContext passing it
the connection string. Finally, drop the OnConfiguring method.

2. We now need to create a test class in the UnitTests project, in a file called
   TransactionTests.cs:

```
using Xunit;
using BusinessLogic;
using DataAccess;
using System;
using System.Data;
using Microsoft.EntityFrameworkCore;
using Microsoft.EntityFrameworkCore.Storage;
namespace UnitTests
{
  public class TransactionTests : BaseTests
  {
    [Fact]
    public void
      CanUseExplicitTransactionsInCommands()
    {
      //Arrange
      using (var ctx = new BlogContext(
        Configuration["Data:Blog:ConnectionString"]))
      using (var tx =
        ctx.Database.BeginTransaction())
      {
        var con = ctx.Database.GetDbConnection();
        var cmd = con.CreateCommand();
```

```
cmd.CommandText = "SELECT @@TRANCOUNT";
cmd.Transaction = tx.GetDbTransaction();
//Act
var transactions = (int) cmd.ExecuteScalar();
//Assert
Assert.True(transactions == 1);
          }
        }
      }
    }
```

3. The base class for unit tests should also go in the `UnitTests` project and be called `BaseTests`:

```
using Microsoft.Extensions.Configuration;
namespace UnitTests
{
  public abstract class BaseTests
  {
    protected BaseTests()
    {
      var configurationBuilder = new
        ConfigurationBuilder();
      configurationBuilder
        .AddJsonFile("appSettings.json");
      Configuration = configurationBuilder.Build();
    }
    protected IConfiguration Configuration { get; set; }
  }
}
```

4. Finally, add the following connection string to the `appsettings.json` file:

```
{
    "Data": {
        "Blog": {
            "ConnectionString":"Server=(local)\\SQLEXPRESS;
            Database=Blog; Integrated Security=SSPI;
            MultipleActiveResultSets=true"
        }
    }
}
```

For Entity Framework 6, we would add this connection string to the `Web.config` file, under the `connectionStrings` section, with the name `Blog`. Of course, do change the connection string to match your system settings, for example, the name of the SQL Server instance (`SQLEXPRESS`, in this example).

How it works...

We create an explicit transaction by calling `DatabaseFacade.BeginTransaction`. To get hold of the Entity Framework context's underlying connection, we call the `GetDbConnection` extension method, which will return a `DbConnection` instance. Now, because we started an explicit transaction on this connection, every command that is sent to the database in the course of this transaction needs to take the transaction object, which is why we store this object—obtained through the `GetDbTransaction` extension method—in the **Transaction** property of `DbCommand`, even for operations that do not change the data in the database. If we didn't do that, we would end up with an exception.

There's more...

Entity Framework's behavior will be the same as usual; we only need to be concerned with explicit SQL calls that we may be doing. It is possible to create several nested transactions, as can be done in databases; we just need to hold references to all of the transactions (`DbTransaction` instances) and manually manage them.

See also

In this chapter:

*   ► *Using explicit transactions*

Implementing optimistic concurrency in SQL Server

Another way to deal with simultaneous changes to a database is implementing optimistic concurrency control. Unlike transactions—the pessimistic approach—with optimistic concurrency we assume that things will work out fine, so we have no need for explicit control mechanisms (transactions). In this chapter, we will see a solution for SQL Server.

Getting ready

We will be using the NuGet Package Manager to install Entity Framework Core 1 package, `Microsoft.EntityFrameworkCore`. We will also be using a SQL Server database for storing the data, so we will also need `Microsoft.EntityFrameworkCore.SqlServer`.

Finally, `xunit` is the package we will be using for the unit tests and `dotnet-text-xunit` adds tooling support for Visual Studio. Notice that the `UnitTests` project is a .NET Core App 1.0 (netcoreapp1.0), that `Microsoft.EntityFrameworkCore.Design` is configured as a build dependency and `Microsoft.EntityFrameworkCore.Tools` is set as a tool.

Open **Using EF Core Solution** from the included source code examples.

Execute the database setup script from the code samples included for this recipe. This can be found in the `DataAccess` project within the `Database` folder.

How to do it...

We will make use of SQL Server's ROWVERSION (previously known as TIMESTAMP) data type to implement optimistic concurrency:

1. First, we create a `Blog.cs` file containing a `Blog` class, in the `DataAccess` project:

```
using System;
using System.ComponentModel.DataAnnotations;
namespace BusinessLogic
{
    public class Blog
    {
        public int BlogId { get; set; }
        public string Name { get; set; }
        public DateTime CreationDate { get; set; }
        public string Url { get; set; }
        [Timestamp]
        public byte [] RowVersion { get; private set; }
    }
}
```

2. Add this unit test class to the `UnitTests` project in a `ConcurrencyTests.cs` file:

```csharp
using Xunit;
using DataAccess;
using System.Linq;
using Microsoft.EntityFrameworkCore;
using System;
namespace UnitTests
{
    public class ConcurrencyTests : BaseTests
    {
        [Fact]
        public void CanUseSqlServerOptimisticConcurrency()
        {
            //Arrange
            using (var ctx = new BlogContext(
            Configuration["Data:Blog:ConnectionString"]))
            {
                var blog = ctx.Blogs.First();
                var con = ctx.Database.GetDbConnection();
                var cmd = con.CreateCommand();
                cmd.CommandText = "UPDATE Blogs SET Name =
                    Name + '_modified_'";
                blog.Name = "something to trigger a
                    change";
                //Act
                cmd.ExecuteNonQuery();
                //Assert
                try
                {
                    ctx.SaveChanges();
                }
                catch
                {
                    Assert.True(true);
                }
            }
        }
    }
}
```

3. The base class for unit tests should also go in the `UnitTests` project and be called `BaseTests`:

```
using Microsoft.Extensions.Configuration;
namespace UnitTests
{
  public abstract class BaseTests
  {
    protected BaseTests()
    {
      var configurationBuilder = new
        ConfigurationBuilder();
      configurationBuilder
        .AddJsonFile("appSettings.json");
      Configuration = configurationBuilder.Build();
    }
    protected IConfiguration Configuration { get; set; }
  }
}
```

4. Finally, let's add the following connection string to the `appsettings.json` file:

```
{
    "Data": {
        "Blog": {
            "ConnectionString":"Server=(local)\\SQLEXPRESS;
            Database=Blog; Integrated Security=SSPI;
            MultipleActiveResultSets=true"
        }
    }
}
```

> For Entity Framework 6, we would add this connection string to the `Web.config` file, under the `connectionStrings` section, with the name `Blog`. Of course, do change the connection string to match your system settings, for example, the name of the SQL Server instance (SQLEXPRESS, in this example).

How it works...

The `TimestampAttribute` attribute is used to tell SQL Server—through Entity Framework, of course—to use the column of the property it is applied to as a `ROWVERSION` column, for optimistic concurrency control purposes. This is what this means:

- ▸ When generating the database, set `ROWVERSION` as the column's type
- ▸ The `ROWVERSION` data type maps, in .NET, to an opaque array of bytes, not to any type related to date and time
- ▸ Ignore any changes made to the property (in fact, we even defined the setter as private to make it harder)
- ▸ When Entity Framework loads a record of an entity using optimistic concurrency, it will fetch the optimistic concurrency column and hydrate the mapped property, as it does with all the other mapped properties; these values will be kept in the context's cache, also known as first level cache
- ▸ If there is need to update a record for a loaded entity using optimistic concurrency, Entity Framework will use the optimistic concurrency's property value (managed by Entity Framework, don't forget) in all `UPDATE` and `DELETE` operations involving the record, not just its primary key
- ▸ If the optimistic concurrency value sent by Entity Framework does not match the one present in the database, because the database was updated by a third party, then the affected records will be `0`, and EF will throw a `DbUpdateConcurrencyException` exception

Simply put, when Entity Framework needs to update a record, it will issue SQL similar to the following (highly simplified):

```
UPDATE [dbo].[Blogs]
SET [Name] = @p0
WHERE [BlogId] = @p AND [RowVersion] = @p2
```

Notice the `RowVersion` column being used in the comparison expression next to the `BlogId` (primary key).

 ROWVERSION is a SQL Server-specific mechanism, but other databases have similar mechanisms. For example, look for `ORA_ROWSCN` in Oracle or `TIMESTAMP` in MySQL with the `DEFAULT` and `ON UPDATE` options.

There's more...

Instead of using the `TimestampAttribute`, we could have used code configuration, as per this example:

```
protected override void OnModelCreating(ModelBuilder
    modelBuilder)
{
  modelBuilder
    .Entity<Blog>()
    .Property(p => p.RowVersion)
    .IsConcurrencyToken();
  base.OnModelCreating(modelBuilder);
}
```

 You will see in several locations the ROWVERSION data type being referred to as TIMESTAMP. The fact is, they are synonyms, and TIMESTAMP used to be the common name for it, but Microsoft wanted to make it explicit that this time has nothing to do with dates and times; you cannot use ROWVERSION/TIMESTAMP columns to infer any kind of sequential order or creation date/time.

You may ask yourself: what can we do in the case of an optimistic concurrency control failure? Well, if one happened, we know for sure that the database values have changed, and no longer match the values stored in the context cache. There are two possible solutions.

Database wins

We discard our current modified values and instead use the current database ones. The best way to do this is to set the state for our entity as `Detached` and get it again from the database:

```
//load the entity
var blog = ctx.Blogs.Single(b => b.BlogId == 1);
//make changes to the entity and try to save it
//mark the entity as detached, to remove it from cache
ctx.Entry(blog).State = EntityState.Detached;
//reload the entity
blog = ctx.Blogs.Single(b => b.BlogId == 1);
```

Client wins/last one wins

We push the values we have into the database, discarding any modified values there. This is not so easy to achieve because Entity Framework will prevent us from doing it. It is possible, though: it is a matter of getting from the database the current values for the properties that are doing the concurrency check, updating the first level cache, and attempting to save changes again.

See also

In this chapter:

▸ *Implementing optimistic concurrency in a database-agnostic way*

Implementing optimistic concurrency in a database-agnostic way

In the previous chapter, we saw how to use a SQL Server-specific solution to a common problem in database development—implementing optimistic concurrency control. This time, we will see how we can extend it to other databases, and to more than one columns.

Getting ready

We will be using the NuGet Package Manager to install Entity Framework Core 1 package, `Microsoft.EntityFrameworkCore`. We will also be using a SQL Server database for storing the data, so we will also need `Microsoft.EntityFrameworkCore.SqlServer`.

Finally, `xunit` is the package we will be using for the unit tests and `dotnet-text-xunit` adds tooling support for Visual Studio. Notice that the `UnitTests` project is a .NET Core App 1.0 (netcoreapp1.0), that `Microsoft.EntityFrameworkCore.Design` is configured as a build dependency and `Microsoft.EntityFrameworkCore.Tools` is set as a tool.

Open **Using EF Core Solution** from the included source code examples.

Execute the database setup script from the code samples included for this recipe. This can be found in the `DataAccess` project within the `Database` folder.

How to do it...

We will mark a couple of properties as optimistic concurrency tokens, but we won't be using SQL Server's `ROWVERSION` feature, so that our solution works on any database:

1. First, we create a `Blog.cs` file containing a `Blog` class in the `DataAccess` project:

```
using System;
using System.ComponentModel.DataAnnotations;
namespace BusinessLogic
{
  public class Blog
  {
        public int BlogId { get; set; }
    [ConcurrencyCheck]
        public string Name { get; set; }
    [ConcurrencyCheck]
```

```
            public DateTime CreationDate { get; set; }
            public string Url { get; set; }
        }
    }
```

2. Add this unit test class to the `UnitTests` project in a `ConcurrencyTests.cs` file using `Xunit`:

```csharp
using Xunit;
using DataAccess;
using System.Linq;
using Microsoft.EntityFrameworkCore;
using System;
namespace UnitTests
{
    public class ConcurrencyTests : BaseTests
    {
        [Fact]
        public void CanUseOptimisticConcurrency()
        {
            //Arrange
            using (var ctx = new BlogContext(
                Configuration["Data:Blog:ConnectionString"]))
            {
                var blog = ctx.Blogs.First();
                var con = ctx.Database.GetDbConnection();
                var cmd = con.CreateCommand();
                cmd.CommandText = "UPDATE Blogs SET Name = Name +
                    '_modified_'";
                blog.Name = "something to trigger a change";
                //Act
                cmd.ExecuteNonQuery();
                //Assert
                try
                {
                    ctx.SaveChanges();
                }
                catch(Exception ex)
                {
                    Assert.True(ex is
                    DbUpdateConcurrencyException);
                }
            }
        }
    }
}
```

3. The base class for unit tests should also go in the `UnitTests` project and be called `BaseTests`:

```
using Microsoft.Extensions.Configuration;
namespace UnitTests
{
  public abstract class BaseTests
  {
    protected BaseTests()
    {
    var builder = new ConfigurationBuilder()
    .AddJsonFile("appsettings.json");
    Configuration = builder.Build();
    }
    protected IConfiguration Configuration
      { get; private set; }
  }
}
```

4. Finally, let's add the following connection string to the `appsettings.json` file:

```
{
    "Data": {
        "Blog": {
            "ConnectionString":"Server=(local)\\SQLEXPRESS;
            Database=Blog; Integrated Security=SSPI;
            MultipleActiveResultSets=true"
        }
    }
}
```

> For Entity Framework 6, we would add this connection string to the `Web.config` file, in the `connectionStrings` section, with the name `Blog`. Of course, do change the connection string to match your system settings, for example, the name of the SQL Server instance (SQLEXPRESS, in this example).

How it works...

Because we have a number of properties marked with `ConcurrencyCheckAttribute`, all of its values will be used in `UPDATE` and `DELETE`. The differences to the SQL Server-specific solution that uses `TimestampAttribute` are as follows:

▸ `ConcurrencyCheckAttribute` works on any database server, not just SQL Server

- ▶ It can be applied to any number of properties, all of which will be used in the WHERE clause of UPDATE and DELETE
- ▶ Unlike ROWVERSION columns, these are transparent and their values can be set and viewed at any time

When Entity Framework detects that a loaded entity has changed since it was loaded, and it has been asked to persist these changes (SaveChanges was called), it will try to execute SQL as follows:

```
UPDATE [dbo].[Blogs]
SET [Name] = @p0, [CreationDate] = @p1, [Url] = @p2
WHERE [BlogId] = @p3
AND [Name] = @p4 AND [CreationDate]= @p5
```

If the number of affected records is not 1, Entity Framework will throw a DbUpdateConcurrencyException.

There's more...

It is possible to use fluent configuration instead of attributes, if we do not want to pollute our model:

```
protected override void OnModelCreating
   (ModelBuilder modelBuilder)
{
  modelBuilder
    .Entity<Blog>()
    .Property(p => p.Name)
    .IsConcurrencyToken();
  modelBuilder
    .Entity<Blog>()
    .Property(p => p.CreationDate)
    .IsConcurrencyToken();
  base.OnModelCreating(modelBuilder);
}
```

It is safe to use [ConcurrencyCheck] instead of [Timestamp].

See also

In this chapter:

- ▶ *Implementing optimistic concurrency in SQL Server*

5
Querying

In this chapter, we will cover the following topics:

- ▸ Executing client-side functions in LINQ queries
- ▸ Mixing SQL with LINQ queries
- ▸ Getting entities from the local cache
- ▸ Creating filtered collections
- ▸ Creating reusable queries
- ▸ Querying on shadow properties
- ▸ Implementing the query object pattern
- ▸ Using Dynamic LINQ

Introduction

This chapter will be all about getting data from a database using Entity Framework Core. We will explore what Entity Framework Core has to offer, including features not commonly found in other ORMs, such as the ability to mix LINQ with SQL and the usage of shadow properties.

Granted, querying is probably the most common activity you do with an Object-Relational tool such as Entity Framework, or, for that matter, with any data exploration tool.

Applications need data to display or use, and they need it to come fast. Caching data is usually a good thing, performance-wise, and we talk about it here.

Sometimes, we need to run similar queries with just minor adjustments. That's where the **Query Object** pattern kicks in, as well as LINQ reusable queries.

On the other hand, not all kinds of queries that can be expressed in SQL can be performed using LINQ. Entity Framework allows us to have a bit of both worlds, and even combine the comfort of LINQ with the power of SQL.

Also, we cover here some ways by which parts of the data – or actual queries – can be hidden from the developers, possibly to avoid tampering or to enforce certain business rules.

Executing client-side functions in LINQ queries

There have always been two kinds of LINQ in .NET: LINQ to Objects, and all the others. Pun aside, the fact is that there are two fundamentally different LINQ implementations and sometimes we don't even realize that. There's the one that applies to `IEnumerable<T>` instances, and is executed in memory at once—LINQ to Objects—and then there is a myriad of others that are instead interpreted from expressions originating from `IQueryable<T>` instances and then translated to a specific dialect, such as SQL, and only executed when requested. Their syntaxes are exactly the same, and we can only tell them apart if we know the source. Here is an example:

```
var blogs = from blog in Blogs
where blog.Name.Contains("Development")
select blog;
```

Depending on whether `Blogs` is an implementation of `IQueryable<Blog>` or `IEnumerable<Blog>`, you will get one implementation or the other. Now, let's consider that this code is going to be translated to SQL for the SQL Server engine. In this case, the LINQ interpreter needs to know how to translate the `Contains` method (besides all the rest of the expressions, of course), and different engines will have different translations. This does not happen with LINQ to Objects, because the expression is immediately translated into a call to the `String` class `Contains` method. Because expressions are checked at compile time, the only real requirement is that they comply to the C# language, and thus compile, but that does not mean that the LINQ interpreter will know or be able to produce proper SQL (in this example). For example, say you have some `ComputeHash` extension method over the `String` class; the following code will compile, but then it will crash at runtime:

```
var blogs = from blog in Blogs
where blog.Name.ComputeHash() == 0
select blog;
```

It will crash, that is, in the pre-Core version, as we shall see!

Getting ready

We will be using the NuGet Package Manager to install the Entity Framework Core 1 package, `Microsoft.EntityFrameworkCore`. We will also be using a SQL Server database for storing the data, so we will also need `Microsoft.EntityFrameworkCore.SqlServer`.

Finally, `xunit` is the package we will be using for the unit tests and `dotnet-text-xunit` adds tooling support for Visual Studio. Note that the `UnitTests` project is a .NET Core App 1.0 (netcoreapp1.0), that `Microsoft.EntityFrameworkCore.Design` is configured as a build dependency and `Microsoft.EntityFrameworkCore.Tools` is set as a tool.

Open **Using EF Core Solution** from the included source code examples.

Execute the database setup script from the code samples included for this recipe. This can be found in the `DataAccess` project within the `Database` folder.

How to do it...

This example will show how to call an extension method in a LINQ query that will only be evaluated at the client side, that is, after the query results are materialized:

1. Create a class file called `Blog` in a `Blog.cs` file in the `BusinessLogic` project:

```
using System;
namespace BusinessLogic
{
    public class Blog
    {
        public int BlogId { get; set; }
        public string Name { get; set; }
        public DateTime CreationDate { get; set; }
        public string Url { get; set; }
    }
}
```

2. Now, create a C# data context class, call it `BlogContext`, and put it in the `DataAccess` project:

```
using System;
using Microsoft.EntityFrameworkCore;
using Microsoft.EntityFrameworkCore.Infrastructure;
using BusinessLogic;
namespace DataAccess
{
  public class BlogContext : DbContext
  {
    private readonly string _connectionString;
```

```
      public BlogContext(string connectionString)
      {
        _connectionString = connectionString;
      }
      public DbSet<Blog> Blogs { get; set; }
      protected override void OnConfiguring(
      DbContextOptionsBuilder optionsBuilder)
      {
        optionsBuilder
        .UseSqlServer(_connectionString);
        base.OnConfiguring(optionsBuilder);
      }
    }
  }
```

 For Entity Framework 6, replace the `Microsoft.EntityFrameworkCore` namespaces with `System.Data.Entity` and call the base constructor of `DbContext`, passing it the connection string. Finally, drop the `OnConfiguring` method.

3. We now add a static class that will hold some extension methods. Call it `StringExtensions` and have it stored in a `StringExtensions.cs` file in the `UnitTests` project:

```
namespace UnitTests
{
    public static class StringExtensions
    {
        public static int ComputeHash(this string str)
        {
            var hash = 0;
            foreach (var ch in str)
            {
                hash += (int) ch;
            }
            return hash;
        }
    }
}
```

4. Now, let's add a unit test in the UnitTests project, in a file called LinqTests.cs:

```csharp
using Xunit;
using DataAccess;
using System;
using System.Linq;

namespace UnitTests
{
  public class ObjectQueryTests : BaseTests
  {
    [Fact]
    public void CanQueryUsingObject()
    {
      //Arrange
      using (var ctx = new
        BlogContext(Configuration["Data:Blog:ConnectionString"]))
      {
        //Act
        var query = new BlogsQuery(ctx);
        query.LowerDate = DateTime.Today.AddDays(-7);
        query.HigherDate = DateTime.Today.AddDays(-1);
        query.Name = ".NET";
        query.MaxItems = 3;
        var blogs = (ctx as IQueryExecutor).Execute(query);

        //Assert
        Assert.NotEmpty(blogs);
        Assert.True(blogs.Count() <= 3);
        Assert.All(blogs, blog =>
        {
          Assert.Contains(".NET", blog.Name);
          Assert.True(blog.CreationDate >=
            DateTime.Today.AddDays(-7));
          Assert.True(blog.CreationDate <=
            DateTime.Today.AddDays(-1));
        });
      }
    }
  }
}
```

5. We will need the base class for the unit tests, `BaseTests`, which should also go in the `UnitTests` project:

```
using Microsoft.Extensions.Configuration;;
namespace UnitTests
{
  public abstract class BaseTests
  {
    protected BaseTests()
    {
      var configurationBuilder = new
       ConfigurationBuilder();
      configurationBuilder
      .AddJsonFile("appSettings.json");
      Configuration = configurationBuilder.Build();
    }
    protected IConfiguration Configuration { get; set; }
  }
}
```

6. Finally, add the following connection string to the `appsettings.json` file:

```
{
    "Data": {
        "Blog": {
            "ConnectionString":"Server=(local)\\SQLEXPRESS;
            Database=Blog; Integrated Security=SSPI;
            MultipleActiveResultSets=true"
        }
    }
}
```

> For Entity Framework 6, we would add this connection string to the `Web.config` file, under the `connectionStrings` section, with the name `Blog`. Of course, do change the connection string to match your system settings, for example, the name of the SQL Server instance (`SQLEXPRESS`, in this example).

How it works...

When Entity Framework Core analyzes the LINQ expression it is given, it goes through all its nodes and eventually finds a method call that it does not know how to translate to the underlying data source (remember that it may not be a relational data source and hence not use SQL). In this case, what it does is, it does the translation exactly as if the method call wasn't there, and, if the property (or properties) is present in the projected results, it then calls the method on the retrieved results.

See also

In this chapter:

▶ *Mixing SQL with LINQ queries*

Mixing SQL with LINQ queries

Another great new feature in Entity Framework Core is the ability to intertwine LINQ and SQL. This means that we can have SQL that returns results that can be turned into entities, and after this SQL is run, we are back to strong typing and can add additional LINQ clauses.

Getting ready

We will be using the NuGet Package Manager to install the Entity Framework Core 1 package, `Microsoft.EntityFrameworkCore`. We will also be using a SQL Server database for storing the data, so we will also need `Microsoft.EntityFrameworkCore.SqlServer`.

Finally, `xunit` is the package we will be using for the unit tests and `dotnet-text-xunit` adds tooling support for Visual Studio. Note that the `UnitTests` project is a .NET Core App 1.0 (netcoreapp1.0), that `Microsoft.EntityFrameworkCore.Design` is configured as a build dependency, and `Microsoft.EntityFrameworkCore.Tools` is set as a tool.

Open **Using EF Core Solution** from the included source code examples.

Execute the database setup script from the code samples included for this recipe. This can be found in the `DataAccess` project within the `Database` folder.

How to do it...

We are going to run some custom SQL and then turn it into a LINQ query:

1. Execute the following SQL into your SQL Server instance, in the `Blog` database:

```
CREATE PROCEDURE dbo.GetBlogs
AS
SELECT b.*
FROM dbo.Blogs
```

2. Create a class file called `Blog` in a `Blog.cs` file in the `BusinessLogic` project:

```
namespace BusinessLogic
{
    public class Blog
    {
        public int BlogId { get; set; }
        public string Name { get; set; }
        public DateTime CreationDate { get; set; }
        public string Url { get; set; }
    }
}
```

3. Now, create a C# data context class, call it `BlogContext`, and put it in the `DataAccess` project:

```
using System;
using Microsoft.EntityFrameworkCore;
using Microsoft.EntityFrameworkCore.Infrastructure;
using BusinessLogic;
namespace DataAccess
{
  public class BlogContext : DbContext
  {
    private readonly string _connectionString;
    public BlogContext(string connectionString)
    {
      _connectionString = connectionString;
    }
    public DbSet<Blog> Blogs { get; set; }
    protected override void OnConfiguring(
      DbContextOptionsBuilder optionsBuilder)
    {
      optionsBuilder
      .UseSqlServer(_connectionString);
      base.OnConfiguring(optionsBuilder);
```

```
        }
      }
    }
```

 For Entity Framework 6, we would add this connection string to the `Web.config` file, under the `connectionStrings` section, with the name `Blog`. Of course, do change the connection string to match your system settings, for example, the name of the SQL Server instance (`SQLEXPRESS`, in this example).

4. Now, let's add a unit test in the `UnitTests` project, in a file called `LinqTests.cs`:

```csharp
using Xunit;
using DataAccess;
using System.Linq;
using Microsoft.EntityFrameworkCore;
namespace UnitTests
{
  public class LinqSqlTests : BaseTests
  {
    [Fact]
    public void CanFilterAfterSql()
    {
      //Arrange
      using (var ctx = new BlogContext(
       Configuration["Data:Blog:ConnectionString"]))
      {
        //Act
        var blogs = ctx.Blogs
        .FromSql("EXEC dbo.GetBlogs")
        .Where(b => b.Name.Contains("Development"))
        .ToList();
        //Assert
        Assert.NotEmpty(blogs);
      }
    }
    [Fact]
    public void CanSelectAfterSql()
    {
      //Arrange
      using (var ctx = new BlogContext(
       Configuration["Data:Blog:ConnectionString"]))
      {
        //Act
```

```
                var blogNames = ctx.Blogs
                .FromSql("SELECT b.* FROM Blogs b")
                .Select(b => b.Name)
                .ToList();
                //Assert
                Assert.NotEmpty(blogNames);
            }
        }
    }
}
```

5. We will need the base class for the unit tests, `BaseTests`, which should also go in the `UnitTests` project:

```csharp
using Microsoft.Extensions.Configuration;
namespace UnitTests
{
  public abstract class BaseTests
  {
    protected BaseTests()
    {
      var configurationBuilder = new
       ConfigurationBuilder();
      configurationBuilder.AddJsonFile("appSettings.json");
      Configuration = configurationBuilder.Build();
    }
    protected IConfiguration Configuration { get; set; }
  }
}
```

6. Finally, add the following connection string to the `appsettings.json` file:

```json
{
    "Data": {
        "Blog": {
            "ConnectionString":"Server=(local)\\SQLEXPRESS;
            Database=Blog; Integrated Security=SSPI;
            MultipleActiveResultSets=true"
        }
    }
}
```

For Entity Framework 6, we would add this connection string to the `Web.config` file, under the `connectionStrings` section, with the name `Blog`. Of course, do change the connection string to match your system settings, for example, the name of the SQL Server instance (`SQLEXPRESS`, in this example).

How it works...

From the mapped entity collection Blogs, we asked Entity Framework to execute custom SQL, through the `FromSql` method. In one case, it was a call to a stored procedure; in the other, a regular `SQL SELECT`. In both cases, the SQL results were automatically turned into strongly typed (LINQ) object queries, and before they were actually executed—which only happened when `ToList` was called—we added more stuff to the LINQ query, namely, a restriction (`Where`) and a projection (`Select`). All of the filtering and projection took place in the database, not in memory.

There's more...

We can also pass parameters to the `FromSql` method, which will then be passed to the SQL. For example, imagine your stored procedure looked like this instead:

```
CREATE PROCEDURE dbo.GetBlogs
(
    @creationdate DATETIME = NULL
)
AS
    SELECT b.*
    FROM dbo.Blogs b
    WHERE b.CreationDate >= ISNULL(@creationdate, b.CreationDate)
```

You could pass a parameter to match `@creationdate` as this:

```
var blogs = ctx.Blogs
    .FromSql("EXEC dbo.GetBlogs @p0", DateTime.Today)
    .ToList();
```

So, each parameter will look like @p0, @p1, and so on.

See also

In this chapter:

▶ *Executing client-side functions in LINQ queries*

Getting entities from the local cache

When using an **Object-Relational Mapper** (**ORM**) such as Entity Framework, a very important feature to keep in mind is this: when an entity is materialized as the result of executing a query, it is stored in an in-memory cache. This is usually referred to as *First Level Cache*, but Martin Fowler gave it another name: *Identity Map*. In its definition, he said that the purpose of this pattern is to ensure that each object gets loaded only once, by keeping every loaded object in a map. If you think of it, it is a good thing performance-wise, because there's always a cost in instantiating classes and hydrating them from the records obtained from the data source. This is used internally by ORMs, but we can also make use of it to our benefit.

Getting ready

We will be using the NuGet Package Manager to install the Entity Framework Core 1 package, `Microsoft.EntityFrameworkCore`. We will also be using a SQL Server database for storing the data, so we will also need `Microsoft.EntityFrameworkCore.SqlServer`.

Finally, `xunit` is the package we will be using for the unit tests and `dotnet-text-xunit` adds tooling support for Visual Studio. Note that the `UnitTests` project is a .NET Core App 1.0 (netcoreapp1.0), that `Microsoft.EntityFrameworkCore.Design` is configured as a build dependency and `Microsoft.EntityFrameworkCore.Tools` is set as a tool.

Open **Using EF Core Solution** from the included source code examples.

Execute the database setup script from the code samples included for this recipe. This can be found in the `DataAccess` project within the `Database` folder.

How to do it...

In this example we are going to retrieve an entity from the **First Level Cache**.

1. Create a class file called `Blog` in a `Blog.cs` file in the `BusinessLogic` project:

```
using System;
namespace BusinessLogic
{
    public class Blog
    {
        public int BlogId { get; set; }
        public string Name { get; set; }
        public DateTime CreationDate { get; set; }
        public string Url { get; set; }
    }
}
```

2. Now, create a C# data context class, call it `BlogContext`, and put it in the `DataAccess` project:

```csharp
using System;
using Microsoft.EntityFrameworkCore;
using Microsoft.EntityFrameworkCore.Infrastructure;
using BusinessLogic;
namespace DataAccess
{
  public class BlogContext : DbContext
  {
    private readonly string _connectionString;
    public BlogContext(string connectionString)
    {
      _connectionString = connectionString;
    }
    public DbSet<Blog> Blogs { get; set; }
    protected override void OnConfiguring(
    DbContextOptionsBuilder optionsBuilder)
    {
      optionsBuilder
      .UseSqlServer(_connectionString);
      base.OnConfiguring(optionsBuilder);
    }
  }
}
```

 For Entity Framework 6, replace the `Microsoft.`
`EntityFrameworkCore` namespaces with `System.Data.`
`Entity` and call the base constructor of `DbContext`, passing it
the connection string. Finally, drop the `OnConfiguring` method.

3. Now, let's add a unit test in the `UnitTests` project, in a file called `CacheTests.cs`:

```csharp
using Xunit;
using BusinessLogic;
using DataAccess;
using System.Linq;
namespace UnitTests
{
  public class CacheTests : BaseTests
  {
```

```
[Fact]
public void CanRetrieveFromCache()
{
  //Arrange
  using (var ctx = new BlogContext(
   Configuration["Data:Blog:ConnectionString"]))
  {
    //Act
    var blogs = ctx.Blogs.ToList();
    //Assert
    var cachedBlogs = ctx.ChangeTracker
      .Entries<Blog>()
      .Select(e => e.Entity);
    Assert.NotEmpty(cachedBlogs);
  }
}
```

4. We will need the base class for the unit tests, BaseTests, which should also go in the UnitTests project:

```
using Microsoft.Extensions.Configuration;
namespace UnitTests
{
  public abstract class BaseTests
  {
    protected BaseTests()
    {
      var configurationBuilder = new
       ConfigurationBuilder();
      configurationBuilder
      .AddJsonFile("appSettings.json");
      Configuration = configurationBuilder.Build();
    }
    protected IConfiguration Configuration { get; set; }
  }
}
```

5. Finally, add the following connection string to the `appsettings.json` file:

```
{
    "Data": {
        "Blog": {
            "ConnectionString":"Server=(local)\\SQLEXPRESS;
            Database=Blog; Integrated Security=SSPI;
            MultipleActiveResultSets=true"
        }
    }
}
```

 For Entity Framework 6, we would add this connection string to the `Web.config` file, under the `connectionStrings` section, with the name `Blog`. Of course, do change the connection string to match your system settings, for example, the name of the SQL Server instance (`SQLEXPRESS`, in this example).

How it works...

The `ChangeTracker` instance in the `DbContext` keeps track of all entities known by that context. These entities might have been recently added or loaded by some query operation. In any case, they are made available by the `Entries<T>` method, which returns an `EntityEntry` (or `EntityEntry<T>`) instance, which in turn wraps the actual entity, as its `Entity` property. The `EntityEntry` class also stores the state of the entity (added, unmodified, deleted, or unknown).

There's more...

The existence of the **First Level Cache** (or **Identity Map**, as you prefer) raises an interesting problem: in all subsequent queries that return the same records from a table, if those records have been materialized into entities and kept in the cache, the same unchanged entities are returned. That is, the ORM makes no attempt to try to update (re-hydrate) the in-memory entity properties from the new record values. The only way to refresh these cached entities is to first remove (evict) them from the cache. We can do this explicitly for a given entity:

```
ctx.Entry(blog).State = EntityState.Detached;
```

We can also do it to all entities of a given type:

```
public static class DbContextExtensions
{
    public static void Evict<T>(this DbContext ctx)
    where T: class
    {
        foreach (var entry in ctx.ChangeTracker.Entries<T>().ToList())
```

```
        {
            ctx.Entry(entry.Entity).State =
            EntityState.Detached;
        }
    }
}
```

See also

In this chapter:

▸ *Creating filtered collections*

Creating filtered collections

Sometimes, you may want to always return entities that match certain restrictions. For example, you may want to return orders that have been processed or are in a particular state. This recipe will explain how we can achieve that.

Getting ready

We will be using the NuGet Package Manager to install the Entity Framework Core 1 package, `Microsoft.EntityFrameworkCore`. We will also be using a SQL Server database for storing the data, so we will also need `Microsoft.EntityFrameworkCore.SqlServer`.

Finally, `xunit` is the package we will be using for the unit tests and `dotnet-text-xunit` adds tooling support for Visual Studio. Note that the `UnitTests` project is a .NET Core App 1.0 (netcoreapp1.0), that `Microsoft.EntityFrameworkCore.Design` is configured as a build dependency and `Microsoft.EntityFrameworkCore.Tools` is set as a tool.

Open **Using EF Core Solution** from the included source code examples.

Execute the database setup script from the code samples included for this recipe. This can be found in the `DataAccess` project within the `Database` folder.

How to do it...

In this recipe, we are going to create a filtered collection by inheriting from a base Entity Framework class and adding additional logic:

1. Create a class named `FilteredDbSet` in `DataAccess`, in a file with the same name:

   ```
   using Microsoft.EntityFrameworkCore;
   using Microsoft.EntityFrameworkCore.Internal;
   ```

```csharp
using Microsoft.EntityFrameworkCore.ChangeTracking;
using System;
using System.Collections.Generic;
using System.Linq;
using System.Linq.Expressions;
namespace DataAccess
{
    public class FilteredDbSet<TEntity> : InternalDbSet<TEntity>
      where TEntity : class
    {
        private readonly Expression<Func<TEntity, bool>> _filter;
        private readonly Func<TEntity, bool> _condition;
        private static DbSet<TEntity> GetDbSet(
        DbContext context)
        {
            return context.Set<TEntity>();
        }
        private static IQueryable<TEntity> GetSource(
        DbContext context,
        Expression<Func<TEntity, bool>> filter)
        {
            var query = context.Set<TEntity>() as
            IQueryable<TEntity>;
            query = query.Where(filter);
            return query;
        }
        private void EnsureMatchesFilter(
        IEnumerable<TEntity> entities)
        {
            foreach (var entity in entities)
            {
                EnsureMatchesFilter(entity);
            }
        }
        private void EnsureMatchesFilter(TEntity entity)
        {
            if (!_condition(entity))
            {
                throw new ArgumentException(
                "Entity does not match the filter");
            }
        }
        protected FilteredDbSet(
```

```
        DbContext context,
        Expression<Func<TEntity, bool>> filter) : base(
        GetSource(context, filter), GetDbSet(context))
        {
            _filter = filter;
            _condition = _filter.Compile();
        }
        public static DbSet<T> Create(
        DbContext context,
        Expression<Func<T, bool>> filter)
        {
            if (filter == null)
            {
                throw new ArgumentNullException("filter");
            }
            return new FilteredDbSet<T>(context, filter);
        }
        public override EntityEntry<TEntity> Add(
        TEntity entity)
        {
            EnsureMatchesFilter(entity);
            return base.Add(entity);
        }
        public override void AddRange(
        IEnumerable<TEntity> entities)
        {
            EnsureMatchesFilter(entities);
            base.AddRange(entities);
        }
        public override void AddRange(
        params TEntity[] entities)
        {
            EnsureMatchesFilter(entities);
            base.AddRange(entities);
        }
        public override EntityEntry<TEntity> Attach(
        TEntity entity)
        {
            EnsureMatchesFilter(entity);
            return base.Attach(entity);
        }
        public override void AttachRange(
        IEnumerable<TEntity> entities)
        {
```

```
            EnsureMatchesFilter(entities);
            base.AttachRange(entities);
        }
        public override void AttachRange(
        params TEntity[] entities)
        {
            EnsureMatchesFilter(entities);
            base.AttachRange(entities);
        }
        public override EntityEntry<TEntity> Update(
        TEntity entity)
        {
            EnsureMatchesFilter(entity);
            return base.Update(entity);
        }
        public override void UpdateRange(
        IEnumerable<TEntity> entities)
        {
            EnsureMatchesFilter(entities);
            base.UpdateRange(entities);
        }
        public override void UpdateRange(
        params TEntity[] entities)
        {
            EnsureMatchesFilter(entities);
            base.UpdateRange(entities);
        }
    }
}
```

2. To make this class easier to use, let us add to the same project a static class with an extension method:

```
using System.Linq;
using Microsoft.EntityFrameworkCore;
using System.Linq.Expressions;
using System;
namespace DataAccess
{
    public static class DbContextExtensions
    {
        public static DbSet<T> FilteredSet<T>(
        this DbContext context,
        Expression<Func<T, bool>> filter)
        {
```

```
                            return FilteredDbSet<T>.Create(context, filter);
                    }
                }
        }
```

3. Create a class file called `Blog` in a `Blog.cs` file in the `BusinessLogic` project:

```csharp
namespace BusinessLogic
{
    public class Blog
    {
        public int BlogId { get; set; }
        public string Name { get; set; }
        public DateTime CreationDate { get; set; }
        public string Url { get; set; }
    }
}
```

4. Now, create a C# data context class, call it `BlogContext`, and put it in the `DataAccess` project:

```csharp
using System;
using Microsoft.EntityFrameworkCore;
using Microsoft.EntityFrameworkCore.Infrastructure;
using BusinessLogic;
namespace DataAccess
{
    public class BlogContext : DbContext
    {
        private readonly string _connectionString;
        public BlogContext(string connectionString)
        {
            _connectionString = connectionString;
            JavaBlogs = FilteredDbSet<Blog>.Create<Blog>
                (this, x => x.Name.Contains("Java"));
            DotNetBlogs = FilteredDbSet<Blog>.Create<Blog>
                (this, x => x.Name.Contains(".NET"));
        }

        public DbSet<Blog> JavaBlogs { get; set; }
        public DbSet<Blog> DotNetBlogs { get; set; }
        public DbSet<Blog> Blogs { get; set; }
        protected override void OnConfiguring(
        DbContextOptionsBuilder optionsBuilder)
        {
            optionsBuilder
            .UseSqlServer(_connectionString);
            base.OnConfiguring(optionsBuilder);
        }
    }
}
```

For Entity Framework 6, we would add this connection string to the `Web.config` file, under the `connectionStrings` section, with the name `Blog`. Of course, do change the connection string to match your system settings, for example, the name of the SQL Server instance (`SQLEXPRESS`, in this example).

5. Now, let's add a unit test in the `UnitTests` project in a file called `FilterTests.cs`:

```
using Xunit;
using BusinessLogic;
using DataAccess;
using System;
using System.Linq;
namespace UnitTests
{
    public class FilterTests : BaseTests
    {
        [Fact]
        public void CanRetrieveFiltered()
        {
            //Arrange
            using (var ctx = new BlogContext(
            Configuration["Data:Blog:ConnectionString"]))
            {
                //Act
                var javaBlogs = ctx.JavaBlogs.ToList();
                //Assert
                Assert.NotEmpty(javaBlogs);
                Assert.All(javaBlogs, blog =>
                Assert.Contains("Java", blog.Name));
            }
        }
        [Fact]
        public void CanPreventInsertion()
        {
            //Arrange
            using (var ctx = new BlogContext(
            Configuration["Data:Blog:ConnectionString"]))
            {
                //Act
                var blog = new Blog
                {
```

```
                    Name = "A Blog",
                    CreationDate = DateTime.Today,
                    Url = http://a.url
                };
                //Assert
                Assert.Throws<ArgumentException>(() =>
                    ctx.JavaBlogs.Add(blog));
            }
        }
    }
}
```

6. We will need the base class for the unit tests, BaseTests, which should also go in the UnitTests project:

```
using Microsoft.Extensions.Configuration;
namespace UnitTests
{
    public abstract class BaseTests
    {
        protected BaseTests()
        {
            var configurationBuilder = new ConfigurationBuilder();
            configurationBuilder.AddJsonFile("appSettings.json");
            Configuration = configurationBuilder.Build();
        }
        protected IConfiguration Configuration { get; set; }
    }
}
```

7. Finally, add the following connection string to the appsettings.json file:

```
{
    "Data": {
        "Blog": {
            "ConnectionString":"Server=(local)\\SQLEXPRESS;
            Database=Blog; Integrated Security=SSPI;
            MultipleActiveResultSets=true"
        }
    }
}
```

For Entity Framework 6, we would add this connection string to the `Web.config` file, under the `connectionStrings` section, with the name `Blog`. Of course, do change the connection string to match your system settings, for example, the name of the SQL Server instance (`SQLEXPRESS`, in this example).

How it works...

The `DbSet<T>` generic class plays a very important role in Entity Framework: it is essentially the entry point to the data, both for querying and for inserting new items. It is normally instantiated by the Entity Framework `DbContext` automatically, when the context is created, by inspecting its properties using reflection. We created a new class that inherits from `DbSet<T>`—actually, from the specific class provided by Entity Framework Core, since `DbSet<T>` is abstract—and added some logic to it:

- The source query is filtered
- All of its `Add*` and `Update*` methods check to see if its arguments match the provided filter, otherwise they throw an exception

What we are doing here is overriding this behavior for two specific properties, `JavaBlogs` and `DotNetBlogs`, for which we supply a restriction in the form of a LINQ expression. Each query issued against `JavaBlogs` and `DotNetBlogs` will feature this restriction automatically.

There's more...

All the default behavior will remain the same, but when we query these two collections, the results will appear filtered. We can now add sorting, additional filters, projections, and so on, and the query results will still be cached in First Level Cache. Finally, you will still be able to add entities directly to these collections, provided they match the filter.

See also

In this chapter:

- *Getting entities from the local cache*
- *Creating reusable queries*

Creating reusable queries

In this recipe, we will be working to create reusable queries that are defined outside of the data context and are specific to an object type.

Getting ready

We will be using the NuGet Package Manager to install the Entity Framework Core 1 package, `Microsoft.EntityFrameworkCore`. We will also be using a SQL Server database for storing the data, so we will also need `Microsoft.EntityFrameworkCore.SqlServer`.

Finally, `xunit` is the package we will be using for the unit tests and `dotnet-text-xunit` adds tooling support for Visual Studio. Note that the `UnitTests` project is a .NET Core App 1.0 (netcoreapp1.0), that `Microsoft.EntityFrameworkCore.Design` is configured as a build dependency and `Microsoft.EntityFrameworkCore.Tools` is set as a tool.

Open **Using EF Core Solution** from the included source code examples.

Execute the database setup script from the code samples included for this recipe. This can be found in the `DataAccess` project within the `Database` folder.

How to do it...

We are going to create a couple of extension methods over `IQueryable<T>` that can be called from different locations and are composable:

1. Create a class file called `Blog` in a `Blog.cs` file in the `BusinessLogic` project:

```
namespace BusinessLogic
{
    public class Blog
    {
        public int BlogId { get; set; }
        public string Name { get; set; }
        public DateTime CreationDate { get; set; }
        public string Url { get; set; }
    }
}
```

2. Now, create a C# data context class, call it `BlogContext`, and put it in the `DataAccess` project:

```
using System;
using Microsoft.EntityFrameworkCore;
using Microsoft.EntityFrameworkCore.Infrastructure;
namespace DataAccess
{
    public class BlogContext : DbContext
    {
        private readonly string _connectionString;
        public BlogContext(string connectionString)
```

```
        {
            _connectionString = connectionString;
        }
        public DbSet<Blog> Blogs { get; set; }

        protected override void OnConfiguring(
        DbContextOptionsBuilder optionsBuilder)
        {
            optionsBuilder
            .UseSqlServer(_connectionString);
            base.OnConfiguring(optionsBuilder);
        }
    }
}
```

 For Entity Framework 6, replace the `Microsoft.EntityFrameworkCore` namespaces with `System.Data.Entity` and call the base constructor of `DbContext`, passing it the connection string. Finally, drop the `OnConfiguring` method.

3. We then create a static class for holding our reusable queries. This goes in the `UnitTests` project, in the `BlogQueries.cs` file:

```
using System;
using System.Linq;
using BusinessLogic;
namespace UnitTests
{
    public static class BlogQueries
    {
        public static IQueryable<Blog> FilterByName(
        this IQueryable<Blog> blogs, string name)
        {
            return blogs.Where(x => x.Title.Contains(name));
        }
        public static IQueryable<Blog>
        BlogsCreatedInTheLastWeek(
        this IQueryable<Blog> blogs)
        {
            return blogs.Where(x => x.CreationDate >=
                DateTime.Today.AddDays(-7));
        }
    }
}
```

4. Now, let's add a unit test in the `UnitTests` project, in a file called `ReusableTests.cs`:

```csharp
using Xunit;
using DataAccess;
using System;
using System.Linq;

namespace UnitTests
{
  public class ObjectQueryTests : BaseTests
  {
    [Fact]
    public void CanQueryUsingObject()
    {
      //Arrange
      using (var ctx = new
        BlogContext(Configuration["Data:Blog:ConnectionString"]))
      {
        //Act
        var query = new BlogsQuery(ctx);
        query.LowerDate = DateTime.Today.AddDays(-7);
        query.HigherDate = DateTime.Today.AddDays(-1);
        query.Name = ".NET";
        query.MaxItems = 3;
        var blogs = (ctx as IQueryExecutor).Execute(query);

        //Assert
        Assert.NotEmpty(blogs);
        Assert.True(blogs.Count() <= 3);
        Assert.All(blogs, blog =>
        {
          Assert.Contains(".NET", blog.Name);
          Assert.True(blog.CreationDate >=
            DateTime.Today.AddDays(-7));
          Assert.True(blog.CreationDate <=
            DateTime.Today.AddDays(-1));
        });
      }
    }
  }
}
```

```
                    Assert.All(blogs, blog =>
                    Assert.Contains(".NET", blog.Name)
                    && Assert.True(blog.CreationDate >=
                    DateTime.Today.AddDays(-7)));
            }
        }
    }
}
```

5. We will need the base class for the unit tests, `BaseTests`, which should also go in the `UnitTests` project:

```
using Microsoft.Extensions.Configuration;
namespace UnitTests
{
    public abstract class BaseTests
    {
        protected BaseTests()
        {
            var configurationBuilder = new ConfigurationBuilder();
            configurationBuilder
            .AddJsonFile("appSettings.json");
            Configuration = configurationBuilder.Build();
        }
        protected IConfiguration Configuration { get; set; }
    }
}
```

6. Finally, add the following connection string to the `appsettings.json` file:

```
{
    "Data": {
        "Blog": {
            "ConnectionString":"Server=(local)\\SQLEXPRESS;
            Database=Blog; Integrated Security=SSPI;
            MultipleActiveResultSets=true"
        }
    }
}
```

 For Entity Framework 6, we would add this connection string to the `Web.config` file, under the `connectionStrings` section, with the name `Blog`. Of course, do change the connection string to match your system settings, for example, the name of the SQL Server instance (`SQLEXPRESS`, in this example).

How it works...

Here, we are leveraging a C# language feature called extension methods to layer on our queries without bloating our context with every possible data query. It lets us target a specific type; these queries will only be available on the types that use them, and nowhere else.

Note that we return an `IQueryable<T>` here. This is done to allow us to compose multiple statements together before translating them into an SQL statement that will be executed. These queries are not executed until a terminal operation is called upon them. `ToList`, `ToArray`, `Count`, `Any`, `First`, `FirstOrDefault`, `Single`, and `SingleOrDefault` are the most common terminal operations.

There's more...

When using extension methods, there are some things to keep in mind so you create a consistent and valuable library of queries.

Extension methods

Extension methods allow us to extend behavior onto a type without modifying that type or any of its inheritance chain. These methods are brought into scope at the namespace level. Therefore, we must add the `using` statement to have access to them.

Naming conflict

We can use extension methods to extend behavior to an existing type, but not to override it. The compiler gives priority to instance methods. Therefore, it will never call an extension method with the same signature as an instance method unless we call it explicitly (as in `ExtensionClass.ExtensionMethod(parameter)`). It is also possible, though strongly discouraged, to have two extension methods with the same name, same parameters, and both in scope.

LINQ queries (not LINQ to Objects) are not executed immediately. This means that we can play with them a bit before we actually need their results. For example, we can have code along these lines:

```
//cast to IQueryable<Blog>
var query = ctx.Blogs.AsQueryable();
if (someLogic)
{
    //add some restriction
    query = query.AddSomeFiltering();
}
else
{
    //add another restriction
```

```
            query = query.AddOtherFiltering();
    }
    //add paging (max records) and show page 0
    query = query.AddPaging(0);
    //we're happy with the query, let's execute it
    var results = query.ToList();
```

Here, I am using some hypothetical `AddSomeFiltering`, `AddOtherFiltering`, and `AddPaging` methods, but I think you get the idea.

See also

In this chapter:

- ▸ *Creating filtered collections*
- ▸ *Implementing the query object pattern*

Querying shadow properties

You heard about shadow properties in *Chapter 2, Mapping Entities*. In a nutshell, a shadow property is one that belongs to the model, maps to a database column, but has no counterpart in the POCO class: it stays in the shadows. They are useful because, since we do not see them, we can't (easily) tamper with them. But alas, if they do not exist, they cannot be (easily) queried. In this recipe, we will see how.

Getting ready

We will be using the NuGet Package Manager to install the Entity Framework Core 1 package, `Microsoft.EntityFrameworkCore`. We will also be using a SQL Server database for storing the data, so we will also need `Microsoft.EntityFrameworkCore.SqlServer`.

Finally, `xunit` is the package we will be using for the unit tests and `dotnet-text-xunit` adds tooling support for Visual Studio. Note that the `UnitTests` project is a .NET Core App 1.0 (netcoreapp1.0), that `Microsoft.EntityFrameworkCore.Design` is configured as a build dependency and `Microsoft.EntityFrameworkCore.Tools` is set as a tool.

Open **Using EF Core Solution** from the included source code examples.

Execute the database setup script from the code samples included for this recipe. This can be found in the `DataAccess` project within the `Database` folder.

How to do it...

We will create a model and define a shadow property for it, which we will then query:

1. Create a class file called `Blog` in a `Blog.cs` file in the `BusinessLogic` project:

```
namespace BusinessLogic
{
    public class Blog
    {
        public int BlogId { get; set; }
        public string Name { get; set; }
        public string Url { get; set; }
    }
}
```

2. Now, create a C# data context class, call it `BlogContext`, and put it in the `DataAccess` project:

```
using Microsoft.EntityFrameworkCore;
using System.Linq;
using BusinessLogic;
using System;
namespace DataAccess
{
    public class BlogContext : DbContext
    {
        private readonly string _connectionString;
        public BlogContext(string connectionString)
        {
            _connectionString = connectionString;
        }
        public DbSet<Blog> Blogs { get; set; }

        public override int SaveChanges(
        bool acceptAllChangesOnSuccess)
        {
            foreach (var entry in ChangeTracker
            .Entries<Blog>()
            .Where(x => x.State == EntityState.Added))
            {
                entry.Property("CreationDate").CurrentValue =
                DateTime.UtcNow;
            }
```

```
            return base
            .SaveChanges(acceptAllChangesOnSuccess);
        }
        protected override void OnModelCreating(
        ModelBuilder modelBuilder)
        {
            modelBuilder
            .Entity<Blog>()
            .Property(typeof(DateTime), "CreationDate")
            .IsRequired(true);
            base.OnModelCreating(modelBuilder);
        }
        protected override void OnConfiguring(
        DbContextOptionsBuilder optionsBuilder)
        {
            optionsBuilder
            .UseSqlServer(_connectionString);
            base.OnConfiguring(optionsBuilder);
        }
    }
}
```

 For Entity Framework 6, replace the `Microsoft.`
`EntityFrameworkCore` namespaces with `System.Data.`
`Entity` and call the base constructor of `DbContext`, passing it the
connection string. Finally, drop the `OnConfiguring` method.

3. Now, let's add a unit test in the `UnitTests` project, in a file called `ShadowTests.`
`cs`:

```
using Xunit;
using DataAccess;
using System;
using System.Linq;
using Microsoft.EntityFrameworkCore;
namespace UnitTests
{
    public class ShadowTests : BaseTests
    {
        [Fact]
        public void CanQueryShadowProperties()
        {
```

```
            //Arrange
            using (var ctx = new BlogContext(
            Configuration["Data:Blog:ConnectionString"]))
            {
                //Act
                var blogs = ctx.Blogs
                .Where(b => EF.Property<DateTime>(b,
                  "CreationDate")
                  >= DateTime.Today.AddDays(-7))
                .ToList();
                //Assert
                Assert.NotEmpty(blogs);
            }
        }
    }
}
```

4. We will need the base class for the unit tests, `BaseTests`, which should also go in the `UnitTests` project:

```
using Microsoft.Extensions.Configuration;
namespace UnitTests
{
    public abstract class BaseTests
    {
        protected BaseTests()
        {
            var configurationBuilder = new ConfigurationBuilder();
            configurationBuilder
            .AddJsonFile("appSettings.json");
            Configuration = configurationBuilder.Build();
        }
        protected IConfiguration Configuration { get; set; }
    }
}
```

5. Finally, add the following connection string to the `appsettings.json` file:

```
{
    "Data": {
        "Blog": {
            "ConnectionString":"Server=(local)\\SQLEXPRESS;
            Database=Blog; Integrated Security=SSPI;
            MultipleActiveResultSets=true"
        }
    }
}
```

For Entity Framework 6, we would add this connection string to the `Web.config` file, under the `connectionStrings` section, with the name `Blog`. Of course, do change the connection string to match your system settings, for example, the name of the SQL Server instance (`SQLEXPRESS`, in this example).

How it works...

We configure a shadow property—one that has no physical counterpart—in the `OnModelCreating` method of `DbContext`; in this example, it is a mandatory `DateTime` property called `CreationDate`. When the context is about to save its entries (`SaveChanges`), we iterate through all the added `Blog` entities and we set the `CreationDate` property using a special syntax. For querying, all we need to do is to make use of the EF static class `Property` method, passing it a generic parameter of the desired type, so that we have strong typing.

There's more...

Reusable queries can also make use of shadow properties using this exact same technique (`EF.Property`).

See also

In this chapter:

- ▸ *Creating reusable queries*
- ▸ *Implementing the query object*

Implementing the query object pattern

In this recipe, we will be implementing the **Query Object** pattern on top of Entity Framework Core to leverage maximum reuse without surfacing queryable collections to the consuming developers. The **Query Object** pattern allows encapsulating and making parameterizable queries without actually exposing what it does.

Getting ready

We will be using the NuGet Package Manager to install the Entity Framework Core 1 package, `Microsoft.EntityFrameworkCore`. We will also be using a SQL Server database for storing the data, so we will also need `Microsoft.EntityFrameworkCore.SqlServer`.

Finally, `xunit` is the package we will be using for the unit tests and `dotnet-text-xunit` adds tooling support for Visual Studio. Note that the `UnitTests` project is a .NET Core App 1.0 (netcoreapp1.0), that `Microsoft.EntityFrameworkCore.Design` is configured as a build dependency, and `Microsoft.EntityFrameworkCore.Tools` is set as a tool.

Open **Using EF Core Solution** from the included source code examples.

Execute the database setup script from the code samples included for this recipe. This can be found in the `DataAccess` project within the `Database` folder.

How to do it...

We will create a query object class and a query executor interface and implementation, which will be the `DbContext` class:

1. Create a class file called `Blog` in a `Blog.cs` file in the `BusinessLogic` project:

    ```
    namespace BusinessLogic
    {
        public class Blog
        {
            public int BlogId { get; set; }
            public string Name { get; set; }
            public string Url { get; set; }
            public DateTime CreationDate { get; set; }
        }
    }
    ```

2. The query object base class should go into the `DataAccess` project in a `QueryObject.cs` file:

    ```
    using System.Linq;
    namespace DataAccess
    {
        public abstract class QueryObject<T>
        {
            public int MaxItems { get; set; }
            public int FirstItemIndex { get; set; }
            public abstract IQueryable<T> ToQuery();
        }
    }
    ```

3. Here's our `IQueryExecutor` interface. Here, we are only concerned about the `Execute` method that takes a `QueryObject` instance. This code should go into a file called `IQueryExecutor.cs` in the `DataAccess` project:

```
using System.Collections.Generic;
namespace DataAccess
{
    public interface IQueryExecutor
    {
        IEnumerable<T> Execute<T>(QueryObject<T> query);
    }
}
```

4. Now, create a C# data context class, call it `BlogContext`, and put it in the `DataAccess` project. Notice how it implements our `IQueryExecutor` interface:

```
using System;
using System.Collections.Generic;
using System.Linq;
using Microsoft.EntityFrameworkCore;
using Microsoft.EntityFrameworkCore.Infrastructure;
using Microsoft.EntityFrameworkCore;
using BusinessLogic;
namespace DataAccess
{
    public class BlogContext : DbContext, IQueryExecutor
    {
        private readonly string _connectionString;
        public BlogContext(string connectionString)
        {
            _connectionString = connectionString;
        }
        public DbSet<Blog> Blogs { get; set; }
        public IEnumerable<T> Execute<T>(
        QueryObject<T> query)
        {
            return query
            .ToQuery()
            .ToList();
        }
        protected override void OnConfiguring(
        DbContextOptionsBuilder optionsBuilder)
        {
            optionsBuilder
            .UseSqlServer(_connectionString);
            base.OnConfiguring(optionsBuilder);
```

```
            }
        }
    }
```

 For Entity Framework 6, replace the `Microsoft.
EntityFrameworkCore` namespaces for `System.Data.
Entity` and call the base constructor of `DbContext`, passing
it the connection string. Finally, drop the `OnConfiguring` method.

5. A particular query object class for retrieving all blogs containing a certain name and
    created in a given time frame, `BlogsQuery`, should be located in the `DataAccess`
    project:

```csharp
using Xunit;
using DataAccess;
using System;
using System.Linq;

namespace UnitTests
{
    public class ObjectQueryTests : BaseTests
    {
        [Fact]
        public void CanQueryUsingObject()
        {
            //Arrange
            using (var ctx = new
                BlogContext(Configuration["Data:Blog:ConnectionString"]))
            {
                //Act
                var query = new BlogsQuery(ctx);
                query.LowerDate = DateTime.Today.AddDays(-7);
                query.HigherDate = DateTime.Today.AddDays(-1);
                query.Name = ".NET";
                query.MaxItems = 3;
                var blogs = (ctx as IQueryExecutor).Execute(query);

                //Assert
                Assert.NotEmpty(blogs);
                Assert.True(blogs.Count() <= 3);
                Assert.All(blogs, blog =>
                {
                    Assert.Contains(".NET", blog.Name);
                    Assert.True(blog.CreationDate >=
                        DateTime.Today.AddDays(-7));
                    Assert.True(blog.CreationDate <=
                        DateTime.Today.AddDays(-1));
                });
            }
```

```
        }
      }
    }
```

6. Now, let's add a unit test in the `UnitTests` project, in a file called `ObjectQueryTests.cs`:

```csharp
using Xunit;
using DataAccess;
using System;
using System.Linq;

namespace UnitTests
{
  public class ObjectQueryTests : BaseTests
  {
    [Fact]
    public void CanQueryUsingObject()
    {
      //Arrange
      using (var ctx = new
        BlogContext(Configuration["Data:Blog:ConnectionString"]))
      {
        //Act
        var query = new BlogsQuery(ctx);
        query.LowerDate = DateTime.Today.AddDays(-7);
        query.HigherDate = DateTime.Today.AddDays(-1);
        query.Name = ".NET";
        query.MaxItems = 3;
        var blogs = (ctx as IQueryExecutor).Execute(query);

        //Assert
        Assert.NotEmpty(blogs);
        Assert.True(blogs.Count() <= 3);
        Assert.All(blogs, blog =>
        {
          Assert.Contains(".NET", blog.Name);
          Assert.True(blog.CreationDate >=
            DateTime.Today.AddDays(-7));
          Assert.True(blog.CreationDate <=
            DateTime.Today.AddDays(-1));
        });
      }
    }
  }
}
```

7. We will need the base class for the unit tests, `BaseTests`, which should also go in the `UnitTests` project:

```csharp
using Microsoft.Extensions.Configuration;
namespace UnitTests
{
    public abstract class BaseTests
    {
        protected BaseTests()
        {
            var configurationBuilder = new ConfigurationBuilder();
            configurationBuilder
            .AddJsonFile("appSettings.json");
            Configuration = configurationBuilder.Build();
        }
        protected IConfiguration Configuration { get; set; }
    }
}
```

8. Finally, add the following connection string to the `appsettings.json` file:

```json
{
    "Data": {
        "Blog": {
            "ConnectionString":"Server=(local)\\SQLEXPRESS;
            Database=Blog; Integrated Security=SSPI;
            MultipleActiveResultSets=true"
        }
    }
}
```

For Entity Framework 6, we would add this connection string to the `Web.config` file, under the `connectionStrings` section, with the name `Blog`. Of course, do change the connection string to match your system settings, for example, the name of the SQL Server instance (`SQLEXPRESS`, in this example).

How it works...

A **Query Object** contains all the properties it needs to perform a query. We defined a base abstract class that basically offers paging properties; in the concrete implementation, the `BlogsQuery` takes a `DbContext` in its constructor and a few extra properties (`HigherDate`, `LowerDate`, and `Name`). When it is asked to return a query (`ToQuery`), it takes all of these properties into account and builds the appropriate query, which may be arbitrarily complex. The context only needs to execute this query and materialize it.

 Note that the purpose of the Query Object pattern is not to be extensible or composable, like LINQ, for example. It is meant to return one thing precisely.

There's more...

Use the **Query Object** instead of the **Repository** pattern because it is much more flexible: just think that for any new query you want to implement, you would need to add another method to the repository interface and implementation. If you don't know about the **Repository** pattern, it allows you to abstract possibly complex logic behind a simple façade where all queries look like collections returned by query methods.

See also

In this chapter:

> ▸ *Creating reusable queries*

The Repository pattern: `http://martinfowler.com/eaaCatalog/repository.html`.

Using dynamic LINQ

The `IQueryable<T>` interface offers interesting possibilities for composing queries with some degree of dynamism. However, sometimes that is enough. Imagine, for example, that you want to filter by some text expression or order by a property for which you only have the name. Enter Dynamic LINQ: a means to combine strongly typed LINQ queries with text expressions. Let's see how it works.

Getting ready

We will be using the NuGet Package Manager to install the Entity Framework Core 1 package, `Microsoft.EntityFrameworkCore`. We will also be using a SQL Server database for storing the data, so we will also need `Microsoft.EntityFrameworkCore.SqlServer`.

Finally, `xunit` is the package we will be using for the unit tests and `dotnet-text-xunit` adds tooling support for Visual Studio. Note that the `UnitTests` project is a .NET Core App 1.0 (netcoreapp1.0), that `Microsoft.EntityFrameworkCore.Design` is configured as a build dependency and `Microsoft.EntityFrameworkCore.Tools` is set as a tool.

To use the Dynamic LINQ functionality in .NET Core, we need the `System.Linq.Dynamic.Core` NuGet package.

Open **Using EF Core Solution** from the included source code examples.

Execute the database setup script from the code samples included for this recipe. This can be found in the `DataAccess` project within the `Database` folder.

How to do it...

We are going to use Dynamic LINQ to execute queries with some parameters coming as text.

1. Create a class file called `Blog` in a `Blog.cs` file in the `BusinessLogic` project:

```
namespace BusinessLogic
{
    public class Blog
    {
        public int BlogId { get; set; }
        public string Name { get; set; }
        public string Url { get; set; }
        public DateTime CreationDate { get; set; }
    }
}
```

2. Now, create a C# data context class, call it `BlogContext`, and put it in the `DataAccess` project:

```
using System;
using System.Collections.Generic;
using System.Linq;
using Microsoft.EntityFrameworkCore;
using Microsoft.EntityFrameworkCore.Infrastructure;
using Microsoft.EntityFrameworkCore;
using BusinessLogic;
namespace DataAccess
```

```
{
    public class BlogContext : DbContext
    {
        private readonly string _connectionString;
        public BlogContext(string connectionString)
        {
            _connectionString = connectionString;
        }
        public DbSet<Blog> Blogs { get; set; }
        protected override void OnConfiguring(
        DbContextOptionsBuilder optionsBuilder)
        {
            optionsBuilder
            .UseSqlServer(_connectionString);
            base.OnConfiguring(optionsBuilder);
        }
    }
}
```

 For Entity Framework 6, replace the `Microsoft.EntityFrameworkCore` namespaces with `System.Data.Entity` and call the base constructor of `DbContext`, passing it the connection string. Finally, drop the `OnConfiguring` method.

3. Now, let's add a unit test in the `UnitTests` project, in a file called `DynamicLinqTests.cs`:

```
using Xunit;
using DataAccess;
using System;
using System.Linq;

namespace UnitTests
{
  public class ObjectQueryTests : BaseTests
  {
    [Fact]
    public void CanQueryUsingObject()
    {
      //Arrange
      using (var ctx = new
        BlogContext(Configuration["Data:Blog:ConnectionString"]))
      {
        //Act
        var query = new BlogsQuery(ctx);
        query.LowerDate = DateTime.Today.AddDays(-7);
```

```
query.HigherDate = DateTime.Today.AddDays(-1);
query.Name = ".NET";
query.MaxItems = 3;
var blogs = (ctx as IQueryExecutor).Execute(query);

//Assert
Assert.NotEmpty(blogs);
Assert.True(blogs.Count() <= 3);
Assert.All(blogs, blog =>
{
  Assert.Contains(".NET", blog.Name);
  Assert.True(blog.CreationDate >=
    DateTime.Today.AddDays(-7));
  Assert.True(blog.CreationDate <=
    DateTime.Today.AddDays(-1));
});
            }
         }
      }
}
```

4. We will need the base class for the unit tests, `BaseTests`, which should also go in the `UnitTests` project:

```
using Microsoft.Extensions.Configuration;
namespace UnitTests
{
    public abstract class BaseTests
    {
        protected BaseTests()
        {
            var configurationBuilder = new ConfigurationBuilder();
            configurationBuilder
            .AddJsonFile("appSettings.json");
            Configuration = configurationBuilder.Build();
        }
        protected IConfiguration Configuration { get; set; }
    }
}
```

5. Finally, add the following connection string to the `appsettings.json` file:

```
{
    "Data": {
        "Blog": {
            "ConnectionString":"Server=(local)\\SQLEXPRESS;
            Database=Blog; Integrated Security=SSPI;
            MultipleActiveResultSets=true"
        }
    }
}
```

For Entity Framework 6, we would add this connection string to the `Web.config` file, under the `connectionStrings` section, with the name `Blog`. Of course, do change the connection string to match your system settings, for example, the name of the SQL Server instance (`SQLEXPRESS`, in this example).

How it works...

Microsoft, a long time ago, made available a set of extensions to LINQ that take strings instead of strongly typed expressions. Stef Heyenrath (`https://github.com/StefH`) ported this code to .NET Core (`https://github.com/StefH/System.Linq.Dynamic.Core`) and made it available as a NuGet package (`https://www.nuget.org/packages/System.Linq.Dynamic.Core/`). This is pretty cool and offers exciting possibilities: imagine, for example, that you are receiving the sort order for a query from the web, as a query string parameter, for example. You don't have a strongly typed LINQ query for the property, only a string. Otherwise, you want to be able to concatenate strings to build restrictions.

Note that I'm not talking here about SQL; it's still LINQ, but in string format. All it needs is to add a reference to the `System.Linq.Dynamic.Core` namespace and all the extension methods taking strings are immediately available.

There's more...

You can make arbitrarily complex stringified LINQ queries using this approach and choose whether to pass parameters or have values directly in the string. Even the methods that are normally available in the property types—such as the ones in the String class that can be turned into SQL—are still available.

6

Advanced Scenarios

In this chapter, we will cover the following topics:

- ▶ Generating entities from the database
- ▶ Implementing multitenancy
- ▶ Strongly typed bulk operations
- ▶ Handling soft deletes
- ▶ Adding logging
- ▶ Capturing the audit data
- ▶ Retrieving entity metadata
- ▶ Improving MVC applications
- ▶ Hooking infrastructure services
- ▶ Using other databases

Introduction

This chapter will cover more advanced features of Entity Framework Core. These include some scenarios that more seasoned users will miss.

One of these scenarios is bulk updates and deletes. After some basic usage of an ORM, users will easily find out that it doesn't make much sense to load entities just for deleting or modifying them. We will make use of an external library to make it possible.

If you have a big model, with possibly tens of tables, you will definitely want to generate the class model automatically, and sure enough, Entity Framework Core can do it.

Multitenancy is very popular nowadays, and we will see how we can implement it on the data side of things.

Soft deletes and auditing come in handy when we cannot afford to drop records from the database and wish to see who was the last person who changed a record.

Finally, logging is a must have, and can save us ours of debugging.

We'll see all of this and more; hope you find it instructive!

Generating entities from the database

Entity Framework Core 1.0 supports two different workflows:

  ▶ **Code first**: Entities are first generated as code and only then is the database generated. This follows the **Domain Driven Design** (**DDD**) approach.

  ▶ **Database first**: We already have a database and we want to generate entities for it.

The first approach was made popular when Entity Framework 4.1 "Code First" was released. The idea here is that we, as C# developers, understand code better than anything, and so we model our entities as code. It is left for Entity Framework to produce the database objects (tables, relations, and so on) that will enable it to persist our data in an almost transparent way.

But what happens when you have an existing (legacy or otherwise) database, perhaps consisting of hundreds of tables? Or you have this super cool UML tool that generates the database from a model? It is troublesome, to say the least, to generate all C# entities by hand in Visual Studio, so the option is to have some tool generate coded entities to match all these objects. Enter EF Core scaffolding.

Scaffolding is the process by which the database is inspected and **Plain Old CLR Object** (**POCO**) classes are produced that match the structure of the database objects automatically. This way you do not have to be worried about any spelling mistakes or about forgetting something: as long as the tables have the appropriate constraints–primary and foreign keys–everything works pretty well.

Getting ready

We will be using the NuGet Package Manager to install the Entity Framework Core 1 package, `Microsoft.EntityFrameworkCore`. We will also be using a SQL Server database to store the data, so we will also need `Microsoft.EntityFrameworkCore.SqlServer`. Because we will be using scaffolding, we also need `Microsoft.EntityFrameworkCore.SqlServer.Design` and `Microsoft.EntityFrameworkCore.Design`.

Open **Using EF Core Solution** from the included source code examples.

Make sure you have PowerShell 5 installed. It is available free of charge for a number of Windows editions from 7 upwards. Get it here: `https://www.microsoft.com/en-us/download/details.aspx?id=50395`.

Execute the database setup script from the code samples included for this recipe. This can be found in the `DataAccess` project within the `Database` folder.

How to do it...

We will be generating C# POCO entities that match our database:

1. Open a command prompt and navigate to the folder where you have the `Scaffold` project and run the following command:

    ```
    dotnet ef dbcontext scaffold "Data Source=.\SQLEXPRESS;
    Integrated Security=SSPI; Initial Catalog=Blog;" Microsoft.
    EntityFrameworkCore.SqlServer
    ```

    Of course, do replace the connection string for one that's appropriate to your system.

2. Examine the generated files, for example, `Blog.cs`:

    ```
    using System;
    using System.Collections.Generic;
    namespace Scaffold
    {
        public partial class Blog
        {
            public Blog()
            {
                Post = new HashSet<Post>();
            }
            public int BlogId { get; set; }
            public string Name { get; set; }
            public DateTime CreationDate { get; set; }
            public string Url { get; set; }
            public virtual ICollection<Post> Post { get; set; }
        }
    }
    ```

3. You will notice a couple of things:

    □   Collections are not pluralized (for example, `Post` instead of Posts) and are instantiated in the public constructor as `HashSets<>`

    □   All classes are created as `partial`

    □   Navigation properties and collections are marked as `virtual`

How it works...

The Entity Framework tooling inspects the database whose connection string was passed as the first parameter to scaffold (`"Data Source=..."`) using the provider passed as the second parameter (`Microsoft.EntityFrameworkCore.SqlServer`). It looks for all tables, their columns and keys, and then outputs the corresponding C# POCO entities. When it does so, it produces partial classes, so that you can easily extend the entities without the changes being lost if you regenerate them from the database. The virtual modifier is kind of pointless right now, because Entity Framework Core 1.0 does not have lazy loading, but it doesn't do any harm, and may come in handy in the future.

There's more...

You can extend the classes generated by creating new files, probably with a similar name, and adding the same classes to them bearing the `partial` keyword:

```
using System;
using System.Collections.Generic;
using System.Linq;
namespace Scaffold
{
    public partial class Blog
    {
        public TimeSpan Age
        {
            get
            {
                return DateTime.UtcNow - CreationDate;
            }
        }
        public IEnumerable<Post> RecentPosts
        {
            get
            {
                return Post.Where(p => p.Date >=
                    DateTime.UtcNow.AddDays(-7));
            }
        }
    }
}
```

This might go, for example, in a `Blog.Extensions.cs` file, as it contains additional methods to the `Blog` class.

Implementing multitenancy

Multitenancy is the ability by which an application can act (and seem) different when observed in different ways. Think, for example, of a website that displays a different look and feel when it is accessed as `http://abc.com` or `http://xyz.net`. Here, we are talking about the same physical site having two different domain names bound to it, `abc.com` and `xyz.net`, which are the tenants.

When it comes to relational databases, there are essentially three techniques for achieving multitenancy:

- ▶ **Separate database**: Each tenant's data is kept in a separate database instance, with a different connection string for each; the multitenant system should pick automatically the one appropriate for the current tenant as shown in the following figure:

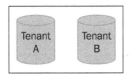

Separate databases

- ▶ **Separate schema**: The same database instance is used for all the tenants' data, but each tenant will have a separate schema; not all RDBMSs support this properly, for example, SQL Server doesn't, but Oracle does. When I say SQL Server doesn't support this, I don't mean to say that it doesn't have schemas, it's just that it does not offer an isolation mechanism, unlike Oracle, and it isn't possible to specify, per query or per connection, the schema to use by default.

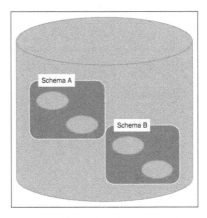

Separate schemas

▶ **Partitioned data**: The data for all tenants is kept in the same physical instance and schema, and a partitioning column is used to differentiate tenants; it is up to the framework to issue proper SQL queries that filter data appropriately.

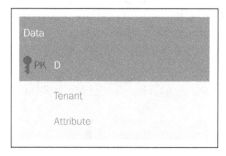

Partitioned data

Entity Framework Core supports all of these techniques. We won't go into which one is better; all have their pros and cons. For the sake of our discussion, let's imagine we have some service that returns the current tenant's ID.

Getting ready

We will be using the NuGet Package Manager to install the Entity Framework Core 1 package, `Microsoft.EntityFrameworkCore`. We will also be using a SQL Server database to store the data, so we will also need `Microsoft.EntityFrameworkCore.SqlServer`.

For the web interfaces, there will also be a need for the `Microsoft.AspNetCore.Http` and `Microsoft.AspNetCore.Http.Abstractions`.

Open **Using EF Core Solution** from the included source code examples.

Execute the database setup script from the code samples included for this recipe. This can be found in the `DataAccess` project within the `Database` folder.

How to do it...

We will be implementing some infrastructure classes that will help with configuring multitenancy:

1. Add a file called `MultitenantEntity.cs` with the following content to the `BusinessLogic` project:

```
using System;
namespace BusinessLogic
{
    public class MultitenantEntity : IMultitenant
```

```
        {
            public int Id { get; set; }
            public string Name { get; set; }
        }
    }
```

2. Add a marker interface called `IMultitenant` also to `BusinessLogic`, in a file with the name `IMultitenant.cs`:

```
namespace BusinessLogic
{
    public interface IMultitenant { }
}
```

3. Add a `MultitenantConfiguration` class to the `DataAccess` project:

```
using Microsoft.EntityFrameworkCore;
using BusinessLogic;
namespace DataAccess
{
    public abstract class MultitenantConfiguration
    {
        public static MultitenantConfiguration Provider
        { get; set; }
        protected MultitenantConfiguration(
        IMultitenantAccessor accessor)
        {
            Accessor = accessor;
        }
        public IMultitenantAccessor Accessor
        { get; private set; }
        public abstract void Use(
        DbContextOptionsBuilder optionsBuilder);
        public abstract void Use(
        ModelBuilder modelBuilder);
    }
}
```

4. The `IMultitenantAccessor` interface defines the contract for getting the current tenant, and it should look like this in the `DataAccess` project):

```
namespace DataAccess
{
    public interface IMultitenantAccessor
    {
        string GetCurrentTenantId();
    }
}
```

5. A simple implementation of the `IMultitenantAccessor` interface would be like this:

```
using System.Linq;
using Microsoft.AspNetCore.Http;
namespace DataAccess
{
    public class HostHeaderMultitenantAccessor :
      IMultitenantAccessor
    {
        private readonly IHttpContextAccessor _accessor;
        public HostHeaderMultitenantAccessor(
            IHttpContextAccessor accessor)
        {
            _accessor = accessor;
        }
        public string GetCurrentTenantId()
        {
            var context = _accessor.HttpContext;
            var parts =
                context.Request.Host.Host.Split('.');
            return parts.ElementAt(parts.Length - 2) + "."
                + parts.Last();
        }
    }
}
```

6. Now add a class to the `DataAccess` project that will implement the **Partitioned Data** approach and call it `PartitionedDataConfiguration.cs`:

```
using System.Linq;
using System.Reflection;
using Microsoft.EntityFrameworkCore;
using BusinessLogic;

namespace DataAccess
{
  public class PartitionedDataConfiguration :
    MultitenantConfiguration
  {
    public const string MultitenantColumn = "TenantId";
    public PartitionedDataConfiguration(IMultitenantAccessor
      accessor) : base(accessor)
    {
    }

    public override void Use(DbContextOptionsBuilder
      optionsBuilder)
    {
```

```
    }

    public override void Use(ModelBuilder modelBuilder)
    {
      var tenantId = Accessor.GetCurrentTenantId();
      foreach (var entity in modelBuilder.Model.GetEntityTypes().
        Where(e => typeof(IMultitenant).IsAssignableFrom(e.ClrType)))
      {
        modelBuilder
          .Entity(entity.ClrType)
          .HasDiscriminator(MultitenantColumn, typeof(string))
          .HasValue(tenantId);
      }
    }
  }
}
```

7. Now, do the **Separate Database** implementation,
   `SeparateDatabaseConfiguration.cs`:

```
using System;
using Microsoft.EntityFrameworkCore;
using Microsoft.Extensions.Configuration;

namespace DataAccess
{
  public class SeparateDatabaseConfiguration :
    MultitenantConfiguration
  {
    private readonly IConfiguration _configuration;
    private readonly string _connectionStringTemplate;
    private readonly Func<IMultitenantAccessor, string>
      _connectionStringProvider;

    public SeparateDatabaseConfiguration(IMultitenantAccessor
      accessor, IConfiguration configuration, string
      connectionStringTemplate) : base(accessor)
    {
      _configuration = configuration;
      _connectionStringTemplate = connectionStringTemplate
        ??  "Data:{0}:ConnectionString";
    }

    public SeparateDatabaseConfiguration(IMultitenantAccessor
      accessor,  Func<IMultitenantAccessor, string>
      csProvider) : base(accessor)
    {
      _connectionStringProvider = csProvider;
```

```
          }

          private string GetConnectionString()
          {
            var connectionString = string.Empty;
            if (_configuration != null)
            {
              var tenantId = Accessor.GetCurrentTenantId();
              var template = string.Format(_connectionStringTemplate,
              tenantId);
              connectionString = _configuration[template];
            }
            else if (_connectionStringProvider != null)
            {
              connectionString = _connectionStringProvider(Accessor);
            }
            return connectionString;
          }

          public override void Use(DbContextOptionsBuilder
            optionsBuilder)
          {
            var connectionString = GetConnectionString();
            optionsBuilder.UseSqlServer(connectionString);
          }

          public override void Use(ModelBuilder modelBuilder)
          {
          }
        }
      }
```

8. Finally, let's do the implementation for **Separate Schema**, which should go in a
   SeparateSchemaConfiguration.cs file, in the DataAccess project:

```
using System.Linq;
using System.Reflection;
using Microsoft.EntityFrameworkCore;
using BusinessLogic;

namespace DataAccess
{
  public class SeparateSchemaConfiguration :
    MultitenantConfiguration
  {
    public SeparateSchemaConfiguration(
      IMultitenantAccessor accessor) : base(accessor)
    {
```

```
    }
    public override void Use(DbContextOptionsBuilder
      optionsBuilder)
    {
    }
    public override void Use(ModelBuilder modelBuilder)
    {
      var tenantId = Accessor.GetCurrentTenantId();
      foreach (var entity in
        modelBuilder.Model.GetEntityTypes().Where
        (e => typeof(IMultitenant).
        IsAssignableFrom(e.ClrType)))
      {
        modelBuilder
          .Entity(entity.ClrType)
          .ForSqlServerToTable(modelBuilder
            .Model.FindEntityType(entity.ClrType)
            .SqlServer().TableName, tenantId);
      }
    }
  }
}
```

9. Next, we add a context (`MultitenantContext`) to the `DataAccess` project:

```
using BusinessLogic;
using Microsoft.EntityFrameworkCore;

namespace DataAccess
{
  public class MultitenantContext : DbContext
  {
    private readonly string _connectionString;

    public MultitenantContext(DbContextOptions
      options) : base(options)
    {
    }

    public MultitenantContext(string connectionString)
    {
      _connectionString = connectionString;
    }

    public DbSet<MultitenantEntity> MultitenantEntities
      { get; set; }
```

```
      protected override void
        OnConfiguring(DbContextOptionsBuilder optionsBuilder)
      {
        optionsBuilder.UseSqlServer(_connectionString);
        MultitenantConfiguration.Provider?
          .Use(optionsBuilder);
        base.OnConfiguring(optionsBuilder);
      }

      protected override void OnModelCreating
        (ModelBuilder modelBuilder)
      {
        MultitenantConfiguration.Provider?.Use(modelBuilder);
        base.OnModelCreating(modelBuilder);
      }
    }
  }
}
```

How it works...

We created a base class for representing the different multitenant strategies:
`MultitenantConfiguration`. It also holds a static reference for the current strategy in use
(`Provider`) and two abstract methods, both named `Use`; these are meant to be called in the
two places in the `DbContext` life cycle, `OnModelCreating` and `OnConfiguring`, where we
can act upon the configuration of the context:

  ▶ `OnConfiguring`: We can select the database provider (not relevant here, as we will
    stick with SQL Server) and the connection string that is specific to that provider

  ▶ `OnModelCreating`: We can inspect and change the data model and its mapping to
    the data store

Before we use the context, we need to make sure that we register the tenant identification
strategy (`IMultitenantAccessor`) implementation of our choice. For web applications,
we're probably going to choose one that gets the tenant from the host header. The sample
`HostHeaderMultitenantAccessor` does just that; for a domain of `abc.com` it returns
`abc`, that is, it strips off the top level domain part plus any additional sub-domains that there
may be. Of course, you can pick a totally different strategy.

This strategy will be fed to a `MultitenantConfiguration` instance, which will be
conveniently kept in the `Provider` static property. In our `MultitenantContext`,
we will make sure to call the `Use` methods of `MultitenantConfiguration` in both
`OnConfiguring` and `OnModelCreating`. Not all strategies require this, but since we do not
know which ones do, we're better off this way. Notice the `?` syntax: if the `Provider` property
is null, nothing will be called.

These strategies work like this:

- ▸ `PartitionedDataConfiguration`: This checks all the mapped entities that implement the marker interface, `IMultitenant`, and add a `WHERE` restriction over a non-mapped column `TenantId` that will hold the current tenant's ID (for example, `TenantId = 'abc'`)

- ▸ `SeparateDatabaseConfiguration`: This returns a different connection string depending on the current tenant ID

- ▸ `SeparateSchemaConfiguration`: For each mapped entity implementing `IMultitenant`, set its schema to be the current tenant ID (for example, `abc.MyEntity`, `xyz.MyEntity`)

There's more...

When it comes to web tenant identification strategies, we have a myriad of choices:

- ▸ Host header (like in this example)
- ▸ Query string parameter
- ▸ Hardcoded per requesting domain/IP range

We won't focus on these; normally, the host header is the one we want.

As for the multitenant configuration, it is certainly possible to think of options other than different schema, databases, or discriminating columns, but these are usually sufficient.

Strongly typed bulk operations

Entity Framework Core 1.0 supports two query options:

- ▸ SQL
- ▸ LINQ

LINQ, of course, is the preferred query language in the .NET world. It has the great advantage that it is compiled to .NET and is strongly typed, meaning most errors are detected at compile time. The drawback is that it cannot be used for anything other than querying, that is, it cannot do updates, inserts, or deletes.

However, because of the great extensibility hooks that are present in Entity Framework Core, it is indeed possible to turn strongly typed LINQ queries into updates and deletes. In particular, Pomelo Foundation has implemented a library for doing just that.

Getting ready

We will be using the NuGet Package Manager to install the Entity Framework Core 1 package, `Microsoft.EntityFrameworkCore`. We will also be using a SQL Server database to store the data, so we will also need `Microsoft.EntityFrameworkCore.SqlServer`. We will also need `Pomelo.EntityFrameworkCore.Lolita.SqlServer` for the strongly typed bulk API.

Finally, `Xunit` is the package we will be using for the unit tests, and `dotnet-text-Xunit` adds tooling support for Visual Studio. Notice that the `UnitTests` project is a .NET Core App 1.0 (netcoreapp1.0), that `Microsoft.EntityFrameworkCore.Design` is configured as a build dependency, and `Microsoft.EntityFrameworkCore.Tools` is set as a tool.

Open **Using EF Core Solution** from the included source code examples.

Execute the database setup script from the code samples included for this recipe. This can be found in the `DataAccess` project within the `Database` folder.

How to do it...

We will create unit tests for doing strongly typed bulk operations using the Pomelo API:

1. Create an entity class `MyEntity` in a similar named file in the `BusinessLogic` project:

    ```
    using System;
    namespace BusinessLogic
    {
        public class MyEntity
        {
            public int Id { get; set; }
            public string Name { get; set; }
            public DateTime Date { get; set; }
        }
    }
    ```

2. Next, we add a context called `MyContext` to the `DataAccess` project:

    ```
    using Microsoft.EntityFrameworkCore;
    using BusinessLogic;
    namespace DataAccess
    {
      public class MyContext : DbContext
      {
        private readonly string _connectionString;
        public MyContext
    ```

```
            (DbContextOptions options): base(options)
        {
        }
        public MyContext(string connectionString)
        {
            _connectionString = connectionString;
        }
        public DbSet<MyEntity> MyEntities { get; set; }
        protected override void OnConfiguring(
        DbContextOptionsBuilder optionsBuilder)
        {
            optionsBuilder.UseSqlServerLolita();
            optionsBuilder.UseSqlServer(_connectionString);
            base.OnConfiguring(optionsBuilder);
        }
    }
}
```

3. Create a unit tests file, `StronglyTypedTests.cs`, in the `UnitTests` project:

```
using BusinessLogic;
using DataAccess;
using Microsoft.EntityFrameworkCore;
using System.Linq;
using Xunit;

namespace UnitTests
{
    public class StronglyTypedTests : BaseTests
    {
        [Fact]
        public void CanDelete()
        {
            //Arrange
            using (var ctx = new
                MyContext(Configuration["Data:Blog:ConnectionString"]))
            {
                //Act
                ctx.MyEntities.Add(new MyEntity { Name = "test" });
                ctx.SaveChanges();
                var result = ctx.MyEntities.Where(b =>
                    b.Name == "test").Delete();

                //Assert
                Assert.True(result == 1);
```

```
      }
    }

    [Fact]
    public void CanUpdate()
    {
      //Arrange
      using (var ctx = new MyContext
        (Configuration["Data:Blog:ConnectionString"]))
      {
        //Act
        ctx.MyEntities.Add(new MyEntity { Name = "test" });
        ctx.SaveChanges();
        var result = ctx.MyEntities.Where(b =>
          b.Name == "test").SetField(b =>
          b.Date).AddDays(1).Update();

        //Assert
        Assert.True(result == 1);
      }
    }
  }
}
```

4. We will need the base class for the unit tests, `BaseTests`, which should also go in the `UnitTests` project:

```
using Microsoft.Framework.Configuration;
namespace UnitTests
{
  public abstract class BaseTests
  {
    protected BaseTests()
    {
        var configurationBuilder = new
          ConfigurationBuilder();
        configurationBuilder
          .AddJsonFile("appSettings.json");
        Configuration = configurationBuilder.Build();
    }
    protected IConfiguration Configuration { get; set; }
  }
}
```

5. Finally, add the following connection string to the `appsettings.json` file and make sure the file is copied to the output folder upon build:

```
{
    "Data": {
        "Blog": {
            "ConnectionString":"Server=(local)\\SQLEXPRESS;
                Database=Blog; Integrated Security=SSPI;
                    MultipleActiveResultSets=true"
        }
    }
}
```

 For Entity Framework 6, we would add this connection string to the `Web.config` file, under the `connectionStrings` section, with the name `Blog`. Of course, do change the connection string to match your system settings; for example, the name of the SQL Server instance (`SQLEXPRESS`, in this example).

How it works...

Notice how we, in the `OnConfiguring` method, make a call to `UseSqlServerLolita`. This is what makes strong typing bulk operations possible. We see two kinds of bulk operation:

▶ **Deletes**: The `Delete` method is called on top of a LINQ expression, which can even be the `DbSet<T>` property, any `IQueryable<T>` will do; it returns the number of affected records (deleted rows)

▶ **Updates**: Here there are two possibilities:
  ❑ Updating a column to a constant value
  ❑ Updating a column to an expression possibly based on the column itself

In any case, the `Update` method always returns the number of affected records (updated rows)

The `Delete` and `Update` "terminal" methods, similar to `ToList`, `ToArray`, `Count`, `First`, `FirstOrDefault`, `Single`, `SingleOrDefault`, and so on, take a LINQ expression waiting to be executed and do so, turning the LINQ expression into SQL, executing it in the database and returning the number of records affected by it.

Our example for strongly typed deletes picks an entity property, `Date`, from entities where its value is before the current date, and adds one day to it.

The actual process of generating SQL from a LINQ expression is quite complex. If you are curious, you can have a look at the code for Lolita in GitHub: `https://github.com/ PomeloFoundation/Lolita`.

Handling soft deletes

Soft deletes is a handy database technique by which you never (or almost never) delete records from your database. Instead, you mark these records as deleted and when you query these records, you always filter out those marked as such. In this recipe, we will see how we can get this working in Entity Framework Core. We will leverage concepts introduced in previous chapters, such as shadow properties.

Getting ready

We will be using the NuGet Package Manager to install the Entity Framework Core 1 package, `Microsoft.EntityFrameworkCore`. We will also be using a SQL Server database to store the data, so we will also need `Microsoft.EntityFrameworkCore.SqlServer`.

Finally, `xunit` is the package we will be using for the unit tests, and `dotnet-text-xunit` adds tooling support for Visual Studio. Notice that the `UnitTests` project is a .NET Core App 1.0 (netcoreapp1.0), that `Microsoft.EntityFrameworkCore.Design` is configured as a build dependency and `Microsoft.EntityFrameworkCore.Tools` is set as a tool.

Open **Using EF Core Solution** from the included source code examples.

Execute the database setup script from the code samples included for this recipe. This can be found in the `DataAccess` project within the `Database` folder.

How to do it...

Let's build a class model suitable for demonstrating soft deletes:

1. Create an entity class called `MyEntity` in a similarly named file in the `BusinessLogic` project (the `ISoftDeletable` definition comes next):

```
using System;
namespace BusinessLogic
{
    public class MyEntity : ISoftDeletable
    {
        public int Id { get; set; }
        public string Name { get; set; }
```

```
        }
    }
```

2. Now, for the interface that will be used to mark entities as soft-deletable, add
    `ISoftDeletable` to the `BusinessLogic` project:

```
namespace BusinessLogic
{
    public interface ISoftDeletable
    {
    }
}
```

3. Next, we add a context called `SoftDeleteContext` to the `DataAccess` project, in
    a file named `SoftDeleteContext.cs`:

```
using Microsoft.EntityFrameworkCore;
using BusinessLogic;
using System.Linq;
using System.Reflection;

namespace DataAccess
{
  public class SoftDeleteContext : DbContext
  {
    private readonly string _connectionString;
    public SoftDeleteContext(DbContextOptions
      options) : base(options)
    {
    }

    public SoftDeleteContext(string connectionString)
    {
      _connectionString = connectionString;
    }

    public DbSet<MyEntity> MyEntities { get; set; }
    public override int SaveChanges()
    {
      foreach (var entry in ChangeTracker.Entries()
        .Where(e => e.State == EntityState.Deleted))
      {
        if (entry.Entity is ISoftDeletable)
        {
          entry
            .Property("IsDeleted")
            .CurrentValue = true;
          entry.State = EntityState.Modified;
```

```
          }
        }
        return base.SaveChanges();
      }


      protected override void
        OnModelCreating(ModelBuilder modelBuilder)
      {
        foreach (var entity in
          modelBuilder.Model.GetEntityTypes())
        {
          if (typeof(ISoftDeletable).IsAssignableFrom
            (entity.ClrType))
          {
            modelBuilder
              .Entity(entity.ClrType)
              .HasDiscriminator("IsDeleted", typeof(bool))
              .HasValue(false);

            modelBuilder
              .Entity(entity.ClrType)
              .Property(typeof(bool), "IsDeleted")
              .IsRequired(true)
              .HasDefaultValue(false);

            modelBuilder
              .Entity(entity.ClrType)
              .Property(typeof(bool), "IsDeleted")
              .Metadata
              .IsReadOnlyAfterSave = false;
          }
        }

        base.OnModelCreating(modelBuilder);
      }


      protected override void
        OnConfiguring(DbContextOptionsBuilder optionsBuilder)
      {
        optionsBuilder.UseSqlServer(_connectionString);
        base.OnConfiguring(optionsBuilder);
      }
    }
  }
}
```

4. Create a unit tests file, `SoftDeleteTests.cs`, in the `UnitTests` project:

```
using Xunit;
using BusinessLogic;
using DataAccess;
using System;
using Microsoft.Framework.Configuration;
namespace UnitTests
{
    public class SoftDeleteTests : BaseTests
    {
        [Fact]
        public void CanSoftDelete()
        {
            //Arrange
            using (var ctx = new SoftDeleteContext(
            Configuration["Data:Blog:ConnectionString"]))
            {
                //Act
                var entity = new MyEntity { Name = "Test" };
                ctx.MyEntities.Add(entity);
                var inserts = ctx.SaveChanges();
                ctx.Entry(entity).State =
                 EntityState.Detached;
                entity = ctx.MyEntities.First();
                ctx.MyEntities.Remove(entity);
                var deletes = ctx.SaveChanges();
                //Assert
                Assert.True(deletes == 1);
            }
        }
    }
}
```

5. We will need the base class for the unit tests, `BaseTests`, which should also go in the `UnitTests` project:

```
using Microsoft.Framework.Configuration;
namespace UnitTests
{
    public abstract class BaseTests
    {
        protected BaseTests()
        {
            var configurationBuilder = new
                ConfigurationBuilder();
```

```
            configurationBuilder
              .AddJsonFile("appSettings.json");
            Configuration = configurationBuilder.Build();
        }
        protected IConfiguration Configuration { get; set; }
    }
}
```

6. Finally, add the following connection string to the `appsettings.json` file and make sure the file is copied to the output folder upon build:

```
{
    "Data": {
        "Blog": {
            "ConnectionString":"Server=(local)\\SQLEXPRESS;
            Database=Blog; Integrated Security=SSPI;
            MultipleActiveResultSets=true"
        }
    }
}
```

For Entity Framework 6, we would add this connection string to the `Web.config` file, under the `connectionStrings` section, with the name `Blog`. Of course, do change the connection string to match your system settings; for example, the name of the SQL Server instance (SQLEXPRESS, in this example).

How it works...

For all entities that are assignable to `ISoftDeletable`, we configure a discriminator column (`HasDiscriminator`) called `IsDeleted`, which has a default value of `false`. This is going to be used by Entity Framework whenever it tries to query records mapped to this entity, for example:

```
SELECT [m].[Id], [m].[Name]
FROM [MyEntity] AS [m]
WHERE [m].[IsDeleted] = 0
```

This is done automatically for you, and is done regardless of other filter conditions. This `IsDeleted` column is a shadow property, because it is mapped but does not have a corresponding property in the POCO model.

Then we intercept the saving of changes (`SaveChanges` method), we iterate through all entities that are marked as `Deleted` and are `ISoftDeletable`, change its state to `Modified`, and set the value of the `IsDeleted` shadow property to `true`. It's as simple as that!

See also

In this chapter:

- ▸ *Capturing the audit data*
- ▸ *Retrieving entity metadata*

Adding logging

It's sometimes important, namely when things go wrong, to get a glimpse of what's going on inside. For that, we can leverage the logging capabilities of Entity Framework Core: we are presented with a detailed register of what is happening, such as the SQL that is being sent to the database.

Getting ready

We will be using the NuGet Package Manager to install the Entity Framework Core 1 package, `Microsoft.EntityFrameworkCore`. We will also be using a SQL Server database to store the data, so we will also need `Microsoft.EntityFrameworkCore.SqlServer`.

We also need the `Microsoft.Extensions.Logging` and `Microsoft.Extensions.Logging.Console` packages to add logging capabilities.

Open **Using EF Core Solution** from the included source code examples.

Execute the database setup script from the code samples included for this recipe. This can be found in the `DataAccess` project within the `Database` folder.

How to do it...

Let's create a sample context and entity, add logging capabilities, and see what happens when we perform simple operations:

1. Create a `MyEntity` entity class in a similarly named file in the `BusinessLogic` project:

```
using System;
namespace BusinessLogic
{
    public class MyEntity
    {
        public int Id { get; set; }
        public string Name { get; set; }
        public DateTime Date { get; set; }
```

```
        }
    }
```

2. Next, we add a context called `MyContext` to the `DataAccess` project:

```
using Microsoft.EntityFrameworkCore;
using BusinessLogic;
namespace DataAccess
{
    public class MyContext : DbContext
    {
        private readonly string _connectionString;
        public MyContext(DbContextOptions options) :
        base(options)
        {
        }
        public MyContext(string connectionString)
        {
            _connectionString = connectionString;
        }
        public DbSet<MyEntity> MyEntities
        { get; set; }
        protected override void OnConfiguring(
        DbContextOptionsBuilder optionsBuilder)
        {
            optionsBuilder
              .UseLoggerFactory(new LoggerFactory()
              .AddConsole());
            optionsBuilder
              .UseSqlServer(_connectionString);
            base.OnConfiguring(optionsBuilder);
        }
    }
}
```

How it works...

The logging framework of .NET Core, used by Entity Framework Core, consists of the following:

-   **Logger factories**: The top-level registration point. Normally, we can just use the built-in `LoggerFactory` and add logger providers to it.

-   **Logger providers**: These are implementations of `ILoggerProvider` that are registered to the .NET Core provided `ILoggerFactory`.

-   **Actual loggers**: These are `ILogger` implementations returned by a logger provider. These do the actual logging.

A logger is returned for a concrete logger category. Logger categories come from infrastructure class names, the ones that provide the logging information. Because Entity Framework Core is built using a modular, layered approach, some of its operations will come from the datastore-agnostic core (`DbContext`, `InternalQueryCompiler`), others will come from the relational layers (`RelationalCommandBuilderFactory`, `RelationalModelValidator`, `SqlServerQueryCompilationContextFactory`, `SqlServerCompositeMethodCallTranslator`), and finally, others will come from database-specific classes (`SqlServerConnection`).

Each logging entry actually consists of the following:

- **Log Level**: The severity of the log entry, such as `Critical`, `Debug`, `Error`, `Information`, or `Trace`
- **Event Id**: This is a provider-specific code that represents the type of event being logged (more on this in a second)
- **State**: An optional contextual object to pass more information to the logger
- **Exception**: An exception, to use in the case of an error (normally for the `Critical` or `Error`) log levels
- **Formatter**: An optional formatter object to help format the log output, in cases where it is necessary

The event ID is specific to the infrastructure. Some common values are as follows:

ID	Meaning	Sender	State
1	Execute SQL	RelationalCommandBuilderFactory	DbCommandLogData
2	Create database	SqlServerConnection	Database and server names
3	Open connection	SqlServerConnection	Database and server names
4	Close connection	SqlServerConnection	Database and server names
5	Begin transaction	SqlServerConnection	IsolationLevel
6	Commit transaction	SqlServerConnection	IsolationLevel
7	Rollback transaction	SqlServerConnection	IsolationLevel
> 7	Warnings		

In the case of relational data sources, these values are specified in the `RelationalEventId` enumeration.

When we add logging to an Entity Framework context through the `OnConfiguring` method, we start to get things in the logging target of our choice–in this example, it is the console. For example, we issue a query such as this:

```
ctx
.MyEntities
.Where(x => x.Date == DateTime.Today)
.ToList();
```

We're likely to get output like this in the console:

```
info: Microsoft.EntityFrameworkCore.Storage.Internal
        .RelationalCommandBuilderFactory[1]
    Executed DbCommand (2ms) [Parameters=[], CommandType='Text',
       CommandTimeout='30']
          SELECT [x].[Id], [x].[Date], [x].[Name]
          FROM [MyEntities] AS [x]
          WHERE [x].[Date] = @__Today_0
```

Notice that the SQL does not include the actual filtering value (`DateTime.Today`); instead, it references the parameter name that was used. Besides the actual SQL, we can see that the execution took 2 milliseconds.

How do we interpret this? Well, first, we can see the log level, `info` in this case. Then we have the provider class that logged this (the category name), `RelationalCommandBuilderFactory`, and then the event inside [], 1. Finally, we have the actual message, which is specific to the log event parameters (`Executed DbCommand`).

There's more...

Microsoft makes some logging providers for .NET Core available:

Provider	Purpose
Microsoft.Extensions.Logging.Console	Logs all messages with log level equal or greater than information to the console of the current application
Microsoft.Extensions.Logging.Debug	Logs to the debug window of the current attached debugger (like Visual Studio while debugging) with log level equal or greater than information
Microsoft.Extensions.Logging. TraceSource	Writes to all registered trace listeners

And you can also write your own logging provider. You need to create a logging provider factory, register it with an Entity Framework Core context, and it will be used automatically.

Finally, you can change the behavior of certain events–ignore, log, throw an exception–by making a call to `ConfigureWarnings`:

```
optionsBuilder.ConfigureWarnings(
warnings =>
{
    warnings.Ignore(RelationalEventId.OpeningConnection,
        RelationalEventId.ClosingConnection);
    warnings.Throw(RelationalEventId
        .RollingBackTransaction);
});
```

Setting a default can be done too:

```
optionsBuilder.ConfigureWarnings(
warnings =>
{
    warnings.Default(WarningBehavior.Ignore);
    warnings.Log(RelationalEventId.CommitTransaction);
});
```

Capturing the audit data

So, we want to track every time a record was changed. There are several ways to do this, but we'll do it the Entity Framework way, so that we do not depend on any database-specific features–see, for example, the Change Data Tracking feature of SQL Server Enterprise.

The data we're interested in is as follows:

- ▸ Creation timestamp
- ▸ Creation user
- ▸ Last update timestamp
- ▸ Last update user

Getting ready

We will be using the NuGet Package Manager to install the Entity Framework Core 1 package, `Microsoft.EntityFrameworkCore`. We will also be using a SQL Server database to store the data, so we will also need `Microsoft.EntityFrameworkCore.SqlServer`.

We also need the `System.Security.Principal.Windows` package in order to get the current logged-in user.

Finally, `Xunit` is the package we will be using for the unit tests, and `dotnet-text-Xunit` adds tooling support for Visual Studio. Notice that the `UnitTests` project is a .NET Core App 1.0 (netcoreapp1.0), that `Microsoft.EntityFrameworkCore.Design` is configured as a build dependency and `Microsoft.EntityFrameworkCore.Tools` is set as a tool.

Open **Using EF Core Solution** from the included source code examples.

Execute the database setup script from the code samples included for this recipe. This can be found in the `DataAccess` project within the `Database` folder.

How to do it...

We are going to define an audit interface where we will capture the data that we're interested in and then we'll intercept the saving of changes and add the audit data:

1. Create an interface called `IAuditable` in the `BusinessLogic` project with the following content:

```
using System;
namespace BusinessLogic
{
  public interface IAuditable
  {
    string CreatedBy { get; set; }
    DateTime CreatedAt { get; set; }
    string UpdatedBy { get; set; }
    DateTime? UpdatedAt { get; set; }
  }
}
```

2. Now, create a class that is auditable, for example, `MyEntity`, to also be added to the `BusinessLogic` project:

```
using System;
namespace BusinessLogic
{
    public class MyEntity : IAuditable
    {
        public int Id { get; set; }
        public string Name { get; set; }
        public string CreatedBy { get; set; }
        public DateTime CreatedAt { get; set; }
        public string UpdatedBy { get; set; }
        public DateTime? UpdatedAt { get; set; }
    }
}
```

3. Now, we need a context that knows about our entity. We'll call it `MyContext` and store it in a `MyContext.cs` file in the `DataAccess` project:

```
using Microsoft.EntityFrameworkCore;
using System;
using System.Security.Principal;
using BusinessLogic;
namespace DataAccess
{
  public class MyContext : DbContext
```

```
    {
      private readonly string _connectionString;
      public MyContext(DbContextOptions options) :
        base(options)
      {
      }
      public MyContext(string connectionString)
      {
        _connectionString = connectionString;
      }
      public Func<string> UserProvider { get; set; }
        = () => WindowsIdentity.GetCurrent().Name;
      public Func<DateTime> TimestampProvider { get; set; }
        = () => DateTime.UtcNow;
      public DbSet<MyEntity> MyEntities { get; set; }
      protected override int SaveChanges()
      {
        foreach (var entry in this.ChangeTracker.Entries()
          .Where(e => e.State == EntityState.Added ||
            e.State == EntityState.Modified))
        {
          if (entry.Entity is IAuditable)
          {
            var auditable = entry.Entity as IAuditable;
            if (entry.State == EntityState.Added)
            {
              auditable.CreatedBy = UserProvider();
              auditable.CreatedAt = TimestampProvider();
            }
            else
            {
              auditable.UpdatedBy = UserProvider();
              auditable.UpdatedAt = TimestampProvider();
            }
          }
        }
        return base.SaveChanges();
      }
      protected override void OnConfiguring(
        DbContextOptionsBuilder optionsBuilder)
      {
        optionsBuilder.UseSqlServer(_connectionString);
        base.OnConfiguring(optionsBuilder);
      }
    }
  }
```

4. Create a unit tests file, `AuditableTests.cs`, in the `UnitTests` project:

```
using Xunit;
using BusinessLogic;
using DataAccess;
using System;
using Microsoft.Framework.Configuration;
namespace UnitTests
{
    public class AuditableTests : BaseTests
    {
        [Fact]
        public void CanAudit()
        {
            /Arrange
            using (var ctx = new MyContext(
            Configuration["Data:Blog:ConnectionString"]))
            {
                ctx.UserProvider = () => "creator";
                ctx.TimestampProvider = () =>
                    new DateTime(2016, 1, 1);
                //Act
                ctx.MyEntities.Add(new MyEntity { Name = "test" });
                ctx.SaveChanges();
                var entity = ctx.MyEntities.First(b =>
                    b.Name == "test");
                var createdBy = entity.CreatedBy;
                var createdAt = entity.CreatedAt;
                entity.Name += "_modified";
                ctx.UserProvider = () => "updater";
                ctx.TimestampProvider = () => DateTime.Today;
                ctx.SaveChanges();
                entity = ctx.MyEntities.First(b =>
                    b.Id == entity.Id);
                var updatedBy = entity.UpdatedBy;
                var updatedAt = entity.UpdatedAt;
                //Assert
                Assert.Equal("creator", createdBy);
                Assert.Equal(new DateTime(2016, 1, 1), createdAt);
                Assert.Equal("updater", updatedBy);
                Assert.Equal(DateTime.Today, updatedAt);
            }
        }
    }
}
```

5. We will need the base class for the unit tests, `BaseTests`, which should also go in the `UnitTests` project:

```
using Microsoft.Framework.Configuration;
namespace UnitTests
{
  public abstract class BaseTests
  {
    protected BaseTests()
    {
      var configurationBuilder =
        new ConfigurationBuilder();
      configurationBuilder.AddJsonFile("appSettings.json");
      Configuration = configurationBuilder.Build();
    }
    protected IConfiguration Configuration { get; set; }
  }
}
```

6. Finally, add the following connection string to the `appsettings.json` file and make sure the file is copied to the output folder upon build:

```
{
    "Data": {
        "Blog": {
            "ConnectionString":"Server=(local)\\SQLEXPRESS;
            Database=Blog; Integrated Security=SSPI;
            MultipleActiveResultSets=true"
        }
    }
}
```

> For Entity Framework 6, we would add this connection string to the `Web.config` file, under the `connectionStrings` section, with the name `Blog`. Of course, do change the connection string to match your system settings; for example, the name of the SQL Server instance (`SQLEXPRESS`, in this example).

How it works...

We have a context in which we defined two provider functions: one for retrieving the current user (`UserProvider`), and the other for retrieving the current timestamp (`TimestampProvider`). These are both initialized to sensible values: the name of the current Windows user in the first case and the current date and time in UTC coordinates for the latter. We do it this way so that we can easily change the way the current user or timestamp is retrieved, without having to change the context class.

When it is time to save changes, we iterate through all the entities pending saving and we figure out those that are either added or modified. For the first ones, we set the creation audit properties, and for the others, we set the updating ones.

 The UpdatedAt property in the IAuditable interface is set to nullable because, of course, a record may have not been updated yet.

See also

In this chapter:

▶ *Handling soft deletes*

▶ *Retrieving entity metadata*

Retrieving entity metadata

When you create an Entity Framework context, you map a domain model to a data store. Specifically, in the case of relational databases, you assign the following:

▶ Classes to tables

▶ Properties to columns

▶ References to foreign keys

Of course, in normal usage, you normally don't need to worry about these mappings; you just query the POCO domain model and that's it. But if you need to write SQL for more advanced queries, you are left with two options:

▶ You know exactly the database names of all the tables and columns (keep in mind that the class Person can be mapped to, say, PERSON, PEOPLE, PERSON_DETAIL, PERSON_DETAILS, and so on)

▶ You obtain this information dynamically at runtime

If you want to be safe, you will stick to the second option and obtain all the information you need whenever you need it; this way, you know you're not wrong. That's what this chapter is about, after all!

Getting ready

We will be using the NuGet Package Manager to install the Entity Framework Core 1 package, Microsoft.EntityFrameworkCore. We will also be using a SQL Server database to store the data, so we will also need Microsoft.EntityFrameworkCore.SqlServer.

Finally, `Xunit` is the package we will be using for the unit tests, and `dotnet-text-Xunit` adds tooling support for Visual Studio. Notice that the `UnitTests` project is a .NET Core App 1.0 (netcoreapp1.0), that `Microsoft.EntityFrameworkCore.Design` is configured as a build dependency and `Microsoft.EntityFrameworkCore.Tools` is set as a tool.

Open **Using EF Core Solution** from the included source code examples.

Execute the database setup script from the code samples included for this recipe. This can be found in the `DataAccess` project within the `Database` folder.

How to do it...

Let's write some extension methods for getting the metadata information for the model dynamically:

1. Create a static class called `ModelExtensions` in the `DataAccess` project with the following content:

```
using Microsoft.EntityFrameworkCore;
using Microsoft.EntityFrameworkCore.Metadata;
using Microsoft.EntityFrameworkCore.Metadata.Internal;
using System;
using System.Linq.Expressions;
namespace DataAccess
{
  public static class ModelExtensions
  {
    //Key
    public static string [] GetPrimaryKeyProperties<T>(
       this IModel model)
    {
      return model
        .FindEntityType(typeof(T))
        .FindPrimaryKey()
        .Properties
        .Select(x => x.Name)
        .ToArray();
    }
    public static string [] GetProperties<T>
       (this IModel model)
    {
      return model
        .FindEntityType(typeof(T))
        .GetProperties()
        .Select(x => x.Name)
        .ToArray();
```

```
        }
        public static string[] GetNavigationProperties<T>
           (this IModel model)
        {
          return model
            .FindEntityType(typeof(T))
            .GetNavigations()
            .Select(x => x.Name)
            .ToArray();
        }
        //Table
        public static string GetTableName<T>(this IModel model)
        {
          return GetTableName(model, typeof(T));
        }
        public static string GetTableName(this IModel model,
          Type entityType)
        {
          return GetTableName(model, entityType.Name);
        }
        public static string GetTableName(this IModel model,
           string entityName)
        {
          return model
            .AsModel()
            .FindEntityType(entityName)
            .Relational()
            .TableName;
        }
        //Discriminator
        public static object GetTableDiscriminatorValue<T>
           (this IModel model)
        {
          return GetTableDiscriminatorValue(model, typeof(T));
        }
        public static object GetTableDiscriminatorValue(
           this IModel model, Type entityType)
        {
          return GetTableDiscriminatorValue
            (model, entityType.Name);
        }
        public static object GetTableDiscriminatorValue
           (this IModel model, string entityName)
        {
          return model
```

```
        .AsModel()
        .FindEntityType(entityName)
        .Relational()
        .DiscriminatorValue;
}
public static string GetTableDiscriminatorColumnName<T>
    (this IModel model)
{
    return GetTableDiscriminatorColumnName
        (model, typeof(T));
}
public static string GetTableDiscriminatorColumnName
    (this IModel model, Type entityType)
{
    return GetTableDiscriminatorColumnName
        (model, entityType.Name);
}
public static string GetTableDiscriminatorColumnName
    (this IModel model, string entityName)
{
    return model
        .AsModel()
        .FindEntityType(entityName)
        .Relational()
        .DiscriminatorProperty
        .Relational()
        .ColumnName;
}
//Schema
public static string GetTableSchema<T>
    (this IModel model)
{
    return GetTableSchema(model, typeof(T));
}
public static string GetTableSchema
    (this IModel model, Type entityType)
{
    return GetTableSchema(model, entityType.Name);
}
public static string GetTableSchema
    (this IModel model, string entityName)
{
    return model
        .AsModel()
        .FindEntityType(entityName)
```

```
        .Relational()
        .Schema;
}
//Database
public static string GetDatabaseName(this IModel model)
{
  return model.AsModel().Relational().DatabaseName;
}
public static string GetDatabaseDefaultSchema
    (this IModel model)
{
  return model.AsModel().Relational().DefaultSchema;
}
//Column
public static string GetColumnName<T>
    (this IModel model, Expression<Func<T,
      object>> property)
{
  var member = property.Body as MemberExpression;
  if (member == null)
  {
    throw new ArgumentException(
      "Invalid property expression", "property");
  }
  return GetColumnName(model,
      member.Member.DeclaringType, member.Member.Name);
}
public static string GetColumnName
    (this IModel model, Type entityType,
      string propertyName)
{
  return model
    .AsModel()
    .FindEntityType(entityType)
    .FindProperty(propertyName)
    .Relational()
    .ColumnName;
}
public static string GetColumnDefaultValueSql<T>
    (this IModel model, Expression<Func<T,
      object>> property)
{
  var member = property.Body as MemberExpression;
  if (member == null)
  {
```

```
        throw new ArgumentException(
          Invalid property expression", "property");
    }
    return GetColumnDefaultValueSql
      (model, member.Member.DeclaringType,
        member.Member.Name);
}
public static string GetColumnDefaultValueSql
    (this IModel model, Type entityType, string
      propertyName)
{
  return model
    .AsModel()
    .FindEntityType(entityType)
    .FindProperty(propertyName)
    .Relational()
    .DefaultValueSql;
}
public static object GetColumnDefaultValue<T>
    (this IModel model, Expression<Func<T,
      object>> property)
{
  var member = property.Body as MemberExpression;
  if (member == null)
  {
    throw new ArgumentException(
      "Invalid property expression", "property");
  }
  return GetColumnDefaultValue(model,
    member.Member.DeclaringType, member.Member.Name);
}
public static object GetColumnDefaultValue
    (this IModel model, Type entityType, string
      propertyName)
{
  return model
    .AsModel()
    .FindEntityType(entityType)
    .FindProperty(propertyName)
    .Relational()
    .DefaultValue;
}
public static string GetColumnType<T>
    (this IModel model,Expression<Func<T,
      object>> property)
{
```

```
    var member = property.Body as MemberExpression;
    if (member == null)
    {
      throw new ArgumentException(
        "Invalid property expression", "property");
    }
    return GetColumnType(model,
      member.Member.DeclaringType, member.Member.Name);
}
public static string GetColumnType
   (this IModel model, Type entityType,
      string propertyName)
{
  return model
    .AsModel()
    .FindEntityType(entityType)
    .FindProperty(propertyName)
    .Relational()
    .ColumnType;
}
public static int? GetColumnMaxLength<T>
   (this IModel model, Expression<Func<T,
      object>> property)
{
  var member = property.Body as MemberExpression;
  if (member == null)
  {
    throw new ArgumentException(
      "Invalid property expression", "property");
  }
  return GetColumnMaxLength(model,
    member.Member.DeclaringType, member.Member.Name);
}
public static int? GetColumnMaxLength
   (this IModel model, Type entityType,
      string propertyName)
{
  var annotation = model
    .AsModel()
    .FindEntityType(entityType)
    .FindProperty(propertyName)
    .FindAnnotation("MaxLength");
    return (annotation != null) ?
      Convert.ToInt32(annotation.Value) :
    (int?)null;
```

```
        }
        public static bool? IsColumnRequired<T>
          (this IModel model, Expression<Func<T,
            object>> property)
        {
          var member = property.Body as MemberExpression;
          if (member == null)
          {
            throw new ArgumentException(
              "Invalid property expression", "property");
          }
            return IsColumnRequired(model,
              member.Member.DeclaringType,
                member.Member.Name);
        }
        public static bool? IsColumnRequired(this IModel model,
          Type entityType, string propertyName)
        {
          return !model
            .AsModel()
            .FindEntityType(entityType)
            .FindProperty(propertyName)
            .IsColumnNullable();
        }
      }
    }
```

2. Create an entity, `MyEntity`, in the `BusinessLogic` project, in a file called `MyEntity.cs`:

```
namespace BusinessLogic
{
    public class MyEntity
    {
        public int Id { get; set; }
        public string Name { get; set; }
    }
}
```

3. We'll also need a context to match `MyContext`, in the `DataAccess` project as well:

```
using Microsoft.EntityFrameworkCore;
using BusinessLogic;
namespace DataAccess
{
  public class MyContext : DbContext
  {
```

```
      private readonly string _connectionString;
      public MyContext(DbContextOptions options) :
          base(options)
      {
      }
      public MyContext(string connectionString)
      {
          _connectionString = connectionString;
      }
      public DbSet<MyEntity> MyEntities { get; set; }
      protected override void OnConfiguring(
          DbContextOptionsBuilder optionsBuilder)
      {
          optionsBuilder.UseSqlServer(_connectionString);
          base.OnConfiguring(optionsBuilder);
      }
    }
  }
}
```

4. Create a unit tests class, `MetadataTests`, in the `UnitTests` project with the following content:

```
using Xunit;
using BusinessLogic;
using DataAccess;
using System;
using Microsoft.Framework.Configuration;
namespace UnitTests
{
  public class MetadataTests : BaseTests
  {
    [Fact]
    public void CanGetMetadata()
    {
      //Arrange
      using (var ctx = new SoftDeleteContext(
          Configuration["Data:Blog:ConnectionString"]))
      {
        //Act
        var id = ctx.Model
            .GetPrimaryKeyProperties<MyEntity>();
        var props = ctx.Model.GetProperties<MyEntity>();
        var tableName = ctx.Model.GetTableName<MyEntity>();
        var columnName = ctx.Model.GetColumnName<MyEntity>
            (x => x.Name);
        var columnMaxLength =
```

```
        ctx.Model.GetColumnMaxLength<MyEntity>
            (x => x.Name);
    var isColumnRequired =
        ctx.Model.IsColumnRequired<MyEntity>
            (x => x.Name);
    //Assert
    Assert.Equal("Id", id);
    Assert.NotNull(props);
    Assert.Equal("Name", columnName);
    Assert.Equal(null, columnMaxLength);
    Assert.Equal(false, isColumnRequired);
        }
      }
    }
}
```

5. We will need the base class for the unit tests, `BaseTests`, which should also go in the `UnitTests` project:

```
using Microsoft.Framework.Configuration;
namespace UnitTests
{
  public abstract class BaseTests
  {
    protected BaseTests()
    {
      var configurationBuilder = newConfigurationBuilder();
      configurationBuilder.AddJsonFile("appSettings.json");
      Configuration = configurationBuilder.Build();
    }
    protected IConfiguration Configuration { get; set; }
  }
}
```

6. Finally, add the following connection string to the `appsettings.json` file and make sure the file is copied to the output folder upon build:

```
{
    "Data": {
        "Blog": {
            "ConnectionString":"Server=(local)\\SQLEXPRESS;
            Database=Blog; Integrated Security=SSPI;
            MultipleActiveResultSets=true"
        }
    }
}
```

For Entity Framework 6, we would add this connection string to the `Web.config` file, under the `connectionStrings` section, with the name `Blog`. Of course, do change the connection string to match your system settings; for example, the name of the SQL Server instance (`SQLEXPRESS`, in this example).

How it works...

Entity Framework makes available all of the domain model in the `Model` property. This class is prototyped as `IModel`, but it is actually a subset of `Model`. Its methods, such as `FindEntityType()` and `GetEntityTypes()`, grant access to the metadata of the domain model, which includes all the definitions of each mapped class, such as the following:

- Mapped table name and schema
- Mapped columns, their names and other information, such as maximum length and nullability
- Mapped properties, including identifiers and navigation properties

It's important to notice that Entity Framework is agnostic when it comes to datastores, so the information it exposes may not be very specific. So, in this case, we are looking for information that is specific to relational databases, hence the `Relational()` extension method call; otherwise, you'd have to do the cast by hand, and what's worse, need to know what to cast to!

There's more...

As an exercise, try iterating through all the entities returned by the `GetEntityTypes` method and see what meaningful information you can extract!

See also

In this chapter:

- *Handling soft deletes*
- *Capturing the audit data*

Improving MVC applications

Granted, most of us who will be writing applications for .NET Core will be writing web applications. This is not only because there aren't really any other application frameworks for .NET Core–no Windows Forms or WPF–but because web applications seem to have taken over. So, it pays to know how to integrate Entity Framework Core with web apps.

We will be looking at the following:

▶ Registering and injecting data contexts into MVC controllers, view components, and views

▶ Passing additional configuration to the data context

Getting ready

We will be using the NuGet Package Manager to install the Entity Framework Core 1 package, `Microsoft.EntityFrameworkCore`. We will also be using a SQL Server database to store the data, so we will also need `Microsoft.EntityFrameworkCore.SqlServer`.

Since we will be working with web applications, we will need to add the appropriate packages: `Microsoft.AspNetCore.Mvc`, `Microsoft.AspNetCore.Server.Kestrel`, and `Microsoft.AspNetCore.Server.IISIntegration`. Mind you, these are added automatically by the Visual Studio template for ASP.NET Web Core applications.

Open **Using EF Core Solution** from the included source code examples.

Execute the database setup script from the code samples included for this recipe. This can be found in the `DataAccess` project within the `Database` folder.

How to do it....

Until now, we have had to manually build instances of the data contexts to use. Because web applications are not manually instantiated, we have a problem...or maybe not!

ASP.NET MVC Core is built around the concepts of **Inversion of Control** (**IoC**) and **Dependency Injection** (**DI**). Basically, these tell us to delegate the creation of concrete classes to specialized libraries and instead just ask them for the interface or base class that describes the functionality that we want to use, and to add any dependencies that the concrete classes may have automatically, so that we don't need to do so ourselves.

So, the first thing to do is to register our data contexts; normally, we would do so in the `ConfigureServices` method of the `Startup` class:

```
services
  .AddEntityFrameworkSqlServer()
  .AddDbContext<BlogContext>(opt =>
{
  opt.UseSqlServer(Configuration["Data:Blog:ConnectionString"]);
});
```

So, we are registering all the services that are required for using the SQL Server database with our service provider (`AddEntityFrameworkSqlServer`) and then we're explicitly saying that our data context (`BlogContext`) will use the SQL Server provider (`UseSqlServer`) with a given connection string (`Configuration["Data:Blog:ConnectionString"]`).

For this to work properly, our context needs to help; in particular, it needs to feature a specific public constructor:

```
public class BlogContext : DbContext
{
  public BlogContext(DbContextOptions options) : base(options)
  {
  }
}
```

Of course, it can have more constructors, but it specifically needs one that takes a `DbContextOptions`. The `DbContext` base class knows what to do with it. Notice that using this approach, we don't even need to have an `OnConfiguring` method, because the actual configuration is done outside the context.

Because we are registering our context to the "global" service provider (that comes from the `ConfigureServices` method), it will be available for injection in all MVC components, such as controllers:

```
public class HomeController : Controller
{
  public HomeController(BlogContext blogContext)
  {
    //do something with blogContext
  }
}
```

It's also available for view components:

```
public class MyViewComponent : ViewComponent
{
    public MyViewComponent(BlogContext blogContext)
    {
        //do something with blogContext
    }
}
```

And it's available for tag helpers:

```
public class MyTagHelper
{
    public MyTagHelper(BlogContext blogContext)
    {
        //do something with blogContext
    }
}
```

Finally, its available for views:

```
@inject BlogContext blogContext
```

Also, the AddDbContext method is the place where you can specify additional options, such as logging:

```
services
    .AddEntityFrameworkSqlServer()
    .AddDbContext<BlogContext>(opt =>
{
    opt.EnableSensitiveDataLogging();
    opt.UseLoggerFactory(new LoggerFactory().AddDebug());
    opt.ConfigureWarnings(warnings =>
    {
        warnings.Throw(RelationalEventId.RollingbackTransaction);
    });
    opt.UseSqlServer(Configuration["Data:Blog:ConnectionString"]);
});
```

See also

In this chapter:

▶ *Adding logging*

Hooking infrastructure services

Being modular means, for Entity Framework Core, that a big part of its constituting parts can be addressed and switched separately. This means that we can replace a component that has some functionality for another one that offers enhanced capabilities.

Most of the components of Entity Framework Core have their functionality specified by an interface. Some of these interfaces are as follows:

- ICompiledQueryCacheKeyGenerator
- IConventionSetBuilder
- IDatabaseProviderServices
- IDbContextTransactionManager
- IInternalEntityEntryFactory
- IEntityQueryModelVisitorFactory
- IHistoryRepository
- IMemberTranslator
- IMethodCallTranslator
- IMigrationsAnnotationProvider
- IMigrationsSqlGenerator
- IModelSource
- IModificationCommandBatchFactory
- IQueryCompilationContextFactory
- IQuerySqlGeneratorFactory
- IRelationalAnnotationProvider
- IRelationalConnection
- IRelationalDatabaseCreator
- IRelationalTransactionManager
- IRelationalTypeMapper
- ISqlGenerationHelper
- ISqlServerSequenceValueGeneratorFactory
- ISqlServerUpdateSqlGenerator
- ISqlServerValueGeneratorCache
- IValueGeneratorSelector

And there are more; these are just those added by the `AddEntityFrameworkSqlServer`, `AddRelational`, `AddDbContext`, and `AddQuery` extension methods. We won't go into all of them. You can see that some are specific to SQL Server (starting with `ISqlServer`) and the rest are generic (or specific to relational datasources). For some, it's easy to guess what they do (take, for example, `IRelationalTypeMapper` or `IRelationalConnection`); others are not so simple. Anyway, they all have a role in making Entity Framework Core work.

So, where does Entity Framework Core get these components (or services) from? The answer is the service provider. Each Entity Framework Core context has its own service provider, and, fortunately, we can make it our own by passing an alternative service provider. Normally, we would build one from a `ServiceCollection` instance automatically:

```
var services = new ServiceCollection();
services
    .AddEntityFrameworkSqlServer()
    .AddDbContext<MyContext>()
    .AddSingleton<IEntityStateListener>(
        new CustomStateListener());
```

In this case, we are using the default behavior of having the data context use the services registered in the external service collection. But we can build another service provider and pass it inside `AddDbContext`:

```
services
    .AddEntityFrameworkSqlServer()
    .AddDbContext<MyContext>(opt =>
{
  var svcscopy = new ServiceCollection();
  for (var i = 0; i < services.Count; i++)
  {
    (svcscopy as IList<ServiceDescriptor>)
        .Add(services[i]);
  }
  opt.UseInternalServiceProvider();
});
```

If you want to resolve, or even change, one of the built-in services, just make sure you do it after calling `AddEntityFrameworkSqlServer` or `AddDbContext`, to make sure it's there in the first place!

Using other databases

Entity Framework, being a modern, modular and extensible data access tool, supports several datastores. In fact, starting with Core 1.0, it even has built-in support for non-relational databases. It is expected that Microsoft and third parties will start making non-relational providers available very soon. In the meantime, we already have support for a number of relational databases:

Database	Provider
Microsoft SQL Server	`Microsoft.EntityFrameworkCore.SqlServer`
SQLite	`Microsoft.EntityFrameworkCore.SQLite`
PostgreSQL	`Npgsql.EntityFrameworkCore.PostgreSQL`
In Memory	`Microsoft.EntityFrameworkCore.InMemory`
MySQL	`Pomelo.EntityFrameworkCore.MySql`

These are just some of the providers that are available for free–and also open source–but there are others commercially available, of course. Other providers, such as `EntityFrameworkCore.SqlServerCompact40` by Erik Jensen (`https://github.com/ErikEJ`) or `EntityFramework.IBMDataServer` by IBM, do not support .NET Core yet. MySQL and Oracle are working on their own provider, which will be available for free. Devart already offers paid providers for MySQL, Oracle, PostgreSQL, SQLite, DB2, and SQL Server.

You can always find up-to-date information about available providers on the Entity Framework Core site: `http://ef.readthedocs.io/en/latest/providers`.

How to do it...

In general, most stuff works the same way regardless of the provider in use, but there are some exceptions:

- Some database options, such as the connection string parameters, differ from provider to provider, reflecting the natural differences between database servers.
- The primary key generation strategy is different. Some providers use auto-incrementing columns, while others use sequences.
- Not all providers support the same data types; if you stick to the .NET basic types, you should be safe:
  - String
  - Integers (`short`, `int`, `long`) – unsigned integers should be avoided

- ❑ Floating point (`float`, `double`)
- ❑ `decimal`
- ❑ `bool`
- ❑ `char`
- ❑ `byte` and `byte []`
- ❑ `DateTime`
- ❑ `Guid`

- ▸ Some providers have more query options than others. For example, some providers offer native regular expression matching.

In general, all providers are configured the same way, through a call to `UseXXX()` on the `OnConfiguring` override, as we can see using the NpgSql provider for PostgreSQL:

```
protected void OnConfiguring(DbContextOptionsBuilder optionsBuilder)
{
  optionsBuilder.UseNpgSql(@"Host=localhost; Database=<db>;
      Username=<usr>; Password=<pwd>");
  base.OnConfiguring(optionsBuilder);
}
```

Each provider, of course, will accept slightly different connection strings. If you need to configure additional options, there's also an overload to `UseXXX()` that takes a lambda, such as the `UseRowNumberForPaging` option for SQL Server:

```
optionsBuilder.UseSqlServer(@"Data Source=localhost; Initial
  Catalog=<db>;
  User Id=<usr>; Password=<pwd>",
opt =>
{
  opt.UseRowNumberForPaging();
});
```

And there may well be some extension methods as in this example using the Pomelo provider for MySQL:

```
modelBuilder.ForMySqlUseIdentityColumns();
```

Primary key generation strategies such as auto-increment (in the case of SQL Server and MySQL) and sequences (SQL Server, PostgreSQL, Oracle, and DB2) are defined by the provider. When it comes to actually configuring the sequence to use, we can do it globally (this works on all providers that support sequences):

```
protected void OnModelCreating(ModelBuilder modelBuilder)
{
    modelBuilder
        .HasSequence(name: "SeqName", schema: "shared")
        .StartsAt(1)
        .IncrementsBy(1);
    base.OnModelCreating (modelBuilder);
}
```

We can do it per entity (this example is for PostgreSQL; notice the NEXTVAL and the schema.sequencename syntax):

```
modelBuilder
    .Entity<Product>()
    .Property(p => p.Id)
    .HasDefaultValueSql("NEXTVAL('shared.SeqName')")
    .ValueGeneratedOnAdd();
```

In case you are wondering, sequences will be created as part of the initial database creation automatically.

 As of now, it is not possible to configure auto-increment options in Entity Framework Core.

It is, of course, possible to use client-generated primary keys, such as meaningful codes or GUIDs. That also works in any kind of database, if your business case allows it; it may be a viable option. You just need to tell Entity Framework to not try to generate the key in any way:

```
modelBuilder
    .Entity<Product>()
    .Property(p => p.Id)
    .ValueGeneratedNever();
```

Finally, not all providers support this kind of query, regular expression matching, but NpgSql does (other providers would do it client-side):

```
context
    .Products
    .Where(p => Regex.IsMatch(p.Name, "%brand%"))
    .ToList();
```

Other providers may do other LINQ to SQL translations that their databases support.

So, this is a resume of what we said:

Database	Provider
Microsoft SQL Server	UseSqlServer("<connection string>")
	https://www.connectionstrings.com/sql-server/
SQLite	UseSqlite("<connection string>")
	https://www.connectionstrings.com/sqlite/
PostgreSQL	optionsBuilder.UseNpgsql("<connection string>")
	https://www.connectionstrings.com/npgsql/
In Memory	UseInMemoryDatabase()
MySQL	UseMySql("<connection string>")
	https://www.connectionstrings.com/mysql/

7

Performance and Scalability

In this chapter, we will cover the following topics, all related to improving the performance and/or scalability of Entity Framework Core:

- ▸ Improving the performance of queries
- ▸ Testing and profiling queries
- ▸ Using asynchronous operations
- ▸ Eager loading
- ▸ Using the cache

Introduction

Nobody will bother too much if a web page takes too long to open, or try to access a site that is unresponsive due to too much simultaneous accesses—people will just close it and navigate somewhere else. With the advances in broadband speed in the last few years, people expect to see things rapidly; there's no excuse for slowness. And that's precisely what this chapter is about.

Performance is how fast we get results, and scalability is how well our system behaves if we have lots of simultaneous requests. Not exactly the same, but related.

Let's go through the options we have.

Improving the performance of queries

We want to get the best performance that we can, from the code/application side of things. When it comes to relational databases, we are interested in optimizing the following:

- Modifications (inserts, updates, deletes)
- Queries

Each has a different solution.

Getting ready

We will be using the NuGet Package Manager to install the Entity Framework Core 1 package, `Microsoft.EntityFrameworkCore`. We will also be using a SQL Server database to store the data, so we will also need `Microsoft.EntityFrameworkCore.SqlServer`. We will also need `Pomelo.EntityFrameworkCore.Lolita.SqlServer` for the strongly typed bulk API.

Open **Using EF Core Solution** from the included source code examples.

Execute the database setup script from the code samples included for this recipe. This can be found in the `DataAccess` project within the `Database` folder.

How to do it...

Let's see how we can improve the performance of our queries.

Modifications

Entity Framework, in any of its versions and like most **ORMs**, is not meant to be used as a bulk import tool, meaning it really shouldn't be used for that and there's nothing really we can do about it. But we can optimize updates and deletes.

Updates

Normally, the flow for doing updates in an ORM is as follows:

1. Retrieve an entity.
2. Make changes to it.
3. Save changes.

But it turns out this is very inefficient: ORMs have to create an instance, hydrate it from the column values returned from the database, and add it to its change tracking service. Imagine we want to do this in bulk, that is, for many records.

There are easy solutions for this:

- Use SQL to apply changes to the database directly
- Use an extension for Entity Framework Core that allows specifying strongly-typed changes

In the first case, we would use something like this:

```
var updatedRecords = ctx
    .Database
    .ExecuteSqlCommand(
    "UPDATE dbo.MyEntities SET Date = {0} WHERE Id = {1}",
      DateTime.Today, 10);
```

 `ExecuteSqlCommand` will return the number of affected records.

We already covered one such extension in the last chapter: it is the `Pomelo. EntityFrameworkCore.Lolita.SqlServer` package, and it allows us to write code such as this:

```
var updatedRecords = ctx
    .MyEntities
    .Where(x => x.Id == 10)
    .SetField(x => x.Date)
    .WithValue(DateTime.Today)
    .Update();
```

 There's no need to call the `SaveChanges` method on `DbContext`, it is done for us through the `Update` extension method. This method will return the number of affected records.

You can see that this is much better in several ways: it's a pure .NET solution with no string constants and no need to know the actual table and column names.

This also works for updates based on the actual data:

```
var updatedRecords = ctx
    .MyEntities
    .Where(x => x.Id == 10)
    .SetField(x => x.Date)
    .AddDays(1)
    .Update();
```

Please keep in mind that this only works if your entity mapping is not using any kind of optimistic concurrency checks, in which case, you have to load each entity before making changes to it.

Deletes

What about deletes? Normally, ORMs follow a similar pattern as updates, but instead of modifying an entity, we mark it as deleted. But, as for updates, there is no need to actually load the full entity into the context. We can do it like this, for a single entity delete:

```
ctx.MyEntities.Remove(new MyEntity { Id = 10 });
var deletedRecords = ctx.SaveChanges();
```

 If there isn't actually any record with the given ID, you will get an exception, so be warned!

For bulk updates, we can use SQL:

```
var deletedRecords = ctx
    .Database
    .ExecuteSqlCommand(
        "DELETE FROM dbo.MyEntities WHERE Id = {0}", 10);
```

Or we can use an extension such as `Pomelo.EntityFrameworkCore.Lolita.SqlServer`:

```
var deletedRecords = ctx
    .MyEntities
    .Where(x => x.Id == 10)
    .Delete();
```

Another very handy optimization has to do with change tracking. All entities loaded by (or explicitly added to) an Entity Framework context are stored in what is called the session or first level cache. When entities are added to this cache, Entity Framework takes a snapshot of its state. When time comes to persist changes to the database–normally when `SaveChanges` is called—the Entity Framework context has to iterate through all of entities in its first level cache and, for each that is not marked as deleted or added, check if it was modified—its current state does not match the one that was taken when the entity was added. If so, then Entity Framework considers that the entity was changed and thus needs to be updated in the database. Now, if we have a big number of entities in the first level cache, it may take some time to check all of them. If we are 100% sure that there are no changes other than additions or deletes (or if we really don't care), we can disable change tracking. To do so, we set `AutoDetectChangesEnabled` to `false`:

```
ctx.ChangeTracker.AutoDetectChangesEnabled = false;
```

If we do so and we want to revert this behavior, for the entities currently in the cache, we need to call `DetectChanges`:

```
ctx.ChangeTracker.DetectChanges();
```

 Just setting `AutoDetectChangesEnabled` to `true` won't work; you also need to call `DetectChanges`.

Queries

When it comes to querying, we normally use LINQ, and it usually does a good job in translating to SQL. But, there are cases where we need to resort to plain SQL, for example, queries that are too complex for LINQ, or when we want to use functions or stored procedures.

SQL

If we want to return data that can be translated to our mapped entities, we can easily use the `FromSql` method:

```
var entities = ctx
    .MyEntities
    .FromSql("EXEC dbo.GetMyEntity @Id = {0}", 10)
    .ToList();
```

Otherwise, for plain data that doesn't have the shape of an entity, it's slightly more work, as we need to handle the data reader, iterate through its results, and fetch the columns we're interested in:

```
var con = ctx.Database.GetDbConnection();
using (var cmd = con.CreateCommand())
{
    var param = cmd.CreateParameter();
    param.ParameterName = "id";
    param.Value = 10;
    cmd.CommandText = "EXEC dbo.GetMyData @Id = @id";
    cmd.Parameters.Add(param);
    if (con.State != ConnectionState.Open)
    {
        con.Open();
    }
    using (var reader = cmd.ExecuteReader())
    {
        while (reader.Read())
        {
            var id = reader.GetInt32(0);
            var name = reader.GetString(1);
```

```
        var timestamp = reader.GetDateTime(2);
        var guid = reader.GetGuid(3);
        var flag = reader.GetBoolean(4);
    }
  }
}
```

 Make sure you dispose of the data reader and command when you no longer need them.

Whenever possible, you should only ask for the data that you effectively need. This has two sides to it:

▸ Using projections to retrieve only the columns that are required

▸ Using paging to return only a small section of the data

Paging in SQL is highly dependent on the server of choice. Even SQL Server offers at least two paging options:

▸ Based on ROW_NUMBER(), which works on any SQL Server version starting from 2008:

```
SELECT [t].[Id], [t].[Name], [t].[Date]
FROM
(
SELECT [x].[Id], [x].[Name], [x].[Date],
ROW_NUMBER() OVER(ORDER BY [x].[Date]) AS
[__RowNumber__]
FROM [MyEntities] AS [x]
) AS [t]
WHERE (([t].[__RowNumber__] > @StartRowNum)
AND (([t].[__RowNumber__] <= (@StartRowNum + @PageSize)) S
```

▸ Based on OFFSET and LIMIT, for SQL Server 2012 and higher:

```
SELECT [x].[Id], [x].[Name], [x].[Date]
FROM [MyEntities] AS [x]
ORDER BY [x].[Date]
OFFSET @StartRowNum ROWS FETCH NEXT @PageSize ROWS ONLY
```

In both examples, @StartRowNum is the index of the first record that should be returned and @PageSize is the number of records to return.

Keep in mind that whenever you want to do paging, you should always specify an order.

Projections are basically done the same way everywhere: we just SELECT the columns we need.

LINQ

If you can live with LINQ, there are a couple of things that you should be aware of.

Any extension methods that you call on your query expression that the provider does not know how to translate to SQL call will be executed client-side.

Second, some provider-specific settings may affect how Entity Framework Core translates the LINQ expressions to SQL. For example, the SQL Server provider has a setting, UseRowNumberForPaging, for controlling whether to use ROW_NUMBER or OFFSET for paging. All relational database providers offer the UseRelationalNulls that can be used to tell Entity Framework how it should generate SQL queries that deal with Nulls:

```
protected override void OnConfiguring(
DbContextOptionsBuilder optionsBuilder)
{
    optionsBuilder.UseSqlServer(_connectionString, opt =>
    {
        opt.UseRelationalNulls();
        //for versions of SQL Server < 2012
        opt.UseRowNumberForPaging();
    });
    base.OnConfiguring();
}
```

 Different providers may offer other options, so do check out the documentation.

Paging in LINQ is done in a standard way:

```
var entities = (from e in ctx.MyEntities orderby e.Date select e)
    .Take(10)
    .Skip(5)
    .ToList();
```

And projections are done in a standard way too:

```
var entityProps = (from e in ctx.MyEntities orderby e.Date select new
{
  e.Name, e.Date })
    .ToList();
```

In this example, we are returning instances of an anonymous class that contains `Name` and `Date` properties. The LINQ to SQL translation will make sure that only these columns are selected.

Finally, let's go back to the first level cache. All entities loaded from Entity Framework as the result of a query (SQL or LINQ) will be stored in the first level cache. If you know that some entities will never have any changes, and therefore do not need to be checked, you can prevent them from being added to the cache by applying the `AsNoTracking` method:

```
var entityProps = (from e in ctx.MyEntities orderby e.Date select e)
    .AsNoTracking()
    .ToList();
```

The default behavior is, of course, to track (add to the cache) all entities, but we can revert it by setting the `QueryTrackingBehavior` property:

```
ctx.ChangeTracker.QueryTrackingBehavior =
QueryTrackingBehavior.NoTracking;
```

In this case, if the default behavior is to not track entities automatically, we can do the opposite to have them being tracked:

```
var entityProps = (from e in ctx.MyEntities orderby e.Date select e)
    .AsTracking()
    .ToList();
```

Disabling the tracking of entities helps in two ways:

▸ Makes queries faster to execute, because each returned entity does not need to be added to a collection after it is instantiated

▸ When the Entity Framework context is about to perform change tracking, there are fewer entities to verify for modifications

 Projected entities are never stored in the first level cache, because they are not considered "complete" entities.

See also

In this chapter:

▸ *Testing and profiling queries*

▸ *Eager loading*

Testing and profiling queries

Sometimes, a query doesn't behave as expected: it either doesn't return what it should or takes longer than desired. When this happens, you need to profile it.

We will talk about four options to test profile your queries:

- Adding logging
- Using a profiler connected to the database to monitor executing queries
- Adding a diagnostics package to monitor your app in real time
- Using a tool to dynamically perform queries and see their results

How to do it...

The next sections will cover tools that will help you in watching the output, measuring the performance, and debugging your queries.

Logging

You have a couple of options when it comes to profiling; first, it is usually helpful to look at the SQL that is being sent to the database. If you enable logging, you can get both the SQL and the time it took to execute. Think of this as the first step in profiling. This is how it goes:

```
protected override void OnConfiguring(
DbContextOptionsBuilder optionsBuilder)
{
    optionsBuilder
        .UseLoggerFactory(new LoggerFactory()
        .AddConsole()
        .AddDebug());
        optionsBuilder.UseSqlServer(_connectionString);
        base.OnConfiguring(optionsBuilder);
}
```

AddConsole is useful for console applications, and AddDebug is useful for web ones. This causes Entity Framework to output any SQL that it produces:

```
info: Microsoft.EntityFrameworkCore.
  Storage.Internal.RelationalCommandBuilderFactory[1]
    Executed DbCommand (2ms) [Parameters=[],
    CommandType='Text',CommandTimeout='30']
      SELECT [x].[Id], [x].[Date], [x].[Name]
      FROM [MyEntities] AS [x]
      WHERE [x].[Date] = @__Today_0
```

You can see in the output, the SQL and the time it took to execute (2 ms).

Database profiler

Sometimes, however, it is not practical or even possible to change the code to add logging and monitor its output. When this happens, another option is to hook directly to the database and see whatever SQL comes in. A good choice is Express Profiler, an open source profiler with .NET code. Express Profiler is available from CodePlex: `https://expressprofiler.codeplex.com/`.

Using Express Profiler is easy: just open it and point to the database you wish to monitor. Then you can observe what is happening:

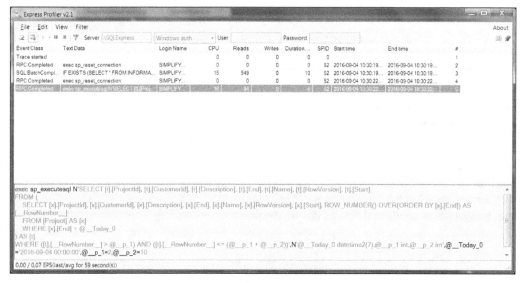

Express Profiler

You can see that it shows all SQL that was sent, even some that you may not be expecting, and a lot of additional information, such as the logged-in user, the CPU usage, duration, and SQL **Server Process ID** (**SPID**). Then you can apply some filters to see only the stuff you're interested in:

Filtering Express Profiler

All in all, an interesting tool for query monitoring.

Real time monitoring

Another very interesting project that we will talk about is **Glimpse**. Glimpse is another open source project, available, `http://getglimpse.com/`, which has a very strong involvement from Microsoft.

Glimpse is not just for monitoring Entity Framework; it provides a number of other useful insights. It has a very small footprint and is very easy to install: just add the `Glimpse.Agent.AspNet.Mvc` and `Glimpse.Server` packages and register its services to the service provider:

```
public void ConfigureServices(IServiceCollection services)
{
    services.AddGlimpse();
    //rest goes here
}
```

And then add the Glimpse middleware to the pipeline:

```
public void Configure(IApplicationBuilder app,
IHostingEnvironment env, ILoggerFactory loggerFactory)
{
    app.UseGlimpse();
    //rest goes here
}
```

After this, the Glimpse bar will be immediately available in your web page:

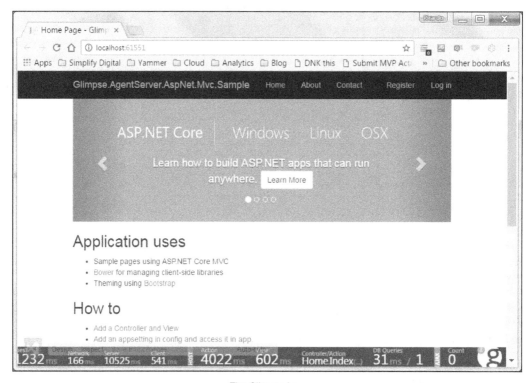

The Glimpse bar

This bar presents a summary of the most useful information, as far as Entity Framework is concerned; it shows how long the queries took (31 ms) and how many records were returned (1). If we want more detailed information, we can click on the Glimpse icon in the top right corner of the screen:

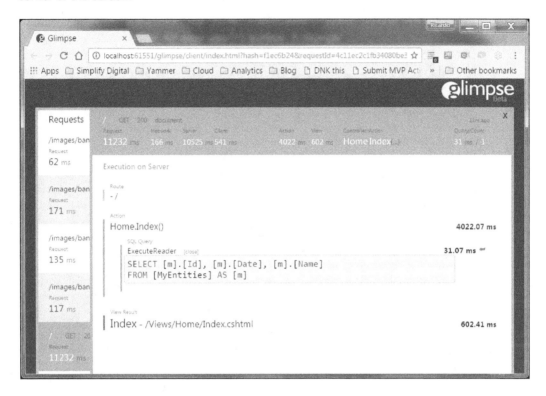

Here, you can see all the queries that have been run as part of the request, but you can check all other resources that were requested as part of the main request. You even get the executed SQL!

Testing

LINQPad is a commercial tool that can be used to play with several LINQ providers, including Entity Framework Core's DbContext implementation. It also offers a free license, which, as can be expected, is not as powerful as the paid one.

After we start LINQPad, we can add connections from several sources. If we choose Entity Framework V7 Driver, select the assembly that contains our data context, choose the data context class from this assembly, and pass it a proper connection string, as shown in the following screenshot:

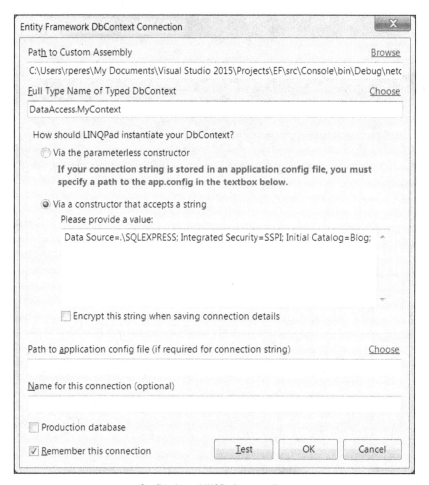

Configuring a LINQPad connection

We can then play with it, like executing any kinds of LINQ queries and seeing its results in a visual way:

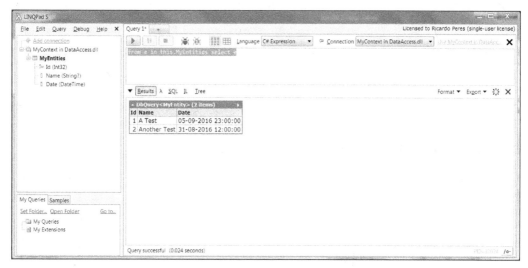

LINQPad queries

I won't go into too much detail about LINQPad, but if you download even the free version, you can see for yourself. You can execute queries dynamically and see the results immediately, with the bonus of also getting the SQL for them.

See also

In this chapter:

- ▶ *Improving the performance of queries*
- ▶ *Eager loading*

Using asynchronous operations

Asynchronous programming can help us avoid performance bottlenecks and enhance the overall responsiveness of our applications. .NET has had support for asynchronous operations since its early days, but version 4.5 took it one step further, with the introduction of the `async` and `await` keywords and related patterns. And, sure thing, the developers of Entity Framework Core took it in consideration when they wrote it: asynchronous operations, both for queries and for modifications.

First, let's get one thing straight: asynchronous operations are not faster than synchronous ones; in fact, they may even be slightly slower because of context switches. The real advantage is that they do not block the current thread of execution, and are therefore more suited for handling multiple simultaneous requests, such as in a web server.

Getting ready

We will be using the NuGet Package Manager to install the Entity Framework Core 1 package, `Microsoft.EntityFrameworkCore`. We will also be using a SQL Server database to store the data, so we will also need `Microsoft.EntityFrameworkCore.SqlServer`.

Open **Using EF Core Solution** from the included source code examples.

Execute the database setup script from the code samples included for this recipe. This can be found in the `DataAccess` project within the `Database` folder.

How to do it...

Asynchronous operations can help in two situations:

- Performing queries for retrieving data
- Making modifications to existing data

Queries

All queries returning records can be made asynchronous by calling an asynchronous terminator. Instead of `ToList`, `ToArray`, `First`, `FirstOrDefault`, `Single`, `SingleOrDefault`, `Count`, and so on, we should use their asynchronous counterparts: `ToListAsync`, `ToArrayAsync`, `FirstAsync`, `FirstOrDefaultAsync`, `SingleAsync`, `SingleOrDefaultAsync`, `CountAsync`, and so on. Here is an example:

```
var entities = await ctx
    .MyEntities
    .Where(x => x.Date <= DateTime.Today)
    .ToListAsync();
```

Just notice the usage of the `await` keyword; it is used to get a synchronous value from an asynchronous method call. `await` can only be used inside methods marked with the `async` keyword, which should return a `Task` or `Task<T>` value.

All asynchronous methods take an optional `CancellationToken` parameter. This parameter, when supplied, provides a way for the caller method to cancel the asynchronous execution:

```
var source = new CancellationTokenSource();
var cancel = source.Token;
cancel.Register(() =>
{
    //cancelled
});
ctx.MyEntities.ToListAsync(cancel);
if (!cancel.WaitHandle.WaitOne(TimeSpan.FromSeconds(5)))
{
    source.Cancel();
}
```

 If you want to perform multiple simultaneous asynchronous queries on the same context at the same time, you need to enable **Multiple Active Result Sets** (**MARS**). See `https://msdn.microsoft.com/en-us/library/ms131686.aspx`.

Modifications

In Entity Framework Core, the only method that applies changes (synchronously) is `SaveChanges`, and, of course, there is an asynchronous version, not surprisingly called `SaveChangesAsync`:

```
var results = await ctx.SaveChangesAsync();
```

Of course, you can also pass a `CancellationToken` as a parameter to `SaveChangesAsync`.

 Having a query running asynchronously doesn't change anything in the SQL or anything else; everything works exactly the same.

See also

In this chapter:

▸ *Improving the performance of queries*

Eager loading

An entity in Entity Framework Core can be associated with other entities in a number of ways:

- ▶ **One-to-one relationship**: Where two entities share a primary key
- ▶ **One-to-many**: An entity has a collection of entities
- ▶ **Many-to-one**: The inverse of one-to-many; an entity has a pointer to another entity

When querying for an entity, Entity Framework does not automatically bring the entities associated with it. This is actually a good thing: depending on how closely related the entities are, asking for one entity could bring with it the entire database!

This doesn't mean, of course, that we can't retrieve, on the same query, all the associated entities that we're interested in: this is called eager loading. In fact, in Entity Framework Core 1, this is of particular importance, since lazy loading is not yet implemented.

 The SELECT N+1 problem is not relevant for Entity Framework Core, since it doesn't (yet) have lazy loading.

Getting ready

We will be using the NuGet Package Manager to install the Entity Framework Core 1 package, Microsoft.EntityFrameworkCore. We will also be using a SQL Server database to store the data, so we will also need Microsoft.EntityFrameworkCore.SqlServer.

Finally, xunit is the package we will be using for the unit tests, and dotnet-text-xunit adds tooling support for Visual Studio. Notice that the UnitTests project is a .NET Core App 1.0 (netcoreapp1.0), that Microsoft.EntityFrameworkCore.Design is configured as a build dependency, and Microsoft.EntityFrameworkCore.Tools is set as a tool.

Open **Using EF Core Solution** from the included source code examples.

Execute the database setup script from the code samples included for this recipe. This can be found in the DataAccess project within the Database folder.

How to do it...

We will be generating C# POCO entities that match our database:

1. Create an entity with the name `Blog` in the `BusinessLogic` project, in a file called `Blog.cs`:

```csharp
using System;
using System.Collections.Generic;

namespace BusinessLogic
{
    public class Blog
    {
       public Blog()
    {
        Posts = new HashSet<Post>();
    }
        public int BlogId { get; set; }
        public string Name { get; set; }
        public DateTime CreationDate { get; set; }
        public string Url { get; set; }
        public virtual ICollection<Post> Posts { get; set; }
    }
}
```

2. And create a file called `Post.cs`, with the following content, in the same project:

```csharp
using System;

namespace BusinessLogic
{
    public class Post
    {
        public int PostId { get; set; }
        public string Title { get; set; }
        public DateTime Timestamp { get; set; }
        public string Body { get; set; }
        public Blog Blog { get; set; }
    }
}
```

3. Now, create a data context called `BlogContext` in the `DataAccess` project:

```
using Microsoft.EntityFrameworkCore;
using BusinessLogic;
using System.Collections.Generic;

namespace DataAccess
{
  public class BlogContext : DbContext
  {
    private readonly string _connectionString;
    public BlogContext(string connectionString)
    {
      _connectionString = connectionString;
    }

    public DbSet<Blog> Blogs { get; set; }

    protected override void OnConfiguring(
      DbContextOptionsBuilder optionsBuilder)
    {
      optionsBuilder
          .UseSqlServer(_connectionString);
      base.OnConfiguring(optionsBuilder);
    }
  }
}
```

 For Entity Framework 6, replace the
`Microsoft.EntityFrameworkCore` namespace with `System.Data.Entity` and call the base constructor of `DbContext` passing it the connection string. Finally, drop the `OnConfiguring` method.

4. A unit test is what follows. Let's call it `EagerLoadingTests` and place it in the `UnitTests` project:

```
using Xunit;
using Microsoft.EntityFrameworkCore;
using System.Linq;
using DataAccess;

namespace UnitTests
{
  public class EagerLoadingTests : BaseTests
  {
    [Fact]
    public void CanEagerLoad()
    {
      //Arrange
```

```
        using (var ctx = new BlogContext
          (Configuration["Data:Blog:ConnectionString"]))
        {
          //Act
          var blogsAndPosts = ctx
            .Blogs
            .Include(b => b.Posts)
            .ToList();

          //Assert
          Assert.NotNull(blogsAndPosts);
          Assert.NotEmpty(blogsAndPosts);
          Assert.All(blogsAndPosts, b =>
            Assert.NotNull(b.Posts));
        }
      }
    }
  }
}
```

5. We will need the base class for the unit tests, `BaseTests`, which should also go in the `UnitTests` project:

```
using Microsoft.Extensions.Configuration;
namespace UnitTests
{
    public abstract class BaseTests
    {
        protected BaseTests()
        {
            var configurationBuilder = new
              ConfigurationBuilder();
            configurationBuilder
            .AddJsonFile("appSettings.json");
            Configuration = configurationBuilder.Build();
        }
        protected IConfiguration Configuration { get; set; }
    }
}
```

6. Finally, add the following connection string to the `appsettings.json` file and make sure the file is copied to the output folder upon build:

```
{
    "Data": {
        "Blog": {
            "ConnectionString":"Server=(local)\\SQLEXPRESS;
            Database=Blog; Integrated Security=SSPI;
            MultipleActiveResultSets=true"
        }
```

```
    }
}
```

 For Entity Framework 6, we would add this connection string to the `Web.config` file, under the `connectionStrings` section, with the name `Blog`. Of course, change the connection string to match your system settings; for example, the name of the SQL Server instance (`SQLEXPRESS`, in this example).

How it works...

By adding an `Include` call to a LINQ expression on a root entity and referencing an entity or collection property, we instruct Entity Framework to load this property as part of the query. When it sees this, Entity Framework will generate SQL with joins to the other tables that are being included:

```
SELECT [b].[BlogId], [b].[Name], [b].[CreationDate], [b].[Url], [p].
[PostId], [p].[Title], [p].[Timestamp], [p].[Body]
FROM [Blog] AS [b]
LEFT JOIN [Post] AS [p] ON [p].[BlogId] = [b].[BlogId]
```

 The `Include` extension method can be used to eagerly load both collections of entities (one-to-many) or entity references (one-to-one or many-to-one). Calling it on a scalar property (one of a base type) has no effect.

Several `include` paths can be specified, but you should ask yourself if you really should do it. This is because the actual data returned is greater than the sum of the individual parts. Just consider these two tables:

BlogId	Name	CreationDate	Url
1	Development With A Dot	2016-08-19	`http://weblogs.asp.net/ ricardoperes`

PostId	BlogId	Title	Body	Timestamp
1	1	First Post	This is the first post	2016-08-19 10:00:00
2	1	Second Post	This is the second post	2016-08-20 16:00:00
3	1	Third Post	This is the third post	2016-09-10 20:00:00

A query over the `Blog` entity and including the `Post` entity might contain the following:

BlogId	Name	CreationDate	Url	PostId	Title	Body	Timestamp
1	Development With A Dot	2016-08-19	http://weblogs. asp.net/ ricardoperes	1	...	...	2016-08-19 10:00:00
1	Development With A Dot	2016-08-19	http://weblogs. asp.net/ ricardoperes	2	...	...	2016-08-20 16:00:00
1	Development With A Dot	2016-08-19	http://weblogs. asp.net/ ricardoperes	3	...	...	2016-09-10 20:00:00

See the problem? Yes, it's *duplication*...when we perform a join between the two tables, we get significant duplication, which means data will take longer to get to the application. This is, of course, not an argument against performing joins, but you should be aware of its implications.

See also

In this chapter:

▸   *Testing and profiling queries*

Using the cache

We already talked about the first level (or session) cache. Basically, all records loaded from an Entity Framework context as the result of a query are added to this cache automatically. So, if we have loaded enough entities, we may have in this cache what we are looking for, without the need to go to the database.

Another kind of cache is sometimes called a second level cache. This kind of cache outlives a data context, meaning different instances of the same context share this cache. What is it good for? Well, it's good for reference data, for example, data that does not change so often. Once this data is loaded into memory, it can be made available to all contexts that need it, no need to query the database again, instantiate all entities, hydrate them, and so on.

We will explore both caches here.

Getting ready

We will be using the NuGet Package Manager to install the Entity Framework Core 1 package, `Microsoft.EntityFrameworkCore`. We will also be using a SQL Server database to store the data, so we will also need `Microsoft.EntityFrameworkCore.SqlServer`.

Next, we will need the `Z.EntityFramework.Plus.EFCore` package. This contains, among others, an implementation of a second level cache.

Finally, `xunit` is the package we will be using for the unit tests, and `dotnet-text-xunit` adds tooling support for Visual Studio. Notice that the `UnitTests` project is a .NET Core App 1.0 (netcoreapp1.0), that `Microsoft.EntityFrameworkCore.Design` is configured as a build dependency, and `Microsoft.EntityFrameworkCore.Tools` is set as a tool.

Open **Using EF Core Solution** from the included source code examples.

Execute the database setup script from the code samples included for this recipe. This can be found in the `DataAccess` project within the `Database` folder.

How to do it...

We will see how we can use both caches, the first level and a second level cache implementation by `Z.EntityFramework.Plus`:

1. Create an entity with the name `MyEntity` in the `BusinessLogic` project, in a file called `MyEntity.cs`:

```
using System;
namespace BusinessLogic
{
    public class MyEntity
    {
        public int Id { get; set; }
        public string Name { get; set; }
        public DateTime Date { get; set; }
    }
}
```

2. We now create an extension method for `DbContext`-derived types. This should go in the `DataAccess` project, in a file called `DbContextExtensions.cs`:

```
using System;
using System.Collections.Generic;
using System.Linq;
using Microsoft.EntityFrameworkCore;
{
    public class DbContextExtensions
    {
        public static IEnumerable<T> Local<T>(
        this DbContext ctx) where T : class
        {
            return ctx
            .ChangeTracker
            .Entries<T>()
            .Select(e => e.Entity);
        }
    }
}
```

3. Now, create a data context called `MyContext` in the `DataAccess` project:

```
using Microsoft.EntityFrameworkCore;
using BusinessLogic;
namespace DataAccess
{
    public static class MyContext : DbContext
    {
        private readonly string _connectionString;
        public MyContext(string connectionString)
        {
            _connectionString = connectionString;
        }

        public DbSet<MyEntity> MyEntities { get; set; }
        protected override void OnConfiguring(
        DbContextOptionsBuilder optionsBuilder)
        {
            optionsBuilder
                .UseSqlServer(_connectionString);
            base.OnConfiguring(optionsBuilder);
        }
    }
}
```

For Entity Framework 6, replace the `Microsoft.EntityFrameworkCore` namespace with `System.Data.Entity` and call the base constructor of `DbContext` passing it the connection string. Finally, drop the `OnConfiguring` method.

4. Now, for a unit test class, let's call it `CacheTests`, and place it in the `UnitTests` project:

```
using Xunit;
using Microsoft.EntityFrameworkCore;
using System;
using System.Linq;
using Microsoft.Extensions.Caching.Memory;
using System.Threading;
using BusinessLogic;
using DataAccess;
using Z.EntityFramework.Plus;

namespace UnitTests
{
  public class CacheTests : BaseTests
  {
    [Fact]
    public void CanQueryFirstLevelCache()
    {
      //Arrange
      using (var ctx = new MyContext
        (Configuration["Data:My:ConnectionString"]))
      {
        //Act
        var entity = new MyEntity
        {
          Name = "Test",
          Date = DateTime.Today
        };
        ctx.MyEntities.Add(entity);
        ctx.SaveChanges();
        ctx.Entry(entity).State = EntityState.Detached;
        var entities = ctx
          .Local<MyEntity>()
          .ToList();
        //Assert
        Assert.NotNull(entities);
        Assert.Empty(entities);
```

```
      ctx.MyEntities.ToList();
      entities = ctx
        .Local<MyEntity>()
        .ToList();
      Assert.NotNull(entities);
      Assert.NotEmpty(entities);
  }
}


[Fact]
public void CanQuerySecondLevelCache()
{
  //Arrange
  var cache = QueryCacheManager.Cache as MemoryCache;
  var query = null as IQueryable<MyEntity>;
  var cacheKey = string.Empty;
  using (var ctx = new MyContext
    (Configuration["Data:My:ConnectionString"]))
  {
    //Act
    var entity = new MyEntity
    {
      Name = "Test",
      Date = DateTime.Today
    };
    ctx.MyEntities.Add(entity);
    ctx.SaveChanges();
    ctx.Entry(entity).State = EntityState.Detached;
    Assert.Equal(0, cache.Count);
    var entities = query
      .FromCache(new MemoryCacheEntryOptions
      {
        SlidingExpiration = TimeSpan.FromSeconds(5)
      });
    cacheKey = QueryCacheManager.GetCacheKey
      (query, new string[0]);
    var isFound = cache.TryGetValue(cacheKey,
      out entities);
    //Assert
    Assert.True(isFound);
    Assert.NotNull(cacheKey);
    Assert.NotNull(entities);
    Assert.NotEmpty(entities);
    Assert.Equal(1, cache.Count);
```

```
        }
        using (var ctx = new MyContext
          (Configuration["Data:My:ConnectionString"]))
        {
          var entities = query.FromCache();
          var isFound = cache.TryGetValue(cacheKey,
            out entities);
          //Assert
          Assert.True(isFound);
          Assert.NotNull(entities);
          Assert.NotEmpty(entities);
          Assert.Equal(1, cache.Count);
          //two minutes
          Thread.Sleep(2 * 60 * 1000);
          isFound = cache.TryGetValue(cacheKey,
            out entities);
          Assert.False(isFound);
        }
      }
    }
  }
```

5. We will need the base class for the unit tests, `BaseTests`, which should also go in the `UnitTests` project:

```
using Microsoft.Extensions.Configuration;
namespace UnitTests
{
    public abstract class BaseTests
    {
        protected BaseTests()
        {
            var configurationBuilder = new
              ConfigurationBuilder();
            configurationBuilder
            .AddJsonFile("appSettings.json");
            Configuration = configurationBuilder.Build();
        }
        protected IConfiguration Configuration { get; set;
    }
}
```

6. Finally, add the following connection string to the `appsettings.json` file and make sure the file is copied to the output folder upon build:

```
{
    "Data": {
        "Blog": {
            "ConnectionString":
                "Server=(local)\\SQLEXPRESS;Database=Blog;
                Integrated Security=SSPI;
                MultipleActiveResultSets=true"
        },
        "My": {
            "ConnectionString":
                "Server=(local)\\SQLEXPRESS;Database=Blog;
                Integrated Security=SSPI;
                MultipleActiveResultSets=true"
        }
    }
}
```

For Entity Framework 6, we would add this connection string to the `Web.config` file, under the `connectionStrings` section, with the name `Blog`. Of course, change the connection string to match your system settings; for example, the name of the SQL Server instance (`SQLEXPRESS`, in this example).

How it works...

The first unit test, `CanQueryFirstLevelCache`, tests the usage of the first level cache: after an item is loaded, it is stored there, and can be queried at any time through the `Entries` method of the `ChangeTracker`. This is all using the built-in functionality.

`CanQuerySecondLevelCache`, on the other hand, makes use of the `Z.EntityFramework.Plus` package to implement a cache that outlives a context. Entries are stored for some amount of time in the cache, and then they expire. Whenever the `FromCache` extension method is used, if the query can be found in the cache, it is returned from there, otherwise, Entity Framework goes to the database, as it usually does.

There's more...

The `Z.EntityFramework.Plus` package offers a lot more than just (if it wasn't enough!) a cache provider. Do have a look at the source code for the project, available at GitHub: https://github.com/zzzprojects/EntityFramework-Plus.

Pitfalls

In this chapter, we are going to cover the following pitfalls–unexpected behaviors of Entity Framework Core:

- ▶ GroupBy executes on the client side
- ▶ Table per class hierarchy requires nullable columns for derived classes
- ▶ References not eagerly fetched are lost
- ▶ Date/time operations are not supported
- ▶ Paging in SQL Server earlier than 2012
- ▶ Database null semantics
- ▶ Migrations and contexts with parameterized constructors
- ▶ Migrations with contexts in different projects
- ▶ Setting the maximum string length
- ▶ Mapping discriminator columns
- ▶ Composite primary keys
- ▶ Refreshing entities
- ▶ Cascading entity deletes

Introduction

In this chapter, we will be looking at some common pitfalls of Entity Framework Core. By pitfall I mean to say some behavior that we are not expecting and which may cause unwanted effects. Not all of these are bugs or implementation problems, it may be just something that we didn't thought of, yet, is here to remind us.

Because Entity Framework Core is quite new – it was a total rewrite of the previous Entity Framework code – some parts of it haven't been implemented, purely because of time constraints. Some of these pitfalls will cease to make sense, hopefully soon, others are just constraints that exist and probably will always exist.

In some cases, it may not be obvious to find out the cause once we fall into one of them, therefore, I hope this appendix will help you in figuring out sooner than later what is going wrong.

GroupBy executes on the client side

The current version of EF Core disregards `GroupBy`.

Problem

We normally use the LINQ `GroupBy` method to group records by some common characteristic, probably with the goal of doing aggregations. In most LINQ implementations, this generates a SQL `GROUPBY`, which is what we want, but, in Entity Framework Core 1.0, this translation is silently ignored, and grouping is instead done on the client-side, after retrieving all records. The problem is, this may bring a lot of records, causing severe performance and memory problems.

Imagine, for example, that you have thousands of products distributed in four colors: blue, red, green, and yellow. You might want to run this query:

```
var productsGrouped = (from p in context.Products
groupby p.Color into g
select new { Color = g.Key, Count = g.Count() })
    .ToDictionary(x => x.Color, x => x.Count);
```

What will happen is, Entity Framework will bring all the thousands of products into the client application and perform the grouping by color and count the products in memory.

How to fix it...

Unfortunately, as of now, we need to use plain SQL for this, which can be a plain SELECT or a stored procedure call. There is no alternative, I'm afraid; we need to do something like the following:

```
//get the ADO.NET connection
var con = context.Database.GetDbConnection();
var productsGrouped = new Dictionary<string, int>();
//create an ADO.NET command attached to the connection
using (var cmd = con.CreateCommand())
{
    cmd.CommandText = "SELECT p.Color, COUNT(1)
    FROM Products p
    GROUP BY p.Color";
    con.Open();
    using (var reader = cmd.ExecuteReader())
    {
        //while there are records to read
        while (reader.Read())
        {
            //read the first column as a string
            var color = reader.GetString(0);
            //read the second column as an integer
            var count = reader.GetInt32(1);
            productsGrouped[color] = count;
        }
    }
}
```

The default implementation, if not understood and dealt with in time, can result in severe performance (lots of records traveling from the database to the client application) and memory (lots of instances being created and hydrated) problems, so be warned!

Table per class hierarchy requires nullable columns for derived classes

When persisting class hierarchies, all properties in derived classes must be nullable.

Problem

A common pattern for representing class hierarchies in relational databases is to use a table that will have columns for each of the base and derived classes. For example, imagine we have a `Vehicle` base class and two derived classes, `LandVehicle` and `AirVehicle`:

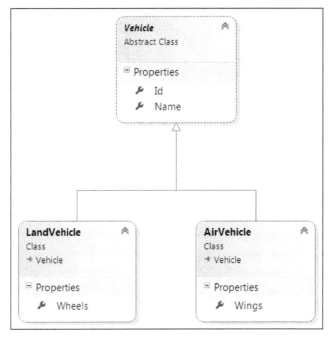

Vehicles class model

Using the Table per class hierarchy (also called single table inheritance), this could be represented as follows:

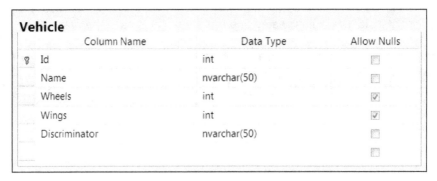

Table per class hierarchy mapping table

You may have noticed that the columns that correspond to the properties in the derived classes-Wheels and Wings-are set to accept nulls. Why is that? Well, since this table has to support a schema for all the possible derived classes, we never know, for each row, which class it will map to. For that reason, all columns that correspond to the properties in derived classes need to be nullable, because otherwise, what value would we store there for the records that correspond to other classes?

Consider the following table per class hierarchy values for example:

ID	Name	Wheels	Wings	Discriminator
1	Helicopter	NULL	0	AirVehicle
2	Car	4	NULL	LandVehicle

How to solve it...

All our properties of value types need to be marked as nullable:

```
public class LandVehicle : Vehicle
{
    public int? Wheels { get; set; }
}
public class AirVehicle
{
    public int? Wings { get; set; }
}
```

This is for nullable value types; since they cannot be null, the built-in conventions will mark the properties as nullable. For reference types, we need to mark them as such explicitly, in the OnModelCreating method:

```
protected override void OnModelCreating(
protected override void OnModelCreating(
DbModelBuilder modelBuilder)
{
    //create the hierarchy
    modelBuilder
    .Entity<Vehicle>()
    .HasDiscriminator()
    .HasValue<LandVehicle>(typeof(LandVehicle).Name)
    .HasValue<AirVehicle>(typeof(AirVehicle).Name);
    //mark Wheels as nullable - not required
    modelBuilder
    .Entity<Vehicle>()
    .Property(x => x.Wheels)
```

```
        .IsRequired(false);
        //mark Wings as nullable – not required
        modelBuilder
        .Entity<AirVehicle>()
        .Property(x => x.Wings)
        .IsRequired(false);
        base.OnModelCreating(modelBuilder);
    }
```

Here we are configuring the class `Vehicle` to have two derived classes, `AirVehicle` and `LandVehicle`, each using as its discriminator value, its own class name. Each property in one of the derived classes is set to `not required` (nullable).

References not eagerly fetched are lost

If you don't explicitly ask for related entities when you load an entity, you won't be able to do it later.

Problem

Object-Relational Mappers (**ORMs**) typically have a feature called **lazy loading**. Lazy loading means that when an entity is loaded from the database, all its relations (one-to-one, one-to-many, many-to-one, many-to-many) do not necessarily need to be loaded too. When they are first accessed, the ORM will issue a query and retrieve the records. This is interesting, because we do not need to pay the extra cost of loading potentially a lot of records if we are not going to use them. On the other hand, it requires that a connection is always available when the lazy properties are first accessed, otherwise their data cannot be retrieved.

So, here's the catch: Entity Framework Core 1.0 does not have lazy loading. It will come in a future version. What happens, then? Let's imagine we have the following class model:

```
using System;
using System.Collections.Generic;
namespace BusinessLogic
{
    public class Blog
    {
        public int BlogId { get; set; }
        public string Name { get; set; }
        public DateTime CreationDate { get; set; }
        public string Url { get; set; }
        public ICollection<Post> Posts { get; set; }
    }
    public class Post
```

```
    {
        public int PostId { get; set; }
        public string Title { get; set; }
        public DateTime Timestamp { get; set; }
        public string Body { get; set; }
        public Blog Blog { get; set; }
        public ICollection<Comment> Comments { get; set; }
    }
}
```

See what happens if you execute a query for the `Blog` class, such as this one:

```
var blogs = ctx.Blogs.ToList();
```

You will retrieve all the blogs in the database, but on each of them, the `Posts` collection will be null, even for those blogs that do have posts! This is an example of a not loaded one-to-many relationship.

How to solve it...

This is caused by the lack of the lazy loading feature. Since Entity Framework wasn't instructed to fetch the associated posts, it won't do it. The solution is to eagerly fetch them in the query:

```
var blogsWithPosts = ctx

    .Blogs
    .Include(b => b.Posts)
    .ToList();
This way, all of the posts will be retrieved alongside the blogs.
```

The same will happen for many-to-one relationships, asking for all posts will not bring along their blogs:

```
var posts = ctx.Posts.ToList();
```

We also need to explicitly ask for the `Blog` property to be included:

```
var postsWithBlogs = ctx
    .Posts
    .Include(p => p.Blog)
    .ToList();
```

If you look at the SQL query that was produced, you will see that it generates a LEFT JOIN clause, bringing together the columns for both the `Blog` and `Posts` tables.

The `Include` extension method can even be used to eagerly load multiple levels, for example:

```
var postsWithBlogsAndComments = ctx
    .Posts
    .Include(p => p.Blog)
    .Include(p => p.Comments)
    .ToList();
```

 Not asking for a relation to be retrieved will cause its corresponding property to be null, so be aware of it.

Date/time operations are not supported

Most direct operations with `DateTime` objects are not supported.

Problem

It is often necessary to produce operations over `DateTime` properties, such as, for example, computing the difference between two columns. In the past (Entity Framework pre-Core), there was a class called `DbFunctions` (https://msdn.microsoft.com/en-us/library/ system.data.entity.dbfunctions(v=vs.113).aspx) that had some useful extension methods that we could use for this.

Unfortunately, as of Entity Framework Core 1, this class is not included. This means that the following queries do not work or will not work as expected–in this example, `AddDays` will be executed client-side, not in the database:

```
var age = ctx
    .Blogs
    .Select(b => DateTime.UtcNow - b.CreationDate)
    .ToList();
var oneWeekAfterCreation = ctx
    .Blogs
    .Select(b => b.CreationDate.AddDays(7))
    .ToList();
```

How to solve it...

For queries that need to perform complex date/time operations in the database side, we need to resort to plain SQL; there is no way around it. For example, the first of these queries could be rewritten as follows:

```
var age = ctx
  .Blogs
  .FromSql("SELECT GETUTCDATE() - CreationDate AS
    CreationDate FROM Blogs")
  .Select(b => b.CreationDate)
  .ToList();
```

And the second could be rewritten as follows:

```
var oneWeekAfterCreation = ctx
  .Blogs
  .FromSql("SELECT DATEADD(day, 7, CreationDate) AS
    CreationDate FROM Blogs")
  .Select(b => b.CreationDate)
  .ToList();
```

Paging in SQL Server earlier than 2012

Beware if you want to use a SQL Server version earlier than 2012 while doing paging.

Problem

At least two features of Entity Framework Core depend on SQL Server 2012:

- ▸ Using sequences to generate primary keys
- ▸ Using OFFSET for pagination

If we are not using SQL Server 2012 or higher, of course, we cannot use these features. The first one is not a problem since we can use IDENTITY columns or manually assigned identifiers, but the second is the default strategy Entity Framework uses for pagination. Type the following LINQ query:

```
var pagedBlogs = ctx
  .Blogs
  .Skip(4)
  .Take(5)
  .OrderBy(b => b.CreationDate)
  .ToList();
```

It will produce SQL similar to this:

```
SELECT [b].[BlogId], [b].[Name], [b].[CreationDate], [b].[Url]
FROM [Blog] AS [b]
ORDER BY [b].[CreationDate]
OFFSET @__b_0 ROWS FETCH NEXT @__b_1 ROWS ONLY
```

How to solve it...

This syntax with `OFFSET... ROWS FETCH NEXT... ROWS ONLY` is only valid for versions of SQL Server equal to or higher than 2012. Fortunately, we can tell Entity Framework to use a compatibility mode that will work from SQL Server 2005 upwards. We just need to set the `UseRowNumberForPaging` configuration setting, probably in the `OnConfiguring` method of our `DbContext`-derived class:

```
protected override void OnConfiguring(
DbContextOptionsBuilder optionsBuilder)
{
    optionsBuilder.UseSqlServer(_connectionString, opt =>
    {
        //use ROW_NUMBER instead of OFFSET
        opt.UseRowNumberForPaging();
    });
    base.OnConfiguring(optionsBuilder);
}
```

After this, the same query will be instead:

```
SELECT [t].[BlogId], [t].[Name], [t].[CreationDate], [t].[Url]
FROM (
    SELECT [b].[BlogId], [b].[Name], [b].[CreationDate], [b].[Url],
ROW_NUMBER() OVER(ORDER BY [b].[CreationDate]) AS [__RowNumber__]
    FROM [Blog] AS [b]
) AS [t]
WHERE ([t].[__RowNumber__] > @__b_0) AND ([t].[__RowNumber__] <=
(@__b_0 + @__b_1))
```

Notice the usage of the `ROW_NUMBER` function and the nested queries.

 You can find a discussion of the two paging techniques in this article: http://social.technet.microsoft.com/wiki/contents/ articles/23811.paging-a-query-with-sql-server.aspx.

Database null semantics

Doing comparisons with NULL can yield unexpected results.

Problem

Relational database engines treat the NULL case differently. NULL is not a value; rather, it is the absence of a value, so the syntax around it is special. To check if a column value is NULL, this is the syntax we use:

```
SELECT * FROM MyTable WHERE MyCol IS NULL
```

Entity Framework, as with other Object-Relational Mappers, has to take this into account. So, what happens if we issue a LINQ query that needs to be executed with a parameter value that may be null? Let's consider this query:

```
var name = GetParameterValue();
var records = ctx
  .MyEntities
  .Where(x => x.Name == name)
  .ToList();
```

By default, it will produce the following SQL:

```
SELECT [x].[Id] AS Id, [x].[Name] AS Name
FROM [dbo].[MyEntities] AS [x]
WHERE ([x].[Name] == @__name_0)
OR (([x].[Name] IS NULL) AND ((@__name_0 IS NULL))
```

This is hardly ideal and it is caused by the fact that, when the SQL is being generated, Entity Framework does not know what value the name parameter will have when the query is executed. If the LINQ query instead uses a literal null, or something clearly different than null, the problem does not occur. Because it doesn't know, it has to be cautious and check, if the values are identical using normal semantics or check if they are both NULL. Unfortunately, this results in some extra work for the database engine.

How to solve it...

If we are 100% sure that the values that we will be using in LINQ comparison queries, we can turn on the UseRelationalNulls flag:

```
protected override void OnConfiguring(
DbContextOptionsBuilder optionsBuilder)
{
    optionsBuilder.UseSqlServer(_connectionString, opt =>
    {
```

```
        //if this is present, use the simple check
        opt.UseRelationalNulls();
    });
    base.OnConfiguring(optionsBuilder);
}
```

If you set this, then the same query will produce this SQL instead:

```
SELECT [x].[Id] AS Id, [x].[Name] AS Name
FROM [dbo].[MyEntities] AS [x]
WHERE [x].[Name] == @__name_0
```

Of course, this will never return any records if the parameter is ever `null`, so be warned.

 In Entity Framework 6.x, this was controlled by the `UseDatabaseNullSemantics` property of the `DbContextConfiguration` class. Refer to the following link:

https://msdn.microsoft.com/en-us/library/system.data.entity.infrastructure.dbcontextconfiguration.usedatabasenullsemantics(v=vs.113).aspx.

Migrations and contexts with parameterized constructors

When using migrations we need to have public parameterless constructors or implement a factory.

Problem

If your context takes parameters in all of its public constructors, then it cannot be used by migrations, since the migrations framework does not know how to instantiate it. The error will be something like "`unable to find the DbContext`", which is far from helpful.

How to solve it...

The solution for this is to have a public context factory class in the same assembly as your migrations assembly. This context factory needs to implement `IDbContextFactory<TContext>` and return a context instance from its `Create` method:

```
public class MyContextFactory : IDbContextFactory<MyContext>
{
    public MyContext Create(DbContextFactoryOptions options)
    {
```

```
        //return a MyContext instance with its parameters
        return new MyContext("<SomeConnectionString>");
    }
}
```

For similar reasons, this class needs to be public and have a public parameterless constructor.

Migrations with contexts in different projects

Problems arise if your context is in a different project than the startup one.

Problem

If you have an entry assembly and an additional project/assembly that contains your DbContext and your model, migrations won't work. This is by design.

For example, you have an assembly called Web and an assembly called DomainModel. The latter contains the DbContext and all the model classes and you are trying to generate a migration from the Web folder using the following:

```
dotnet ef migrations add "Initial version"
```

You could also use a similar one. You will get a "Your target project 'Web' doesn't match your migrations assembly 'DomainModel'" error.

How to solve it...

You either need to pass the --startup-project flag to dotnet, if you run it from the **DomainModel** project:

```
dotnet ef --startup-project ..\Web migrations add "Initial version"
```

Or, from within code, you need to tell Entity Framework which one will be the project containing the startup code:

```
protected override void OnConfiguring(
DbContextOptionsBuilder optionsBuilder)
{
    optionsBuilder.UseSqlServer(_connectionString, opt =>
    {
        //set the migrations assembly
        opt.MigrationsAssembly("Web");
    });
```

```
        base.OnConfiguring(optionsBuilder);
    }
```

 And, by the way, make sure that you include the `Microsoft.`
`EntityFrameworkCore.Design` and `Microsoft.`
`EntityFrameworkCore.Tools` Nuget packages.

Accessing the service provider too soon

Do not access the internal service provider in `OnConfiguring` or `OnModelCreating`.

Problem

The Entity Framework Core context uses a service provider of its own, but it is possible to pass it an external service provider. Having a service provider to hand is appealing, because we can use it to pass any kind of services to the context.

The problem is that most likely, we will be making use of these services in one of the methods that are used to configure the `DbContext`, such as `OnConfiguring` or `OnModelCreating`, but, it turns out, if you try to access the underlying service provider, either the built-in or the passed instance, you will get an "`An attempt was made to use the context while it is being configured`" exception.

How to solve it...

You should pass all services that you will need in the constructor of the `DbContext`-derived class and store them internally. Then you can use them in any of the infrastructure methods, such as `OnConfiguring` or `OnModelCreating`. If you are using Dependency Injection, like you would in a web application, you can even declare these services as their base classes or interfaces and .NET Core will resolve them for you.

You will be able to access the internal service provider after a query is executed or when the `SaveChanges` method is called.

Setting the maximum string length

The right attribute to set the maximum string length is `StringLengthAttribute`.

Problem

We want to define the maximum length of a string column (VARCHAR, and NVARCHAR in SQL Server) in the database using attributes, and there are two choices: `MaxLengthAttribute` or `StringLengthAttribute`.

How to solve it...

The right attribute to use for this is `StringLengthAttribute`. This is the one that Entity Framework will look to when creating the schema:

```
using System.ComponentModel.DataAnnotations;
public class MyEntity
{
    public int Id { get; set; }
    [StringLength(100)]
    public string Name { get; set; }
}
```

 Of course, we can also use fluent mapping for this, but it is not strictly necessary for this simple case.

Mapping discriminator columns

You cannot map discriminator columns.

Problem

When you have a class hierarchy that you want to map to a database table using the **Table per class hierarchy/Single table inheritance** pattern, this table will make use of a discriminator column to figure out the class that each record refers to; this is because the same table will hold records for any of the derived classes of the hierarchy. You may be tempted to add a property for this discriminator column, but you will not succeed, because discriminator columns cannot be mapped.

How to solve it...

You simply cannot map the discriminator column as a property, because doing so might cause the type of the stored record to change from one class to another, and Entity Framework does not let that happen. You can give it any name you want and also give specific values for each subclass, but that's as far as it goes:

```
protected override void OnModelCreating(
DbModelBuilder modelBuilder)
{
    //register a string discriminator column named Type
    //with values for each subclass equal to their type
    modelBuilder
        .Entity<Vehicle>()
        .HasDiscriminator<string>("Type")
        .HasValue<LandVehicle>(typeof(LandVehicle).Name)
        .HasValue<AirVehicle>(typeof(AirVehicle).Name);
    base.OnModelCreating(modelBuilder);
}
```

Composite primary keys

When we have composite primary keys, we need to give them an order.

Problem

In some cases, you may need to have composite primary keys, that is, have a primary key that is composed of not a single column, but many. This is certainly a valid requirement, but, unless you configure it properly, Entity Framework will not work. And something that does not work is mapping attributes:

```
using System;
using System.ComponentModel.DataAnnotations;
using System.ComponentModel.DataAnnotations.Schema;
public class MyClassWithCompositeKey
{
[Key]
    [Column(Order = 0)]
    public int KeyA { get; set; }
[Key]
    [Column(Order = 1)]
public string KeyB { get; set; }
    [Key]
    [Column(Order = 2)]
```

```
public Guid KeyC { get; set; }
}
```

Again, the preceding code will not work; it will be totally ignored by Entity Framework.

How to solve it...

You need to mark all of your properties that make up the primary key with an order number; each will have its own, and you need to use fluent mapping for this:

```
protected override void OnModelCreating(
DbModelBuilder modelBuilder)
{
    //set keys for MyClassWithCompositeKey in order
    modelBuilder
     .Entity<MyClassWithCompositeKey>()
.HasKey("KeyA", "KeyB", "KeyC");
    base.OnModelCreating(modelBuilder);
}
```

This is, sadly, another shortcoming of Entity Framework Core 1 that we expect to see fixed in a future release.

Refreshing entities

Because of the first level cache, reloading an entity with modified database values will not refresh it.

Problem

Entity Framework Core, like other Object-Relational Mappers, uses something called a **First Level Cache** (also known as **Identity Map**) to keep track of the entities that it knows about. These are entities that were loaded from the database or ones that have been marked for persistence. This, in general, can be regarded as an optimization: when Entity Framework loads the same record over and over again, it does not need to instantiate the entity's class and hydrate it with the values coming from the database.

The problem is, what if the entity's record changes in the database and we wish to refresh the ones we have? For example, this won't work:

```
//retrieve an entity from the database
var myEntity = ctx.MyEntities.First();
//the entity's record changes in the database
//retrieve the entity again
//unchanged: is returned from the first level cache
myEntity = ctx.MyEntities.First();
```

How to solve it...

The way to solve this is to first detach it from the context, which effectively means removing it from the first level cache, like this:

```
//retrieve an entity from the database
var myEntity = ctx.MyEntities.First();
//the entity's record changes in the database
//detach the entity
ctx.Entry(myEntity).State = EntityState.Detached;
//retrieve the entity again
myEntity = ctx.MyEntities.First();
```

This way, you are sure to get the most up-to-date values.

Cascading entity deletes

Cascading deletes, if not configured properly, can cause cycles.

Problem

Cascade delete means that if an entity is deleted, all of its dependent entities will be removed too. This makes sense in those cases where a child cannot exist without its parent; imagine a blog and its posts, for example. This is how Entity Framework deletes these dependent entities:

- If we are using a database engine that supports cascades in constraints (such as SQL Server) and Entity Framework was used to create the database, it will use them
- If the dependent entities are not loaded, they will be deleted with a single DELETE statement
- If we cannot delete them, we can set the relation property to NULL; unfortunately, this has to be done one by one for all the related entities

Problems start to arise if we let Entity Framework set up the cascade constraints in the database and there are cycles, meaning the deletion of a record cascades to other records, possibly in different tables, which in turn will trigger a deletion on a third level table, like in the following diagram:

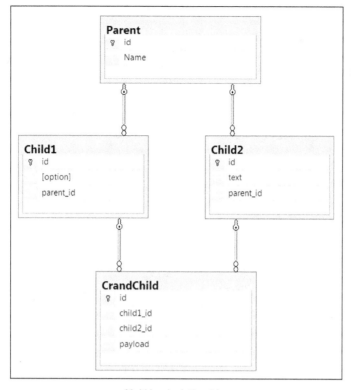

Multi-level relationships

We cannot let SQL Server manage these cascade deletions through foreign key constraints because it would result in an error when the database is created.

How to solve it...

Cascade deletions are enabled by default for required relations but can be configured explicitly. For that, we use the fluent API:

```
protected override void OnModelCreating(
ModelBuilder modelBuilder)
{
    modelBuilder
      .Entity<Parent>()
      .HasMany(c => c.Children2)
      .WithOne(c => c.Parent)
      .OnDelete(DeleteBehavior.SetNull);
    base.OnModelCreating(modelBuilder);
}
```

And we also use this class model:

```csharp
public class Parent
{
    public int Id { get; set; }
    public string Name { get; set; }
    [InverseProperty("Parent")]
    public ICollection<Child1> Children1 { get; set; }
    [InverseProperty("Parent")]
    public ICollection<Child2> Children2 { get; set; }
}
public class Child1
{
    public int Id { get; set; }
    public int Option { get; set; }
    [Required]
    public Parent Parent { get; set; }
    [InverseProperty("Child1")]
    public ICollection<GrandChild> GrandChildren
    { get; set; }
}
public class Child2
{
    public int Id { get; set; }
    public string Text { get; set; }
    public Parent Parent { get; set; }
    [InverseProperty("Child2")]
    public ICollection<GrandChild> GrandChildren
    { get; set; }
}
public class GrandChild
{
    public int Id { get; set; }
    public byte [] Payload { get; set; }
    [Required]
    public Child1 Child1 { get; set; }
    [Required]
    public Child2 Child2 { get; set; }
}
```

Do not pay attention to the names of the classes and their properties; this is just a simple example.

Notice that for the `Child2` class, we do not mark the `Parent` property as required, this is what allows us to use the `SetNull` cascade option. Also, we do not need to specify the cascade delete behavior for all the other relations, this is the default.

So, with this setup, what happens if we delete a `Parent` instance is this:

- If the `Children1` or `Children2` collections have not been loaded, Entity Framework will only remove records from the `Parent` table
- All loaded entities in the `Child1` table that are related with the `Parent` instance (`Children1` collection) are deleted with a single `DELETE` command
- All loaded entities in the `Child2` table that are related with `Parent` (`Children2`) have their `Parent` property set to `NULL` one by one
- If any of the `GrandChildren` collections was loaded, the entries in the `GrandChild` table stored in it will be deleted one by one

Of course, if we want, we can disable cascade deletes altogether:

```
modelBuilder
    .Entity<Child1>()
    .HasMany(c => c.GrandChildren)
    .WithOne(c => c.Child1)
    .OnDelete(DeleteBehavior.Restrict);
```

However, in this case we must not forget to remove the dependent entities before removing the principal one.

Index

www.ingramcontent.com/pod-product-compliance
Lightning Source LLC
LaVergne TN
LVHW081333050326
832903LV00024B/1145

* 9 7 8 1 7 8 5 8 8 3 3 0 9 *